Warm Summers and Cold Winters

Warm Summers and Cold Winters

How Baseball Survived the Korean War

Steven P. Gietschier

BLOOMSBURY ACADEMIC
NEW YORK · LONDON · OXFORD · NEW DELHI · SYDNEY

BLOOMSBURY ACADEMIC
Bloomsbury Publishing Inc, 1359 Broadway, New York, NY 10018, USA
Bloomsbury Publishing Plc, 50 Bedford Square, London, WC1B 3DP, UK
Bloomsbury Publishing Ireland, 29 Earlsfort Terrace, Dublin 2, D02 AY28, Ireland

BLOOMSBURY, BLOOMSBURY ACADEMIC and the Diana logo are
trademarks of Bloomsbury Publishing Plc

First published in the United States of America 2026

Cover design by Enterline Design Services
Cover images © Getty Images/Bettmann, © Everett Collection/Alamy

Bloomsbury Publishing Inc does not have any control over, or responsibility for, any
third-party websites referred to or in this book. All internet addresses given in this
book were correct at the time of going to press. The author and publisher regret
any inconvenience caused if addresses have changed or sites have ceased
to exist, but can accept no responsibility for any such changes.

A catalog record for this book is available from the Library of Congress.

ISBN: HB: 978-1-5381-9388-4
        ePDF: 979-8-2163-9167-8
        eBook: 978-1-5381-9389-1

Typeset by Integra Software Services Pvt. Ltd.
Printed and bound in the United States of America

For product safety related questions contact productsafety@bloomsbury.com.

To find out more about our authors and books visit www.bloomsbury.com
and sign up for our newsletters.

To the memory of the twenty-one men, professional ballplayers
and citizen-soldiers, who gave their lives in service to their
country during the Korean War:

Ace Adamcewicz

Bill Crago

James Ferguson

Leonard Glica

John Hrasch

James Hudgens

Raymond Jankowski

Walter Koehler

John Lazar

Edward Leneve

Jack Leonard

Bob Neighbors

James Pickett

Marcel Poehler

George Reeden

Gilbert Shirk

George Sulliman

Bill Sweiger

Fred Tschudin

Carl Tumlinson

Charles Wilcox

And to the memory of Walter Adelmann,
the depth of whose suffering we can only imagine.

We have said your names again.

Contents

We were issued winter clothes. They were cotton padded pajamas. "Cotton pads," we called them. They were warm and helped against the brutally cold winters of 40–50 degrees below zero. Even with the clothing there were large numbers of POWs with frostbite conditions. In the summer we would have to shed the padded clothing because the summers were just as hot as the winters were cold.

SERGEANT WALTER G. ADELMANN, FORMER MINOR LEAGUE BASEBALL PLAYER

SEVENTH REGIMENT, FIRST CALVARY DIVISION, US ARMY

PRISONER OF WAR, NOVEMBER 6, 1951–AUGUST 13, 1953

Acknowledgments

The completion of this book gives me the chance to thank publicly those who have been particularly instrumental in its development and completion. It is deeply satisfying to do so because no book is the product of just a single person.

All of the following helped make this book better than it would otherwise have been: Marty Appel, Carlos Bauer, Gary Bedingfield, Jon Daniels, Michael Frank, Doron "Duke" Goldman, Michael Haupert, Jeff Jaech, Ron Kaplan, Francis Kinlaw, Cassidy Lent, Clay Luraschi, Chuck McGill, Anne Mintz, Rod Nelson, Andrew North, Jeff Oddo, Mark Pattison, B. W. Radley, Claudette Scrafford, David Smith, Andy Terrick, Dennis VanLangen, and Rick Zucker.

All these people share quite rightly in whatever this book accomplishes and whatever pleasure it gives those who might read it. Any errors or mistakes, of course, remain my responsibility alone.

In a certain sense, undertaking this project allowed me to return to my scholarly roots. Long ago, I completed a dissertation on the home front during the Korean War. My thanks, therefore, go to all my undergraduate professors at Georgetown University and my graduate professors at the Ohio State University who taught me and guided me, with varying degrees of success, as I tried to turn my interest in history into a professional commitment that has nourished me for decades.

Finally, I take great joy in thanking my wife, Donna, for her love and for all she has done for me, including allowing me to retreat into my home office day after day, week after week, and month after month as I pursued the task of turning an idea into a book.

Introduction

This book is a study of how Organized Baseball behaved as a sport and a business during the Korean War years. It considers four seasons, 1950, when the war began, through 1953, when the war ended. Historians tackle their craft in a variety of ways. The choice here is to combine two approaches, heeding narrative chronology but infusing it with an examination of the problems Organized Baseball confronted, including those emanating from the war, while providing background, analysis, and foreshadowing.

The Korean War abides as America's forgotten war. Ask for a list of America's military engagements in the twentieth century, and the answer is liable to include, "Oh, and Korea." Perhaps defining the conflict as a "police action" and not a "war" explains some of this amnesia. Perhaps the result, an armistice without victory or loss, does so as well. The nation's popular culture includes many more books and movies on World War II and the Vietnam War than it does on Korea. Even M*A*S*H, the long-running television show, while set in Korea, was, at least in its first few seasons, an allegory for the United States' involvement in Vietnam.[1]

The hostilities in Korea stand as the first time the modern United States tried to fight a war with one hand tied behind its back, attempting to engage an enemy without significantly disrupting civilian life, providing citizens with both "guns and butter." The American involvement in this protracted conflict that started with a shock and concluded with a whimper imposed peculiar challenges and uneven pressures upon individuals and institutions throughout American society. How Organized Baseball responded on and off the field is this book's focus.

Let me offer one caveat. I am neither a military historian nor a diplomatic historian. I do not intend this work to be situated in either of those fields. Each chapter in this book includes a section summarizing the events of the Korean War as they unfolded during the period the chapter covers. The purpose of these abbreviated essays, unencumbered by the complexities of historiographic debate, is simply to provide a straightforward account of the war to contextualize how and why Organized Baseball behaved as it did.

To set the scene, consider this. Although baseball's history in the immediate post–World War II years has sometimes been characterized as the start of a "golden age," such was not the case. By the time North Korean troops invaded South Korea by crossing the 38th parallel in June 1950, Organized Baseball had already stubbed its corporate toe trying to reintegrate World War II veterans into its labor force, fighting off an attempt at unionization, dealing ham-handedly with a Mexican millionaire's attempt to establish a third major league in his country, and seeing attendance rise to record levels but then begin to tumble.

Owners had hoped for postwar stability and sustained prosperity, but turbulence persisted during the four seasons considered here. The sport's racial integration was far from complete. Americans were moving south and west while major league baseball remained planted in the North and East. Baseball had no strategy for dealing with television. Urban ballparks were growing old and decrepit even as families were abandoning cities for suburbs. Clubs were quite willing to entice young players to sign their first professional contracts by offering them hefty bonuses. In addition, as baseball suffered from a leadership crisis, several players sued the sport over the reserve clause, a congressional subcommittee held hearings to examine the sport's antitrust status, and the military draft, instituted in 1940 and never completely abolished, remained in place, infecting rosters with an unhealthy dose of uncertainty.

The four seasons this book examines saw exciting pennant races in the major leagues, highlighted by the success of the Philadelphia Phillies' Whiz Kids; the debuts of Mickey Mantle and Willie Mays; the "shot heard 'round the world"; and the transformation of the New York Yankees from a perennially good team into a dynasty. The minor leagues concurrently began to struggle, entering a period of decline that would soon threaten their very existence.

No database exists listing the names of every professional baseball player who served in the armed forces during the Korean War. Such a database, if properly constructed, would include both major league players and minor league players in three categories: those whose playing careers were over before they entered the service; those whose careers were interrupted or ended by military service; and those whose service to their country concluded before their playing careers began. A more expansive database might also include managers, coaches, club executives, staff personnel, umpires, and even journalists and broadcasters.

Should the resources ever be marshaled to assemble this database, the result would include the names of well more than a thousand men—and perhaps more than two thousand. At least two hundred-fifty of these citizen-soldiers—perhaps more—played major league baseball. The majority of these men finished serving their country before making the majors; that is, they were minor leaguers when Uncle Sam called. About five dozen were active major leaguers who had their careers interrupted by the war. Almost all of this group returned from service and resumed their careers, but a few did not.

Most ballplayers who served remained in the United States, and many were able to continue playing ball while in the service. Just three active players, Jerry Coleman, Lloyd Merriman, and Ted Williams, all of them also World War II veterans, actually fought in Korea. A fourth, Bob Kennedy, seemed destined to do so before his orders were changed. Bobby Brown, a doctor, was stationed at the Tokyo Army Hospital and spent one month as a surgeon at a field hospital in Korea.

Only one former major leaguer, Bob Neighbors, an infielder with the St. Louis Browns in 1939 and also a World War II veteran, died in Korea. Twenty career minor leaguers entered military service during the war and did not survive. Some were killed in combat. Others died of disease or in accidents. It is reasonable to think that the careers of many other baseball players were truncated or ended by the effects of their military service during the war.

Baseball historical researcher Ron Kaplan asked a number of major league players how military service during these years affected the trajectory of their careers. The memories of some of these men are worth recalling when we contemplate the scourge of this war.

Herb Adams broke into the major leagues in September 1948 with the Chicago White Sox. Drafted in 1950, he was sent to Korea as a combat MP. "I was stationed in Taegu," he recalled, "and in two months I came down with infectious hepatitis. I nearly died in a MASH unit." Sent home in time for spring training in 1953, Adams struggled. "I could hardly run. They demoted me to Triple-A. It took me almost two years to get my legs back," he said, "and I never got another chance in [the] big leagues. Yes, it lost me plenty, and [there were] no celebrations when I got home."[2]

Tony Bartirome played 124 games for the Pittsburgh Pirates in 1952 and spent the next two seasons in the Army. "I was stationed in Berlin," he told Kaplan. "The war wasn't hot, but we were under a lot of pressure because, as you know, Berlin was located behind the Iron Curtain." He added, "When you miss two seasons, you're bound to lose something. I know I lost a step or two, [but] I was proud to serve my country." He also did not play in the majors again.[3]

Catcher Del Crandall made his major league debut in June 1949 with the Boston Braves. He remembered,

> I came to the major leagues at the age of nineteen and spent one-and-a-half years in the majors before going into the service. I feel the time spent in the service helped me mature and overall was good to me. But I was fortunate to be able to play ball both in the States and in Japan. Therefore, [I] came out of the service in good shape.[4]

Vernon Law pitched for the Pirates in 1950 and 1951 before being drafted and missing two seasons. "I was stationed at Ft. Eustis, Virginia," he wrote. "You can't be away from the game for two years without it affecting your arm strength and batting eye. So, yes, it [military service] does affect your ability."[5]

Rudy Minarcin pitched in the minor leagues from 1948 through 1951 before being drafted and stationed at Ft. Eustis. On the day before he was set to leave for Korea to serve as physical training instructor, he fractured his knee and tore his anterior cruciate ligament (ACL) in a touch football game. "I got hurt," he recalled. "I ruined my ACL. I went to a few doctors, and they didn't know about the ACL then. That ruined a good career for me. I never got operated on my knee." But Minarcin persevered. After being discharged, he played in the minors in 1954 and in the majors during parts of the next three seasons.[6]

The White Sox signed catcher J. W. Porter in December 1950, paying him a bonus of $67,500, but he did not make his major league debut until July 1952. Drafted in February 1953, he spent his entire time in the Army at Ft. Ord, California. "The company I was in originally was sent to Korea," he recalled. "About ninety percent of them didn't make it back." When asked if serving in the Army hampered his career, he replied, "The answer is unprintable, so I will simply say, 'Damn betcha.'"[7]

Bob Ross pitched for the Washington Senators in 1950 and 1951 and was drafted during spring training in 1952. He recalled,

The draft call was a great disappointment and probably the major turning point in my thirteen-year career. I spent the first year in the Army in heavy weapons training and playing for the post team at Camp Roberts, California. The second year I was assigned to Special Services and managed and pitched for Ft. Ord in California. . . . Looking back from strictly a baseball career perspective, I would have been better served if I had spent 1947–48 in the service rather than 1952–53 when I was twenty-three years old and ready to pitch in the big leagues and had the opportunity. As they say, 'Timing is everything.'[8]

On June 14, 2000, Commissioner of Baseball Bud Selig and Chairman of the Joint Chiefs of Staff General Henry Shelton, working with the Fiftieth Anniversary of the Korean War Commemoration Committee, laid a wreath at the Tomb of the Unknown Soldier in Arlington National Cemetery to commemorate baseball's contributions to the Korean War effort. Selig read the names of a hundred or so players who served their country during the war. But he paid particular attention to Neighbors, whose brother, Morris, and son, Cam, were present. Selig said, "Cam, I thank you for all that you, your father, and your family have done for your country." In response, Morris said, "Bob was the hero of the family even before World War II. . . . He was and always will be my hero."[9]

Steven P. Gietschier

April 2025

Prologue: A Cold War in Europe, October–December 1949

In the years immediately after World War II, baseball time did not begin on Opening Day, as sportswriter Thomas Boswell would later testify. Nor did it start in early March when players began their workouts in spring training. Instead, each baseball season commenced during the preceding December when the sport's executives from both the minor leagues and the major leagues conducted their annual winter meetings. Sometimes these men—they were all men—sat in official sessions and listened. Often, they huddled for informal chats in suites, hallways, bars, and restaurants. Either way, league presidents, club owners, administrators, managers, journalists, and other hangers-on came together to discuss where their game stood as a sport and as a business, what challenges it faced, and how those challenges might be met. Each year the winter meetings set the course for the season to come.[1]

Occasionally these annual gatherings were held in some sunny spot, giving attendees the chance to throw off the chill of winter and anticipate the warm weather to come. But not in 1949. In that year, the minor leagues, formally organized as the National Association of Professional Baseball Leagues, met in Baltimore at the Lord Baltimore Hotel, twenty-two stories of French Renaissance style topped by a copper mansard roof. For Baltimore civic leaders, the minors' convocation, bringing together representatives of fifty-nine leagues, more than in any previous year, was an opportunity to showcase their city as a future home for a major league team. Mayor Thomas D'Alesandro said so in his opening remarks. There were even a few of the more than 2,500 in attendance who recalled that the Charm City had once been a major league city decades before.[2]

Major league officials also eschewed the chance to bask in the sunshine. They convened in New York's Commodore Hotel, a renowned architectural wonder with two thousand rooms and a main ballroom said to be the largest in any hotel in the world. American League and National League executives brought many concerns with them, but they no longer had to worry whether the new players' pension plan risked insolvency. The plan had gone into effect in April 1947, and barely two years later, clubs learned that because sixty former players already qualified for the maximum benefit, $100 a month beginning at age fifty, a significant and unanticipated deficit loomed. Relief had come in November when Commissioner Albert "Happy" Chandler found a remedy. He announced that he had signed a contract extension for the rights to broadcast the World Series on the radio. Over seven years, the Mutual Broadcasting System and the Gillette Safety Razor Company would be paying Organized Baseball $1,370,000, all of which Chandler earmarked for the pension fund, thus assuring its financial stability.[3]

As baseball's executives entered cars, boarded trains, or perhaps climbed onto airplanes for their trip to these two East Coast cities, they could reflect with satisfaction upon the season just concluded, one that the author of "The Year 1949 in Review" essay in the *Sporting News Baseball Guide and Record Book* called "one of the outstanding years in the history of America's national game." For the first time since 1908, pennant races in both major leagues had remained close throughout the season and were not decided until the contenders played their final games. Off the field, the commissioner made headlines when he healed a wound, tempering justice with mercy by lifting what remained of the five-year bans he had imposed upon the players who had left Organized Baseball and jumped to the Mexican League in 1946.[4]

Prior to the 1949 season, members of the Baseball Writers' Association of America (BBWAA) polled by the *Sporting News* had picked the Brooklyn Dodgers to win the National League pennant and the Boston Red Sox to finish first in the American League. These same voters had predicted that the previous year's pennant winners, the Boston Braves and the Cleveland Indians, would each wind up second in their respective leagues. Only the Dodgers came through. The Red Sox finished second, the Braves, racked by dissension, tumbled to fourth, and the Indians wound up a disappointing third.

Once the St. Louis Cardinals overcame a dreadful 12–17 start by winning twenty-five of their next thirty-seven games, they moved into first place in the National League and battled Brooklyn neck-and-neck throughout the rest of the season. With one week to play, St. Louis led the Dodgers by 1½ games, but the Cardinals lost four of their final five while Brooklyn won three of its final four. On October 2, the season's final day, St. Louis slammed the Chicago Cubs, 13–5, but the Dodgers defeated the Philadelphia Phillies, 9–7 in ten innings, to preserve their one-game lead and avoid a playoff.

Reports that the Braves were not a happy team had surfaced during spring training with most of the alleged discontent directed by players toward manager Billy Southworth. In August, club president Lou Perini convinced Southworth to take a leave of absence under the guise of ill health. The club rallied under coach Johnny Cooney, winning nine of its next twelve, but then fell back again in the standings. When the players decided how to divide their fourth-place winnings from the pool of World Series revenues, they voted to give Southworth only half a share, a vindictive act that Chandler overrode.[5]

Brooklyn's Jackie Robinson, playing in his third major league season since integrating the majors, won the batting title by hitting .342 and was named the league's Most Valuable Player. Ralph Kiner of the Pittsburgh Pirates led the league in home runs with fifty-four, two shy of the league record, and runs batted in with 127. Boston's Warren Spahn won twenty-one games, and the Cardinals' Howie Pollet won twenty. Don Newcombe joined the Dodgers in May, won seventeen games, and was named Rookie of the Year.

In the American League, the New York Yankees under new manager Casey Stengel led the pennant race until the last week when the Red Sox caught and passed them, only to have the Yankees sweep the season's final two games against Boston and eke out a one-game triumph. The Yankees began the season with aging star Joe DiMaggio hobbled by a sore right heel, the residue of bone spur surgery the previous year, and they played shorthanded most of the season. Publicity director Arthur Patterson began counting injuries, but he stopped when he reached seventy-one. Stengel, though, had a deep, talented roster at his disposal, and his skill at platooning players belied his reputation as a well-loved clown.

The Indians, who had won both the pennant and the World Series in 1948 for the first time since 1920, lost seventeen of their first twenty-nine games, a start so bad that Bill Veeck, their showman owner, staged a "second opening day" on May 27 to try to right the ship. Cleveland eventually climbed to second place but finished in third, eight games behind New York. When the Indians were eliminated from the race, Veeck, for whom no stunt was too outrageous, staged a mock funeral for the team's pennant hopes. He and manager Lou Boudreau buried the 1948 pennant in a shallow grave just beyond the centerfield fence as business manager Rudie Schaffer read the last rites from the *Sporting News*, the weekly publication often called the "Bible of Baseball."[6]

Boston's Ted Williams nearly won his third Triple Crown. He led the league in home runs with forty-three and tied teammate Vern Stephens with 159 RBIs, but George Kell of the Detroit Tigers edged him out for the batting title, .3429 to .3427. Five pitchers won twenty or more games, led by Mel Parnell of the Red Sox, who won twenty-five. Williams won the Most Valuable Player award, and Roy Sievers of the St. Louis Browns was named Rookie of the Year.

For the third time in nine years, the Dodgers played the Yankees in the World Series, and for the third time, they lost. "Coaxial cables joined the East and Midwest," wrote scholars James R. Walker and Robert V. Bellamy Jr., "and for the first time all cities with major league teams could view all the World Series contests live" on television, sponsored by Gillette. Those who watched saw an unprecedented feat, a pair of 1–0 shutouts in the first two games. New York's Allie Reynolds beat Newcombe in Game One, and Brooklyn's Preacher Roe defeated Vic Raschi in Game Two. Thereafter, the Yankees won three straight, giving the club its second championship in three years and twelfth overall. Said Stengel after his team's triumph, "Maybe we aren't the greatest team in history, but we finished on top, didn't we? What more can you do? . . . But if we hadn't won, I was ready to step aside and no hard feelings."[7]

By the end of 1949, Americans had come to the grim realization that the peace unfolding after World War II was not the peace for which they had fought. Even before Germany surrendered in May 1945, the Grand Alliance—the United States, Great Britain, and the Soviet Union—had begun to fray. "Of all the world's nations," historian George C. Herring wrote, "only the United States emerged stronger and richer at war's end." Yet, those who anticipated a *Pax Americana*, or even the advent of magazine publisher Henry Luce's "American Century," had their dreams dashed upon the rocky shoals of what soon became known as the Cold War, a term first used by George Orwell and then applied to the postwar world in a speech by American financier and presidential adviser Bernard Baruch.[8]

Scholars have traced the roots of the Cold War back into the nineteenth century when socialism challenged the expansion of the Industrial Revolution in Europe and later when Karl Marx and his followers organized "socialist principles into a fundamental critique of capitalism" that came to be called communism. The clash between industrial capitalism and these critics may have been predictable, but in the early twentieth century two competing worldviews set off this conflict even more starkly.[9]

On the one hand, when Vladimir Lenin engineered the Bolshevik Revolution, he took Marxist principles and applied accelerant to them. Marx had argued that capitalism produced economic inequality and social alienation so great that revolution was inevitable. This was science, he argued, and bound to happen. From this viewpoint, World War I set capitalist nations against one another and was a precursor to the complete downfall of the bourgeoisie. Lenin's *coup d'état* in Russia was his attempt to turn Marxist principles into action, and he believed that revolutionaries in other states would soon seize power and bring Marx's irreversible new world to fruition.[10]

On the other hand, when President Woodrow Wilson led the United States into the war in April 1917, he wanted to make the world "safe for democracy" and capitalism. His sympathies were entirely with the Allied

Powers—France, Great Britain, and Russia—and he urged Congress to intervene against Germany's submarine warfare that had killed civilians and disrupted international shipping, including, but not limited to, arms. Wilson articulated his war aims, the Fourteen Points, in January 1918. He called for self-determination of peoples, freedom of the seas, and a League of Nations to guarantee political independence and territorial integrity. His speech, according to historian John Lewis Gaddis, was "the single most influential statement of an *American* ideology in the 20th century" and "a direct response to the ideological challenge Lenin had posed."[11]

Both Lenin as a Marxist and Wilson as a social democrat laid out a series of principles and goals that transcended a single nation-state to encompass the entire world. Their views were diametrically opposed, and yet the Soviet Union post-Lenin and the United States post-Wilson did not come to blows. On the contrary, once Adolf Hitler's Germany invaded the Soviet Union in June 1941 and Japan attacked the United States in December 1941, the two ideological adversaries joined with Great Britain to put aside their differences and defeat the greater enemy.

Like many alliances, this one was a tense marriage of convenience. It was clear from the beginning that each side sought to destroy the Third Reich and simultaneously advance its own interests. The Soviet Union was committed to defeating Hitler, and Premier Joseph Stalin was certain he needed allies to do so. Yet Stalin trusted that Marxist-Leninist ideology would prevail after the war and that all of Europe would soon be open to communism. Beyond victory, the goals of the United States were much less certain. President Franklin Roosevelt thought that American ideals, including capitalism and democracy, should triumph throughout the world. He also believed that the allies would need to cooperate to shape a peace that would lessen the possibility of future wars.[12]

The Big Three—Stalin, Roosevelt, and British Prime Minister Winston Churchill—met at Yalta, a resort in the Crimea, in February 1945. With the defeat of Germany imminent, they negotiated the future of the war in the Pacific and the shape of the postwar world. Their discussions were testy, and the very word "Yalta" soon came to symbolize the frustrations inherent in those arduous talks. Roosevelt got Stalin to agree to join the United Nations and to enter the war against Japan. Churchill secured a major place in the postwar order for defeated France. Stalin insisted that postwar governments in Eastern Europe be "friendly" to their Communist neighbor. Within a few years, though, as the Soviet Union tightened its grip on Eastern Europe, "Yalta" became a code word for betrayal or at least feckless appeasement. "A sick man [Roosevelt] went to Yalta," Senator William Langer (R-ND) raged, "and gave away much of the world."[13]

When the Big Three met again in Potsdam, a small town near Berlin, two months after Germany's surrender, the cast of characters had changed. Stalin was there, but Roosevelt had died, and Harry Truman was now president of the United States. Moreover, halfway through the conference, British voters ousted Churchill's government, and Clement Atlee, leader of the Labor Party, replaced him as prime minister. Agreement among these three on what to do with Germany, at least in the short term, came quickly: division of the country into four zones of occupation (American, British, French, and Soviet), demilitarization, and denazification, plus returning all the territories Hitler had annexed and shifting Poland's border with Germany to the east. Otherwise, according to historian Odd Arne Westad, "the Potsdam Conference spent a good deal of time avoiding decisions for the future."[14]

Stalin accepted the division of Germany because he was sure that Germans who lived in the western zones would soon move east to live under the Marxist-Leninist government he planned to install. Simultaneously, he kept the Red Army in Eastern Europe, and over time Communist governments took control in country after country throughout the Soviet "sphere of influence." In February 1946, US Foreign Service officer George Kennan composed the "long telegram," a trenchant analysis of Soviet behavior in which he argued that the Stalinist regime's quest for security mandated that the dictator treat the West as hostile and that the West should not offer concessions because they would not be reciprocated. When Kennan published his expanded thoughts a year later, he urged his government to adopt a "long-term, patient but firm and vigilant *containment* of Russian expansive tendencies."[15]

Out of office, Churchill visited the United States in 1946. In a speech at Westminster College in Truman's home state of Missouri, he characterized the new reality in Europe as if an "Iron Curtain" had descended between the West and the Soviet sphere. Truman agreed, and he soon took action that would define American foreign policy throughout the Cold War. When the British government admitted early in 1947 that it could no longer afford to support non-Communist governments in Greece and Turkey, the president announced a program of military and economic assistance that came to be called the Truman Doctrine. In his speech, the president said that it "must be the policy of the United States to support free peoples who are resisting attempted subjugation by armed minorities or outside pressures." According to Gaddis, Truman harkened back to Wilson, saying that the world was now divided between "two ways of life," democracy and authoritarianism.[16]

One way to prevent the spread of communism, the Truman administration believed, was to help devastated Europe recover economically. In June 1947, Secretary of State George Marshall outlined a proposal to do just that. Underlying the Marshall Plan was the belief that American economic assistance would fight hunger and poverty, the breeding grounds for communism, and give Europe a pro-American psychological boost. The United States believed that Stalin and Eastern Europe would reject Marshall Plan aid, and when they did, the relationship between East and West was further strained.[17]

Stalin tried to drive the Western allies out of Berlin, a divided city within the Soviet zone of occupation. When Red Army troops cut off land access to Berlin in June 1948, the United States responded with the Berlin airlift, flying in tons of supplies to the beleaguered city for nearly a year, sometimes at the rate of one airplane every three minutes, and proving to German citizens in the West that the Soviet Union did not have their best interests at heart. The Soviet blockade also persuaded Truman that a military alliance between the United States and countries in Western Europe would be good policy. The result was NATO, the North Atlantic Treaty Organization, established in 1949 with twelve nations as signatories.[18]

The United States, of course, was still the only country to possess the atomic bomb. The Manhattan Project had secretly developed the bomb to use against Germany, but the Nazis surrendered before the bomb was ready. Moreover, Soviet spies had penetrated American security, so when Truman told Stalin about the bomb at Potsdam, the Soviet leader was not surprised. After the war, the president rejected calls to share atomic technology while Stalin pushed his scientists to develop a Soviet bomb as soon as possible. The United States anticipated that the Soviets would succeed in this effort eventually, but it was a shock when the Soviets tested their bomb successfully in August 1949.[19]

As the 1949 winter meetings opened, the agendas for both the minors and the majors included several problems that had confounded Organized Baseball for several years.[20] Perhaps most vexing was the so-called bonus rule, an attempt to dissuade clubs from offering untried players enormous sums of money to sign their first professional contract. Scouts had long used up-front money to persuade young players to sign with them. To give just two examples, the Yankees signed Lou Gehrig in 1923 for a $1,500 bonus plus $400 a month in salary, and the Tigers gave Hank Greenberg a $9,000 package in 1929, $6,000 to sign and another $3,000 promised when he reported after completing college four years later.[21]

Paying huge bonuses became an issue in 1941 when Detroit signed Dick Wakefield from the University of Michigan for $51,000 plus a new car for his father. Other teams took similar, if less extravagant, risks. The Red Sox gave 18-year-old Dick Callahan $15,000 in May 1944. The next year, the Washington Senators signed high school pitcher Dick Weik for $20,000, the Red Sox paid 17-year-old Ted Del Guercio $19,000, and the Phillies gave Lewis West, also 17, $7,500. Substantial sums, yes, and risky, and of these four, only Weik eventually played in the majors.[22]

Club owners found self-restraint nearly impossible. Some stretched beyond their means, offering bonuses out of fear that richer clubs in both the majors and the minors would otherwise corral all the best young players. At the 1946 winter meetings, the majors and the minors tried to curb their own extravagance. They defined a bonus player as one who signed a first contract above certain specified limits: $6,000 for a major league contract, $4,000 for Class Triple-A, and so on down to $800 for Class D. Bonus players would keep this designation throughout their careers, and no club could demote a bonus player without first asking irrevocable waivers. If the waived player was not claimed, he would then be subject to the draft. Commissioner Chandler added teeth to this rule. He declared that any club violating it would be fined, and the player in question would become a free agent.[23]

The rule, tough as it was, did not work, in part because the war had interrupted the flow of talent to the majors. Clubs scrambled to fill rosters; they continued to spend on untried talent; and they found ways to circumvent the regulation. They hid bonuses, paid them out over time, or offered compensation to players' parents. Veteran players complained that bonus players were unproductive and that bonus money deprived veterans of deserved raises. Almost no one was happy, save for the youngsters themselves. Owners amended the bonus rule slightly in 1947, and early in 1949, a study committee proposed three further amendments to tighten the rule, but still the critics were not satisfied. In Baltimore, thirty-two of the minor leagues gave up, voting to repeal the rule entirely, but that simple majority was short of the three-fourths majority needed for passage. The following week, the American League voted for repeal, but the National League did not. Chandler broke the tie by siding with the American League. That sent the matter back to the minors for a second vote by mail in January 1950, but it failed, and the rule, flawed as it was, remained in place. That same month, the Pirates set a record, signing young pitcher Paul Pettit for $100,000.[24]

The minors and the majors did agree on a new rule governing the signing of high school players. Previously, a player who left school without graduating or who did not graduate on time had to wait until the class he was last enrolled in had finished school before he could sign. The new rule, a bit more lenient, allowed a high school player to sign once the class in which he entered high school had graduated.[25]

Like bonuses, how to fashion baseball's relationship with the emerging technology called television perplexed the majors and the minors. In December 1948, *Newsweek* magazine reported that there were more than seven hundred thousand television sets in the United States and forty-six television stations, many of them depending on sports, especially baseball, for programming. John Reed Kilpatrick, president of Madison Square Garden in New York, predicted that games would soon be televised from coast to coast and that local television stations would each evening provide summaries of that day's sporting events.[26]

As the number of television sets and stations grew, major league teams jumped onto the bandwagon quickly. The Yankees blazed the trail, selling their local television rights in 1947 for $75,000. Within two years, fourteen other teams, all except the Pirates, had done the same, with rights fees dependent upon fan appeal and market size. Television sets were expensive—roughly $300 for a large appliance with only a twelve-inch screen—but the chance to watch baseball and other sports from the comfort of one's own home was the driving force behind many families' decision to buy their first set. In 1949, thirty-one stations were televising the games of fifteen major league teams, and a year later, nine of those teams would offer all seventy-seven home games to local viewers.[27]

Although some television stations in minor league cities began to televise the games of the hometown team, the minor leagues as a whole became alarmed when major league games were shown in minor league cities. Frank Shaughnessy, president of the International League, noted that major league telecasts depressed minor league attendance, and he warned that televised baseball, if not controlled in some way, might endanger the minors' future. One club owner put the problem succinctly. "What are you going to do," he asked, "if you have a last-place club and are playing a seventh-place team, with a telecast of the Yankees' game with the Red Sox, or the Dodgers against the Cardinals, available to your fans? The answer is obvious."[28]

Yet restricting telecasts brought baseball unwanted attention from the Department of Justice. In 1946, the major leagues had adopted Rule 1(d), requiring each team to obtain permission before allowing a station to broadcast or telecast its games into any other team's home city. The Justice Department began an investigation into whether this restriction violated antitrust law, and in October 1949, the majors amended Rule 1(d). The new rule, both complicated and contentious, stipulated that each team would have exclusive rights to broadcast and televise games "within the circumference of a circle having a radius of fifty miles, with its center at the baseball park of such baseball club." Beyond this circle, a team could authorize broadcasts and telecasts only when another team located in the proposed broadcast area was not playing.[29]

The minors had little choice but to accede to this amended rule and hope that continued scrutiny by the Justice Department might lead to further modification. Some minor league executives wondered about the fate of minor league teams located within fifty miles of a major league franchise. In fact, Claude B. Davidson, president of the New England League, announced that the 1949 season would be his league's last, and he blamed televised games from Boston and New York. Even though the eight cities in his league had a combined population of more than one million, four clubs had disbanded during the 1949 season and the other four gave up after its conclusion.[30]

One item not on the winter meeting's agenda but still discussed caught the owners by surprise. Commissioner Chandler, believing that he had served his employers well since taking the job in 1945, asked that the major league owners renew his contract, fully two years before its scheduled expiration date in 1952. In this quest, he miscalculated, perhaps because he thought that the support he enjoyed from both players and fans mattered. The owners were of two minds. On the one hand, they voted to raise his salary from $50,000 to $65,000. On the other, they balked at granting an extension so early. They agreed to a new stipulation that no commissioner could be reelected more than eighteen months nor less than twelve months before his term expired. Chandler was left in a valley of uncertainty.[31]

1

A Cold War in Asia, January–March 1950

The question in 1950 was not whether spring training should begin but when it should begin. Under regulations appended to the new uniform player's contract approved in 1946, each club could "require the Player to report for practice at such places as the Club may designate and to participate in such exhibition contests as may be arranged by the Club for a period beginning not earlier than February 15 in 1947 and not earlier than March 1 in 1948 and subsequent years."[1]

In 1947, the New York Yankees jumped out of the starting gate early by flying players to Puerto Rico to commence drills on February 15. The Cleveland Indians, one of two teams training in Arizona, opened camp in Tucson on February 17 but preceded it by inviting players to attend a special hitting school run by Rogers Hornsby a week or so earlier. All other clubs took a more leisurely approach, beginning on February 16 or later with two, the Cincinnati Reds and St. Louis Cardinals, not having their first workouts until March 1.[2]

The next year, even before camps opened, many players and managers spoke out against opening camps on March 1, less than a week before the first exhibition games. New York Giants manager Mel Ott said, "It isn't so much when you start training as how much time you have before your first game. The way things stand, with a March 1 start, we are forced to play our opening exhibition with only five days of preparation." He continued, "The way things shape up currently, we cannot miss running into the prettiest epidemic of sore arms you ever saw."[3]

The Detroit Tigers, too, voiced their opposition to the new rule as they gathered in Lakeland, Florida. "Six days is not enough," manager Steve O'Neill said. "By starting your training season on March 1 and playing your first exhibition game on March 7, you have a lot of lame guys on your hands. It just doesn't work out." Trainer Jack Homel added, "It takes players six days to get rid of their soreness and more than another week to work themselves into playing condition." Pitcher Hal Newhouser declined to complain, saying that he "was in pretty good shape when I got down here, . . . and on the seventh [day] I'm ready to pitch three innings, hoping my control is good," but Al Benton, his veteran teammate, disagreed. "Six days may be all right for some, but not for me. It's too quick."[4]

When major league owners met in St. Louis with each league's elected player representative during the 1948 All-Star Game break, they discussed the March 1 deadline. Some owners wanted it abolished, leaving the start of spring training to individual clubs. Others thought the deadline was a fine thing, but even they agreed that playing games so soon after opening camp was a bad idea. The result was the passage of a new regulation, forbidding any exhibition games until the second weekend in March.[5]

Thus, in 1949, every major league team began spring training on March 1, and for the first time, every club played its first exhibition game on the same date, March 12. Players had asked for a full two weeks of workouts before playing games, but owners wanted to capitalize on the March 12–13 weekend. Some clubs, according to sportswriter Dan Daniel, had also wanted to open camp early, but "it is conceivable," he wrote, "that the contract clause which forces a club to give each training player $25 a week for incidental expenses, as well as high hotel rates, had a lot to do with the retention of the March 1 deadline."[6]

"The rule is a good one," said Brooklyn Dodgers president and general manager Branch Rickey early in 1950. "There is no reason for starting regular training in February." But Rickey wondered aloud whether the Chicago Cubs' plan to take their players on a two-week vacation prior to March 1 or the Yankees' setting up early training for some forty minor league players and inviting a number of veterans to serve as instructors violated the spirit of the rule. "The question arises," said Rickey, "if all this is not cutting corners with regard to the rule forbidding training before March 1."[7]

After Commissioner Happy Chandler ordered the Yankees to pull nine players out of that instructional camp, National League president Ford Frick predicted that the March 1 rule would be dead by 1951. "[Yankees co-owner] Larry MacPhail had flown the Yankees to Panama and Puerto Rico in February 1947, and fear that this practice would become widespread developed among the players of other clubs," Frick said. "However," he added, "the isolated situation which prompted the rule no longer exists. That's how you come out if you pass regulations because of sudden situations which are bound to disappear."[8]

Frick suggested that pitchers needed to be "lumbered up and ready to throw in batting practice when the batters trot out for their first workout." So, when owners and player representatives met in Chicago before the 1950 All-Star Game, they approved a resolution for 1951 that clubs could invite players, especially pitchers and catchers, to come to camp before March 1 but not require them to do so.[9]

When players from the sixteen major league teams assembled at their 1950 training camps—ten in Florida, four in California, and two in Arizona—they confronted a new rule book, a major revision and consolidation that reduced the number of rules from seventy-one, some no more than a single paragraph, to ten, nine playing rules and one covering official scoring, each rule divided into many sections.[10]

Baseball's Playing Rules Committee generally met during each offseason, and at a special meeting in March 1949, Chandler had endorsed the committee's intention to rewrite the entire code. "There are some rules which can stand changing," he said, "especially some minor rules which the two leagues—American and National—interpret differently." Edgar G. Brands, *Sporting News* editor, lent his support to this effort, writing that "Despite charges that the rules are written in arcane language, that a number conflict with each other, that clarification is imperative, and that various league interpretations should be incorporated in the code, reform has been a slow and laborious process."[11]

The rules committee created a subcommittee that met throughout the summer of 1949, produced a report in November, and published the new rule book early in 1950. Brands wrote that "the new playing code . . . reflects concern for standardization, precision, and authority, emphasizes the competitive nature of play on the field but also stresses sportsmanship and demands discipline and reaffirms the dignity and authority of the umpire."[12]

The new rule book introduced Rule 1.00, Objectives of the Game, combining some old material with much that was new. For the first time, basic principles of the game, formerly merely understood, were laid down in print. "Heretofore," wrote the *Sporting News*,

> it was taken for granted that the team making the most runs was the winner of the game, that the object of each team was to win by scoring more tallies, that a game consists of nine innings, and that an inning was that portion of the game during which each team plays both offensively and defensively. These objectives now are explicitly set forth.[13]

Equally important, new Rule 2.00, Baseball Definitions as Used in This Code, provided definitions for sixty-eight terms, arranged alphabetically from "ADJUDGED is a judgment decision by the umpire" to "WIND-UP POSITION is the pitcher's position when he stands facing the batter, his pivot foot on, or in front of and touching the pitcher's plate, and the other foot free."[14]

Some of these definitions incorporated new information; some simply made explicit what had for years been implied; and others did a bit of both. Old Rule 42, for example, said in part: "When the batsman fails to strike at a pitched ball which passes over the plate at the legal height, between knees and shoulder, a strike is called." It became new Rule 2.63—"THE STRIKE ZONE is that space over home plate which is between the batter's arm-pits and the top of his knees when he assumes his natural stance." To drive this point home even more forcefully, the new book included a photograph of Cardinals outfielder Enos Slaughter at bat, with the top and bottom of the strike zone set off by dotted lines.[15]

New Rule 10.00, The Scorer, expanded and clarified old Rules 70 and 71 and supplanted separate sets of instructions used by official scorers in the American and National Leagues. The new rule declared that "the scorer is an actual official of the game he is scoring, is an accredited representative of the League, is entitled to the respect and dignity of his office and shall be accorded full protection by the President of the League." The new rule defined many scoring decisions precisely, including formulae for calculating earned run average, winning percentage, batting average, slugging percentage, and fielding average, and made several substantive changes, including requiring a starting pitcher to finish five innings to be credited with a win.[16]

To help players, coaches, and managers understand the implications of the new rule book, National League umpire Bill Stewart and American League umps Art Passarella and Bill Summers spoke at every spring training camp. When Stewart, a member of the committee that had rewritten the rule book, visited the Indians' camp, he insisted that the new rule lowering the top of the strike zone from the shoulders to the armpits was not a new rule at all. "All we did was to become practical," Stewart said. "We always called strikes in this area. We decided to get it into the book this way so this practice would become standard in the minors and the sandlots, too."[17]

Still, debate over the dimensions of the strike zone continued, and lurking in the background was Rickey's innovative suggestion, not designed to replace or even aid the home plate umpire, but merely to serve as a training device. Sparked by an idea from Brooklyn farmhand Charley Lare, a Princeton graduate, and collaborating with engineers from General Electric, Rickey introduced the Electric Umpire, a gadget that used a series of mirrors and electric eyes to judge whether a pitch had passed through the strike zone. Sportswriter Harold C. Burr added that further research "may enable scouts to determine a standard velocity for major league fastballs," a possibility that Rickey foresaw scouts using to "tell at a second's glance if a minor league prospect's fast one measures up to major league specifications."[18]

The Cold War was not confined to Europe. As the Grand Alliance fractured, questions emerged about the futures of Africa, Latin America, the Middle East, and, most prominently, Eastern Asia, especially China and Japan. The Soviet Union had not declared war on Japan when the Big Three met at Yalta, but Stalin said he would do so within three months after Germany's surrender. Roosevelt and Churchill accepted this promise, anticipating that the Red Army might need to invade Japanese-held Manchuria to help bring the war in the Pacific to an end. In return, Roosevelt and Churchill agreed to redress several Soviet grievances stemming from the 1904–5 Russo-Japanese War.[19]

The successful test of the atomic bomb in July 1945 made the need for Soviet military assistance in China moot. Nevertheless, Stalin declared war on Japan on August 8, and the next day, as the second atomic bomb fell on Nagasaki, his troops invaded Manchuria. After the Japanese surrender, the Soviets took control of the territories promised to them at Yalta, and in a series of moves that Gaddis defined as "more by accident than design," Soviet troops occupied the northern half of the Korean peninsula while American troops occupied the southern half.[20]

The future of postwar Japan appeared to lie with the Allied Council for Japan with representatives from the British Commonwealth, China, the Soviet Union, and the United States, but in truth, wrote historian Mikiso Hane, General Douglas MacArthur, Supreme Commander of the Allied Powers, ran the occupation of Japan as "a one-man show. His forceful leadership, self-assurance, dignified bearing, sense of mission, and sound political sense won him the respect of the Japanese and made his 'reign' a highly successful one." MacArthur, although a conservative on the American political spectrum, engineered a broad program of progressive change, instituting land reform, introducing labor unions and collective bargaining, promoting educational improvements, and advancing equal rights for women. In 1946, American officials allowed professional baseball in Japan, inactive in 1945, to resume. The nation's new constitution, adopted in May 1947, established a representative democratic government under the rule of law, renounced war, and prohibited maintaining armed forces.[21]

After the Big Three left Yalta, the fate of China, a supposed ally partially occupied by Japan and governed, more or less, by the National People's Party (the Nationalists) and Chiang Kai-shek, remained uncertain. At the 1943 Cairo Conference, Roosevelt and Churchill had accepted Chiang as an ally and pledged that Japan would be ejected from territories seized from China and Korea. Roosevelt hoped that a strong China would provide stability in postwar Asia and serve as a bulwark against possible Soviet expansion. Chiang distrusted the United States, though, and his government, riddled with corruption and ineptitude, was hardly up to the task. According to Herring, China "remained a second-class ally whose role was to keep Japanese troops busy until the European war was won." Moreover, the Chinese Nationalists had their own internal problem dealing with the Chinese Communist Party (CCP) led by Mao Tse-tung, who fully intended to take over the government.[22]

The Nationalists had battled the CCP during the 1930s as Mao became a redoubtable leader with a strong following among the Chinese peasantry, keen on land reform. During the war, the CCP fought both the Nationalists and the Japanese and readied itself, assuming Stalin's help, to seize control of the country. After the war, though, Stalin seemed to turn his back on Mao by negotiating a treaty with Chiang that gave the Nationalists control of Manchuria in exchange for Soviet access to the region for military and economic purposes.[23]

Mao felt betrayed, and he sent troops into Manchuria despite Soviet instructions not to do so. Seeing the chances for a stable, pro-America China fading, President Truman sent George Marshall to China as a mediator. Stalin urged Mao to cooperate in these talks, in part because he needed the Nationalists' cooperation in Manchuria and in part because Marxist theory taught him that a Communist revolution could not be successful in agrarian China. Fighting between the Nationalists and the Communists continued. American troops backed Chiang, but Stalin, more concerned about Europe, withdrew from Manchuria in May 1946. That set the stage for a civil war that lasted more than three years. America continued to support the Nationalists, but the Truman administration kept aid flowing not because it believed that Chiang would prevail but rather to protect itself from political attacks from rabid Nationalist supporters in Congress and the media, the so-called China Lobby.[24]

Chiang believed that China could become a modern world power if his army could destroy the CCP and unite the country under his leadership. He pushed hard to make this happen, but the Soviets began to offer some support to Mao's troops—now called the People's Liberation Army (PLA)—and the PLA trapped the Nationalist armies in the northeast region of the country. "Chiang was a man in a hurry," Westad wrote, but he gradually lost popular support. Peasants turned against him as his army grabbed their sons to fight for a cause that had begun to seem hopeless. Landowners abandoned him when Chiang sent his own men into their provinces as rulers. The bourgeoisie resented runaway inflation and government corruption. In 1949, when the

CCP was in control nearly everywhere, few in the working class joined the fight on Chiang's side. Chiang fled to the island of Taiwan, and Mao declared the creation of the People's Republic of China in October 1949. Stalin was still not sure. He called the Chinese revolution "national" rather than "socialist," and he distrusted the CCP for seizing power without much Soviet assistance. Still, when Mao journeyed to Moscow to negotiate an alliance with the Soviets, the Chinese leader got what he wanted.[25]

Americans were shocked by what some called the "loss of China," a country that had once been both an ally and a home for American investment. China, soon called "Red China," was now an ally of America's enemy and was governed, in Truman's words, by a "cut-throat organization [that] will never be recognized by us as the government of China." Moreover, many Americans who had been isolationists before World War II were now resolute Cold Warriors. Among them was a young congressman, Richard Nixon (R-CA), who warned the country about a global Communist threat that the Democratic administration, he said, was ignoring, perhaps treacherously so. "If we are going to combat communism in Greece and Turkey," he said, "should we not also clean house here at home and remove Communists and fellow travelers from positions of power in our government departments and labor unions?"[26]

Facing these international tensions, Organized Baseball tried, as it had during World War II, to play its patriotic part. In January 1949, Senator John Bricker (R-OH) spoke to a meeting of minor league executives in Columbus. Noting his sadness that forty million [*sic*] Chinese might soon be living in a country about to go "into the Communist fold," Bricker asserted that baseball's duty was to help make democracy work by giving every boy a chance to carve out his own career. "Today," he said, "there are youngsters in the Class D leagues who, in a few years, will be stars in the majors." Yet he also warned baseball that its responsibility was great. Officials strive to make money and win pennants, he said, but they must also "teach the boys coming into the game the American way of life."[27]

In July the commissioner went back to his hometown, Corydon, Kentucky, to watch an exhibition game and, as was his wont, to give a speech extolling the game over which he presided. More than three thousand fans joined him as the Corydon semipro team defeated the Owensboro Oilers of the Kitty

League, 5–4. "As long as men are free to play in our baseball fields," Chandler said in his remarks, "I don't think we shall ever be afraid of Russia and her despised communistic ways."[23]

Willing to try something different as 1950 began, Charley and Bill DeWitt, owners of the St. Louis Browns, hired Dr. David Tracy, a psychologist and hypnotist, to help pull their team out of its perennial doldrums. "This is no gag," Charley DeWitt said. "We have several fellows on our club who have an inferiority complex." This was certainly understandable, for the Browns had won only one American League pennant, in 1944, and finished in the first division just eleven other times since moving to St. Louis from Milwaukee in 1902. "I've noticed a certain tenseness among the Browns," said Tracy, who accompanied the team to spring training in Burbank, California. Manager Zack Taylor, who had introduced the DeWitts to Tracy after meeting him during the previous summer, said, "Dr. Tracy will work with the boys during the hours they are not in uniform. This means his work will be done off the field and not during practice or a game."[29]

If winning more ball games was the goal of this experiment, the effort failed. The Browns cut Dr. Tracy loose at the end of May when their record was 8–25. Billed more as a hypnotist than what would later become known as a sports psychologist, Tracy said, "I certainly believe I earned my pay," and Charley DeWitt agreed, but he admitted that "the Browns are terminating their contract with Dr. Tracy as a retrenchment move due to the poor crowds we have been attracting to our home games. This experiment was an expensive proposition, and it is our feeling that we can't continue to enjoy these luxuries unless we draw bigger crowds."[30]

Preparing to pitch in the majors in 1950 meant preparing to adjust to newly configured mounds in several ballparks. Rule 1.09 in the revised code decreed that "the pitcher's plate shall be on a mound 15 inches higher than home plate," but surveys showed eight or perhaps nine of the majors' fourteen ballparks did not meet that standard. Since the previous rule had been less precise, clubs had regularly tailored their mounds to suit their own pitchers, raising them to accentuate the advantage afforded tall pitchers and cutting them down if pitchers threw sidearm. In 1949 only five ballparks—Briggs Stadium in Detroit, Comiskey Park in Chicago, Crosley Field in Cincinnati, Ebbets Field in Brooklyn, and Fenway Park in Boston—had mounds that met the new requirement. Eight other mounds would have to be raised. The peculiar slope of the entire field at Washington's Griffith Stadium was so irregular that owner Clark Griffith, long a proponent of standardization, was given an extra year to bring his mound into compliance.[31]

In February, the National Baseball Hall of Fame announced that ten-year members of the BBWAA had elected no one for induction in the summer. One hundred sixty-seven BBWAA members had cast votes, for no more than ten former players each, but no one had received the required 126 votes or 75 percent of the total. Ott led the tally with 115 votes or 68.9 percent. Bill Terry finished second with 105, and Jimmie Foxx was third with 103. All the top thirty vote getters, save one, were eventually inducted. Thirty-one former players got only one vote, but five of those were later inducted, too. Sportswriter Daniel complained in advance about the results. "If the writers insist on voting for local favorites who obviously do not belong," he wrote, "the onus is on their BBWAA."[32]

Part of every spring's ritual—and 1950 was no exception—was what the *Sporting News* called the "merry contract signing season." Owners were bound to send players contracts by February 1, and upon receipt, players could sign them or send them back and risk being labeled a holdout. In January, Daniel reminded his readers what a holdout was. "Some insist," he wrote, "that any player who returns his contract unsigned with an accompanying beef about salary is a holdout. The officials maintain that no player can be a holdout until March 1. If, on that day, he is unsigned and is not in camp, he is a holdout, the magnates agree." Clubs and holdouts would negotiate, but given the reserve clause in the uniform player contract, there was no doubt who had the upper hand.[33]

The year 1950 had its share of holdouts, including pitchers Ken Heintzelman of the Philadelphia Phillies and Joe Page of the Yankees. Chicago White Sox infielder Cass Michaels returned his unsigned contract five times before getting a raise from $12,000 to $17,500. The Browns' Al Widmar, another holdout, objected when Bill DeWitt threatened him with an ultimatum.

"Unless Widmar accepts our terms, it looks like he'll have to give up baseball," DeWitt said. Widmar shot back, saying, "I'm definitely not going to California [for spring training]. When I talked to Bill on the phone before he went to California, he pointed out that the Browns won only fifty-nine games in 1949 without me and added that they can lose without me this year, too. Well, the way they pay ballplayers, they'll never quit losing."[34]

Daniel also suggested that Jackie Robinson's salary demand, coming off his outstanding 1949 season, might cause the Dodgers to trade him, but Rickey squelched this speculation by signing Robinson for $35,000, making him the highest-paid Dodger. "Of course," Rickey said, "in the case of Robinson, drawing power must be considered." Robinson would earn more in 1950 than Brooklyn's captain, shortstop Pee Wee Reese, and the team's other stars, pitcher Don Newcombe and catcher Roy Campanella.[35]

Other stars made salary news too. Cleveland pitcher Bob Feller agreed to take a pay cut. Ever since 1938, his third season in the majors, Feller's contract had included a bonus clause based on home attendance. In 1948, wrote sportswriter Ed McAuley, Feller made $40,000 in base pay and another $40,000 as a bonus. The following season, he earned the same base salary and pulled down at least $65,000. For 1950, team president Ellis Ryan and general manager Hank Greenberg agreed with Feller's suggestion that he be paid only a flat sum, believed at the time to be between $45,000 and $50,000.[36]

Yankees general manager George Weiss was planning to reduce Joe DiMaggio's salary, but after a talk with co-owners Dan Topping and Del Webb, he changed his mind. In 1949, DiMaggio made $100,000 plus $365 for every plate appearance. Weiss's intention was to reduce the slugger's base pay to $75,000, the maximum cut allowed, and offer a bonus if he played over 130 games. Topping and Webb convinced Weiss to offer DiMaggio a straight $100,000 contract that the aging superstar accepted. DiMaggio's rival, Ted Williams of the Boston Red Sox, probably the best player in the American League, signed his contract for an estimated $125,000, making him the highest-paid player ever.[37]

The National League's best player, the Cardinals' Stan Musial, had no salary dispute. He had signed a two-year contract after the 1948 season for $50,000 annually plus a $5,000 bonus if home attendance exceeded nine hundred thousand. Ralph Kiner of the Pittsburgh Pirates, the league's leading slugger, signed a contract that bypassed Musial's. It called for $65,000, making him the highest-paid player in the league and third overall behind Williams and DiMaggio.[38]

As players reported to spring training, fans learned that the Liberty Broadcasting System would be transmitting major league games on nearly three hundred radio stations in thirty-three states. Liberty, the brainchild of young Gordon McLendon, a Yale graduate with a degree in Asian languages, had started broadcasting games in 1948 over fifty-five stations. In 1949, his network grew to more than a hundred stations in thirteen states. In its first year, Liberty did not broadcast games live. Instead McLendon used a technique called "recreation." He hired agents in major league cities to listen to local games and transmit play-by-play accounts to his Dallas studio. There he would call each game as if it were live, adding colorful sound effects, including crowd noises and the chants of vendors, to simulate the real thing.[39]

Because of Organized Baseball's rule prohibiting the broadcasting of any other game within fifty miles of a club's home without that club's consent, McLendon shied away from live transmission and started his network in Texas and Oklahoma, far away from the majors. In addition, Liberty broadcast day games when most minor league clubs were playing predominantly at night. McLendon disliked these restrictions, and in 1950, he worked out an accommodation with both leagues. He signed a contract with the American League granting him broadcast rights to any game of his choosing on a nonexclusive basis. The National League gave him access to thirty-four exhibition games plus exclusive rights to a certain number of home games for each team, games he had to select by March 1, plus nonexclusive rights to some other games, not specified in advance. And some of Liberty's 1950 games would be broadcast live.[40]

2

A Divided Korea, April–June 1950

The 1950 major league season opened on Tuesday, April 18, with a full slate of eight games. In the National League, beginning its seventy-fifth year of play, the Cincinnati Reds opened at home and lost to the Chicago Cubs, 9–6, with Cubs center fielder Andy Pafko hitting two home runs. The Boston Braves beat the Giants, 11–4, at the Polo Grounds in New York as Warren Spahn pitched a complete game. The Philadelphia Phillies visited Brooklyn and defeated the Dodgers, seeking their third pennant in four years, 9–1. Robin Roberts pitched a complete game for the winners, but Brooklyn's ace, Don Newcombe, lasted only a bit more than one inning. Hosting the first Opening Day night game, the St. Louis Cardinals beat the Pittsburgh Pirates, 4–2.

The American League began its fiftieth season as a major league. The New York Yankees, looking to win their third World Series in four years, slugged past the Red Sox in Boston, 15–10. Each team got fifteen hits, but the Yankees scored nine runs in the eighth inning. Ned Garver pitched a complete game for the St. Louis Browns, who defeated the White Sox, 5–3, at Chicago's Comiskey Park. The Detroit Tigers beat the Cleveland Indians, 7–6, in ten innings, with Dick Kryhoski scoring the winning run on a sacrifice fly, and the Washington Senators, opening at home, scored five runs in the first inning and edged the Philadelphia Athletics, 8–7.

Honoring a rite of spring inaugurated by William Howard Taft in 1910, President Truman threw out the ceremonial first pitch at the Presidential

Opener in Washington. Truman was no stranger to baseball and was a friend of Washington owner Clark Griffith, another Missourian. The president was a fan, albeit not much of a player, from boyhood. "You don't have to weigh 250 pounds to make good in baseball," he said, "and you don't have to be 6' 7" either. I like that. I was a little fellow myself." Even though rain began to fall in the sixth inning, Truman grabbed a light jacket and stayed until the A's made the final out.[1]

Although President Roosevelt had declined to attend any Opening Day games during World War II, Truman, campaigning for vice president in 1944, had watched Game Two of the World Series in St. Louis. After becoming president upon Roosevelt's death in April 1945, he also attended a game at Griffith Stadium on September 2, six days after Japan surrendered, as if to mark the return of peacetime. Thereafter he went to more than a dozen games during his presidency, including a night game on August 17, 1948, in the middle of the strenuous campaign as Truman was running for president for the first time.[2]

The president was ambidextrous. In 1950 he threw two ceremonial pitches, the first with his left hand and the second with his right. He and his family and friends sat in box seats, and he threw from there, aiming at the Senators lined up along the first-base line. Pitcher Joe Haynes caught the first pitch, and outfielder Gil Coan grabbed the second. During the game, Haynes sat on the field adjacent to the box with his glove, there to nab any ball that might threaten the presidential party.[3]

Over the next several weeks, the minor leagues also began their seasons. Minor league baseball, close to dormant throughout the war, had experienced a postwar renaissance. Only twelve minor leagues had played in 1945, but that number jumped to forty-three in 1946, fifty-two in 1947, fifty-eight in 1948, and fifty-nine in 1949. That total nearly held steady for 1950. The Central States League and the Eastern Shore League joined the New England League in going out of business, but the Gulf Coast League started up, and the Provincial League, an independent league in 1948 and 1949, joined the National Association.[4]

At the top of the minor league baseball pyramid stood the three Triple-A leagues, the American Association, the International League, and the Pacific

Coast League (PCL). Each included clubs in cities that would one day seek to be considered "major league," but all of them were hemmed in by the majors' insistence that the major leagues should consist of just two leagues of eight teams each. All three enjoyed jumps in attendance in the immediate postwar years, but the PCL stood above the other two as a league with a distinctive history and a potentially brighter future.

The PCL traced its roots back to the nineteenth century, and it became a member of the National Association as a Class A league in 1904. As the minors grew and the cities within the league increased in size, the PCL became a Double-A league, the highest classification at the time, in 1912, and a Triple-A league in 1946. Blessed with long, warm summers, the PCL played extended seasons, including two hundred games in 1950, and attracted some players good enough to be major leaguers but unwilling to leave West Coast sunshine and perhaps take a cut in salary.

Before the end of World War II, the PCL had argued that it was robust enough to become a third major league. The war put this campaign on hold, but league president Clarence "Pants" Rowland renewed it at the 1945 winter meetings. The majors rejected his proposal, citing, among other reasons, the inadequate size of several PCL ballparks. Rowland pressed his league's case at the next several winter meetings, but each time, the majors said no, even as the fear arose among PCL owners that one or more existing major league clubs might entertain the notion of moving west and poaching their territory.[5]

Attached to the PCL's quest for major league status was the growing dissatisfaction of some owners with the major league player draft, an annual procedure under which the majors could select from each PCL club a player who had as much as four years' experience in Organized Baseball and acquire his contract for a below-market price. PCL owners resented their subordinate status that saw them surrendering talent that they had developed for, as sportswriter Edgar Munzel wrote, "mere pittances." Some suggested leaving Organized Baseball if their grievance was not satisfied. Commissioner Happy Chandler countered that top-flight players might decline to sign with PCL clubs if they knew they could not be drafted, and conservative PCL owners recognized that going outlaw might provide an additional incentive for an existing major league club to move to Los Angeles or San Francisco, the

PCL's two largest cities. Chandler attempted to calm the waters with an April statement promising that the sport's Executive Council would give the PCL's complaint a fair hearing.[6]

As the argument festered, one suggestion emerged that the PCL might remain in the National Association but move to a special status above Triple-A. When Rowland journeyed to Cincinnati for the Executive Council's May meeting, he carried with him an ultimatum, a two-page, five-hundred-word letter signed by all eight PCL owners demanding an answer to the draft question. Yet he left unsatisfied. The council took no formal action on the proposal, persuaded by the National Association that special draft treatment for one league required its permission first. Undeterred, Rowland said he would seek support from National Association president George Trautman, but sportswriter Frank Finch of the *Los Angeles Times* burst the PCL's bubble when he accused the league of "suffering from delusions of grandeur." Finch disputed the league's position that "the draft materially weakened the caliber of Coast league baseball." On the contrary, he said, noting that from 1943 through 1949, thirty-six PCL players had been drafted, and most of them were either back in the league or retired. "Found wanting by the majors," he asked, "do these players give a touch of big-time class to the Coast?"[7]

Several other minor leagues were part of a critique of the new rule book and how its provisions should be applied on the field. International League president Frank Shaughnessy announced in April that his league's umpires had drawn up their own interpretation of the new code and that the Canadian-American, Colonial, Interstate, and Pony Leagues would follow along. Shaughnessy said that "In rewording the rules, the original sense was lost in some of them. A few of the old rules, although admittedly minor, were inadvertently overlooked. . . . And besides, the committee contradicted itself by specifying different rulings on the same plays in different sections of the book."[8]

Drawing the most criticism from players, managers, and fans alike was the balk rule. The old rule specified that a pitcher holding runners on base must stretch and "return to a natural pitcher's position and stop" before delivering a pitch, while the new rule required the pitcher to come "to a stop of one full second." That change had already caused much chaos. Umpires called thirteen balks in the first two exhibition games between the Giants and the Indians, and PCL umps called forty-nine balks during the first week of regular season play. Moreover, the two major leagues differed on what the rule meant, the National League opting to read "one full second" literally while the American League required only a "stop." Said American League president Will Harridge, "Who is to determine the length of a second?"[9]

Chandler responded to this confusion by calling a special meeting of the rules committee for May 4. The *Sporting News* agreed, writing editorially that "the recodification of the playing rules has left some rough spots which need smoothing out." When the committee met, it recommended seventeen minor interpretative changes, including removing some contradictory language. Some of these changes stemmed from Shaughnessy and the minor leagues following his lead, but the new balk rule was left intact.[10]

Dangling from the northeast coast of China and barely more than a hundred miles from Japan lay the Korean peninsula. Once comprised of three kingdoms, Korea had been unified in the late seventh century but was still subject to influence from its neighbors. After the Mongols conquered China, they struck Korea several times and subjugated it in 1258. Just more than a century later, Korea threw off this yoke. The Yi dynasty took control and ruled from 1392 until 1910 although China's dynasties continued to require payments of tribute.[11]

Japan's interest in Korea kicked into high gear after the Meiji restoration in 1868. Eight years later, Japan, bent on imperialism, forced Korea to establish diplomatic and economic relations. Some Koreans saw Japan as a model for reform and modernization, but others, more conservative, looked to China to protect traditional interests. The two interlopers came to blows in the First Sino-Japanese War (1894–95), the result of which marked Japan as a rising military power. After quick Japanese victories on land and at sea, China sued for peace, and by the Treaty of Shimonoseki, the Chinese recognized Korea's independence and ceded several territories to Japan, including the island of Taiwan.[12]

Russia too had an interest in the region and was particularly upset that China's concessions to Japan had included the Liaodong Peninsula, jutting out into the Yellow Sea just west of Korea. The Tsarist government allied itself with France and Germany and forced Japan to give the peninsula back to China, a move the Japanese government used to launch a massive program of military spending. Russia also forged an alliance with China that included a lease on the peninsula. Japan felt its interests being squeezed, and when negotiations with Russia over several issues failed, the Russo-Japanese War erupted in 1904, during which Japan won a series of. stunning victories that rewarded the militarists in its government. President Theodore Roosevelt helped negotiate the peace. The Treaty of Portsmouth recognized Japan's interests in Korea, which became a protectorate and then a colony where, according to one scholar, the Japanese inflicted upon the native population "the hardest and most relentless form of Imperial administration."[13]

The United States also had its eye on Korea, going back to William Seward, whose view of manifest destiny extended to Asia and included some preparations to open Korea to trade and Western culture. This effort led to the Treaty of Chemulpo (1882) that inaugurated diplomatic relations and enabled a negligible amount of trade on a most-favored-nation basis. When Roosevelt cajoled Japan and Russia to the peace table in 1905, the president did not attend the negotiations in person, but he won the 1906 Nobel Peace Prize anyway. The terms of the treaty satisfied neither warring party. Japan won control of Korea but failed to garner the huge financial indemnity it sought. The Japanese public blamed the United States, and anti-peace rioters surrounded the US legation in Tokyo.[14]

Japan imposed military rule upon its new Korean colony. According to Hane, "All the governors-general were either admirals or generals; the military police controlled the police force; and civilian officials, even teachers, carried sabers with them." The authorities sold confiscated farmland to Japanese development companies, and peasants were reduced to tenancy. New laws restricted Korean industry and traditional handicraft production. Koreans held no political rights and were denied freedom of speech and assembly. Armed resistance led to mass imprisonment and executions. When Wilson's call for self-determination of peoples went unheeded at the Versailles peace conference, protests broke out in colonized areas around the world. Koreans in exile and students and Christian leaders within the country staged a mass demonstration for independence on March 1, 1919. The Japanese government labeled the dissidents as rioters, but it took two months for them to quell the resistance.[15]

The movement for Korean independence continued abroad, especially in Hawaii where its leader was Syngman Rhee, a native Korean with an American education including a doctorate from Princeton. He published tirelessly on the cause of Korean nationalism and styled himself the president of Korea in exile. Korean nationalists wanted more than liberation from Japanese oppression. They envisioned a modern, powerful, and virtuous nation, a beacon for other colonized peoples. Rhee articulated a vision for his country that embraced Confucian values, modern technology, and capitalism, and he renounced communism. During World War II, though, Korea played no significant part in Grand Alliance planning. The United States concentrated on allying with Chiang Kai-shek and defeating Japan, and the State Department, according to Westad, considered Rhee a nuisance, useful perhaps only after the war. Even Japan devalued Korea, withdrawing troops from the peninsula to fight elsewhere and impressing Korean women, students, and laborers to work in Japanese factories.[16]

Young Korean Communists developed an alternative vision of what an independent Korea should look like. A few years after Lenin seized power, they formed an underground resistance that drew the attention of the Japanese police. Infighting plagued these groups, as did Stalin's paranoia. In 1928, the Soviet leader shut down the Korean Communist Party and insisted that Korean Communists be educated in the Soviet Union. But, Westad wrote, "during the purges of the 1930s all top Korean Communists in Moscow were arrested and shot, accused of being Japanese spies." Some survived this purge, including Kim Il Sung, born in 1912 and raised in Manchuria in a Presbyterian family. Kim's biography is shrouded in mystery, but he appears to have become a Marxist at seventeen, a member of the CCP at nineteen, and the leader of a band of guerillas fighting against the Japanese soon thereafter. Kim's group did well for a while, but then they moved across the border into the Soviet Union. In 1939 or 1940, he joined a Korean battalion in the Red Army, and he returned to Korea after the war as a Soviet officer.[17]

The Allied plan for postwar Korea was simple: divide the peninsula at the 38th parallel and determine the future later. The United States turned the south over to Rhee, who had some international recognition and an organization that could take control on the ground. The Soviets turned to Kim, not only because he possessed leadership skills but also because they believed he would be subservient. But, like Rhee, he also wanted to lead all of Korea. The United Nations took responsibility for this divided Korea in November 1947 while the United States hoped for reunification and national elections.[18]

Whatever ideas the United Nations, the United States, and the Soviet Union harbored about a unified Korea fell apart as Rhee and Kim refused to budge. Rhee pressured the United States to allow elections in the south only, and the Truman administration gave in. After Mao Tse-tung had gained the upper hand against Chiang, the United States began reimagining both Japan and south Korea as allies against a Communist China. About the same time, Stalin came to believe that a Soviet-controlled north Korea could aid CCP forces fighting in Manchuria. Rhee held elections in the south in May 1948 and proclaimed the Republic of South Korea as a new state in August. Kim followed suit in September, calling his new state the Democratic People's Republic of Korea. The two superpowers approved, both Truman and Stalin apparently believing that the creation of separate states would lessen the chance of war.[19]

Sporadic but intense fighting along the parallel took about one hundred thousand lives, with each side champing at the bit to commence a war for unification. The United States restrained Rhee, and the Soviet Union held back Kim, but the North Korean leader was persistent. According to Westad, shortly after Mao's victory in China, Stalin began to change his mind. Dean Acheson, who succeeded George Marshall as secretary of state, had given a speech in January 1950 in which he declined to include Korea within America's Asian defense perimeter, and Stalin now believed that the United States would not engage in a land war in Asia. Moreover, the Soviet representative in North Korea told Stalin that Kim possessed superior military might that could make for a short war. At 4:00 a.m. (local time) on Sunday, June 25, 1950, the North Koreans attacked across the parallel. When the news reached Army Chief of Staff J. Lawton Collins, he and his wife Gladys were on a weekend retreat in

Maryland. Dressing quickly, grabbing a cup of coffee, and heading for the door, Collins was brought up short by his wife's query, "Does this again mean war?"[20]

For the second year in a row, members of the BBWAA polled by the *Sporting News* before the season picked the Dodgers and the Red Sox as pennant winners. Harold C. Burr of the *Brooklyn Eagle* wrote that the 1950 edition of the Dodgers "shapes up like [a] better squad than last year's National League champions." Most writers picked the Phillies to finish in the middle of the pack, but three Philadelphia writers, Frank Yeutter, Lans McCurley, and Stan Baumgartner, disagreed. Baumgartner, in fact, oozed optimism when Cardinals owner Fred Saigh confronted him during a spring training conversation. Saigh asked scornfully, "And where do you think the Phillies will finish?" The writer, a former major league pitcher, replied, "Why, I think they are going to win the pennant."[21]

Hopes for the Red Sox were less solid. Boston was bruised by having come up short in 1948 and 1949, and while the BBWAA poll landed the club in first again, sportswriters also agreed that the Yankees would provide a formidable challenge. Roger Birtwell noted in the *Boston Globe* that in the seventeen seasons since Tom Yawkey had bought the club and spent a lot of money trying to build a winner, the Sox had won only one pennant, in 1946, but lost the World Series. "The Red Sox of the Yawkey era," he wrote, "will be remembered for their stats rather than their successes." As for New York, Dan Daniel suggested that the club could repeat as pennant winners, but "it could also finish second if Father Time takes [a] fairly good crack at its older personnel."[22]

The Phillies, by contrast, proved that a rich owner could spend freely to rescue a moribund franchise and be successful if good judgment and luck prevailed. Millionaire Robert Carpenter Sr., a member of the DuPont family, had bought the club, which had not won the pennant since 1915, for $400,000 in 1943. He installed his son, Bob Jr., as club president, a move that caused some fans to snicker, but he also hired retired pitcher Herb Pennock as general manager. Pennock came from the Red Sox, but he believed that the best way to build a winner was to invest in young players. Of the eight position players who started for the Phillies in 1950, five had signed their first contract with Philadelphia, and three of their six starting pitchers had received considerable bonuses to do so. These players were all young, and in spring training, sportswriter Harry Grayson dubbed them the Whiz Kids, borrowing the name either from the 1942–43 University of Illinois basketball team or from *The Quiz Kids*, a popular 1940s radio show. In charge was Eddie Sawyer, a graduate of Ithaca College and Cornell and a former minor league outfielder who had seasoned these players in the Phillies' farm system.[23]

The Red Sox, on the other hand, were a veteran team. Three of their starting eight position players had ten or more years of major league experience, and six of these eight were at least thirty years of age. Moreover, six of the starting eight and three starting pitchers had been Red Sox in 1948 when Boston lost a one-game playoff to Cleveland, and five of the eight had been part of the 1946 team that won the pennant and then lost to the Cardinals. The Yankees' roster, too, was stocked with veterans, including first baseman Johnny Mize, shortstop Phil Rizzuto, center fielder Joe DiMaggio, and a quartet of starting pitchers, all of whom were at least thirty years old.

Over the first two months of the season, three National League teams, Brooklyn, Philadelphia, and St. Louis, spent time in first place. After play on Sunday, June 25, the Dodgers led the Phillies by a half-game with the Cardinals in third place, a game behind. The Braves were in fourth place, the Cubs fifth, and the Giants sixth, just 5½ games out of first. Jackie Robinson led the league in batting average (.369), and the Pirates' Ralph Kiner led in home runs with eighteen and runs batted in with fifty-three. The American League had settled into a four-team race for the flag. Detroit was in first place on June 25, New York was second, Cleveland third, and Boston fourth, 7½ games out of first. The Tigers' George Kell led the league in batting average (.368). Ted Williams of the Red Sox led in home runs (twenty-one), and he and teammate Vern Stephens each had seventy runs batted in.

American League president Harridge had rejoiced in spring training that the clubs in his league were selling tickets at a record pace. "All clubs are reporting terrific advance sales," he said. "The Indians are heading for $1,000,000 before the season opens; the Red Sox have around $750,000 in the bank; Detroit had to stop selling season box seats so that game-to-game fans would not be shut out." The league had enjoyed record attendance (11,150,099) in 1948, but had dropped to 10,730,647 a year later, and Harridge declined to predict whether 1950's advance sale would lead to a new record. "Two big factors," he said, "are the early weather and a continuation of the pennant battle into the final month." Harridge's National League counterpart, Ford Frick, was more certain that a general decline in attendance had set in. National League attendance peaked in 1947 at 10,388,470 and had fallen off in each of the following two seasons. Frick predicted that the downward trend would continue. "It isn't going to be anything serious or alarming, just a natural return to normal," he said. "Nevertheless, 7,500,000 still can be regarded as a successful season."[24]

Through June 1, Frick's prediction proved inaccurate. Although there had been twenty-six fewer playing dates than in 1949, due mostly to postponements, total attendance was down a whopping 21.7 percent. Besides the bad weather, clubs blamed rising national unemployment and the growing impact of television for the decline. "With player salaries at an all-time peak, and general overhead more formidable than ever before in the history of baseball," Daniel wrote, "the majority of the sixteen clubs were confronted with problems in bookkeeping and bank balances which they had not been forced to tackle in four years."[25]

The minors were suffering from the same malady. The *Sporting News* noted in April that Harley Phillips, president of the Maryville (CA) club in the Far West League, a club that had drawn a total of 16,784 fans in 1949, would be offering season tickets at ten dollars each, plus two dollars tax, good for all sixty-nine home games. "We can better afford to sell our season tickets at this price," Phillips said, "than we can afford to play to empty seats." Before the month was out, the Pacific Coast League reported huge drop-offs in attendance. The Hollywood Stars drew only 27,271 during the first week of play, and the Los Angeles Angels only 15,926 during the next week. The San Francisco Seals expected 18,000 for Opening Night but attracted only 12,000, and just 6,000 showed up on the season's second night instead of an anticipated 15,000. The culprit, PCL owners declared, was televising too many league games for too little revenue. The San Diego Padres had acted preemptively, reducing the number of televised games to one per week, but the Seals were stuck with a contract mandating two games per week on television for no additional fee beyond what they earned from radio broadcasting. Both Hollywood and Los Angeles were committed to televising every home game, and both clubs regretted it, as the Stars would earn only $35,000 from their 1950 contract. The Oakland Oaks announced that they would televise only Saturday day games, cutting one televised night game per week for which the club received only a hundred dollars.[26]

Television baffled baseball more than radio. Owners had come to understand that broadcasting games on the radio would spur fans to buy tickets and boost attendance. With television, they were not so sure. On June 15, Saigh announced that he would introduce a resolution at the next owners' meeting to ban televising any regular season game in 1951 and for the near future. "The Cardinals believe," he said, "that telecasts should be banned until a check of their effect on attendance can be made." But there was no such reluctance to utilize radio. Saigh had said in April that Cardinals games would be broadcast over a network of seventy-three stations covering an area extending into eleven states and that the broadcast team, former players Dizzy Dean and Gabby Street, would work "directly from the park where the game is being played, doing away with ticker-tape reports of road contests." The Mutual Broadcasting System applied this concept nationally, broadcasting one major league game each day, except Sunday, throughout the season, to an audience estimated at seventy-five million listening over 312 stations. Mutual's president, Frank White, said that the idea for national broadcasts became a reality when he decided to augment national advertisements with local "spot" announcements between innings made available to "lumber and building supply firms, auto agencies, food stores, restaurants, appliance and hardware dealers, furniture merchants, [and] auto accessory dealers."[27]

3

The Police Action and the Pennant Race, July–September 1950

As the 1950 season wound into the summer, players, managers, and fans focused their attention on the significant increase in offense, especially the number of home runs being hit in the majors. On Memorial Day, every team played a doubleheader. Those sixteen games produced 333 hits, 161 walks, 40 home runs, and 191 runs, nearly 12 per game. At the close of play on July 9, the Sunday before the All-Star Game, Ted Williams of the Boston Red Sox and the Cleveland Indians' Al Rosen led the American League with twenty-five home runs each, while Ralph Kiner of the Pittsburgh Pirates led the National League with twenty-four homers. These individual totals were not astounding, but by the end of the season, both leagues would set records for total home runs. American Leaguers would hit 973 home runs, 204 more than in 1949 and 109 above the league record set in 1938. National Leaguers would hit 1,100 home runs, 165 more than the previous league record set in 1949.

Reacting to this offensive barrage, Connie Mack, president and manager of the Philadelphia Athletics, said simply, "Something will have to be done." He noted that, "Pitching has changed in recent years, and not for the better. Eight or ten bases on balls are nothing today—routine, that's all—and the games are too long." Mack went on, saying,

I'm not so old that I think there's only one side to this picture. The ball today seems to have a lot of rabbit in it. . . . Of course, everyone is swinging for the fences these days, but when you come right down to it, there are not many players around who are fitted by nature and build to hit home runs. Yet everybody seems to be doing it.[1]

Observers noticed that the number of home runs seemed to escalate when the supply of balls left over from 1949 was exhausted, and new 1950 balls were put in play. Late in June, though, Luther Coleman, vice president of A. G. Spalding & Bros., the company that made the baseballs for both major leagues, insisted that the way the official ball was made had not changed. "It is conceivable that many reasons lie behind the rise in extra-base hitting in the National and American leagues," he said, "but a change in the texture, mode of manufacture, ingredients and official resiliency of the ball is not one of them."[2]

In Cleveland, skeptics tested Coleman's assertion. A nationally known lab found no measurable difference between the balls from 1949 and the new ones. Emil Bossard, the Indians' groundskeeper, dropped balls from the roof of Municipal Stadium to concrete pavement below. Both new and old bounced to roughly the same height. Indians general manager Hank Greenberg absolved the baseball and instead blamed weather and pitching. "If you'll note," he said, "the sudden multitude of homers has come during these very hot, dry days when the air is light and offers little resistance to the balls." He added, "In regard to the pitching, it must be remembered we had a very cold spring. The pitchers couldn't condition properly and were not accustomed to hot weather. Suddenly the temperatures rose, and they weren't ready for it."[3]

Others agreed with Greenberg that poor pitching was the culprit. New York Yankees general manager George Weiss argued that if Spalding had not already changed the ball, the company should do so now, deadening it to compensate for poor pitching. "Good young hurlers just are not coming up, and what with the ball and other conditions, the situation really is serious," he said. Brooklyn Dodgers general manager Branch Rickey also indicted pitchers. "The pitchers today have read about and experienced the long base-hit so much that they are expecting it to happen every time they get in a jam," he said. "They quail. They flinch. They let up, perhaps unconsciously, when they should be firing it with abandon. They are too careful."[4]

Pitching, of course, was playing a significant role in both pennant races. The Detroit Tigers grabbed first place in the American League early and held it until the Yankees won nine games in a row in mid-May. Manager Red Rolfe told sportswriter Watson Spoelstra that Detroit was counting on its pitchers, including veterans Fred Hutchinson and Hal Newhouser and youngsters Ted Gray and Art Houtteman. New York had good starting pitchers, too—Tommy Byrne, Eddie Lopat, Vic Raschi, and Allie Reynolds—but Casey Stengel's club was burdened by the ineffectiveness of key relief pitcher Joe Page, dubbed "the Fireman." Page earned more than $30,000 in 1950, the highest salary any Yankees pitcher had ever received, but he had reported to spring training out of shape, and his fastball was no longer a reliable weapon. The Tigers regained the lead on June 10 and held a three-game lead over New York at the All-Star break.[5]

The first half of the National League season was a four-team race between the Dodgers, the Boston Braves, the Philadelphia Phillies, and the St. Louis Cardinals. The Braves and the Cardinals enjoyed effective pitching, but the Phillies' young pitchers, Bob Miller, Robin Roberts, and Curt Simmons, excelled. Weiss explained that

> the Phillies furnish an exception. . . . They were able to take their time and farm out pitchers to themselves. . . . We [the Yankees] have to be fighting for the pennant all the time, . . . but other clubs, unused to pennants, can afford to bring up young pitchers and let them get their bumps, and their education in the major league company.

The Dodgers' young pitchers did not rise to the occasion. "Never before in the history of a Branch Rickey club," wrote *Sporting News* publisher Taylor Spink, "have so many bright young pitchers, who seemed to be on the brink of a real major league stardom, suddenly gone bad." At the All-Star break, the Dodgers were in fourth place, 4½ games behind the Phillies.[6]

The seventeenth All-Star Game was played at Chicago's Comiskey Park, the site of the initial All-Star Game in 1933. The 1950 game was the first to be televised nationally, and fans who watched saw an exciting and suspenseful game, the first to go into extra innings, won by the National League, 4–3. The

Nationals opened the scoring with two runs in the second inning, but the Americans countered with one in the third and a pair in the fifth. Kiner led off the top of the ninth inning with a home run that tied the score. There things sat until the top of the fourteenth when the Cardinals' Red Schoendienst hit a home run into the upper deck in left field. In the bottom of the inning, Ferris Fain of the Athletics singled with one out, but then the Yankees' Joe DiMaggio grounded into a game-ending double play. The National League's win was its fifth against a dozen defeats.[7]

Bad weather plagued the first part of the minor league season and exacerbated attendance problems. In fact, halfway through the schedule, nearly every minor league above Class C had seen a decrease in attendance. *Sporting News* editor Edgar G. Brands wrote that "nearly every league reporting losses had a large number of games postponed, some clubs being delayed as much as two weeks in opening the schedule. Unseasonable low temperatures or long rainy periods prevailed in nearly every section of the country." Minor league officials asserted that radio broadcasts and telecasts also cut deeply into attendance. Two league presidents, according to Brands, making a significant observation, "blamed television, in general, and not telecasts of games, for keeping the fans at home."[8]

At the highest level of minor league play, Class Triple-A, all three leagues reported significant losses. In 138 games, the American Association drew 403,986 fans, down from 536,830 in 1949, a 24.7 percent decrease. The International League's gate was down twenty percent with two Opening Days and several Sunday games victimized by rain. In the Pacific Coast League, the Hollywood, Oakland, and Portland clubs' increases were offset by decreases elsewhere, especially in Sacramento and San Francisco. Class Double-A leagues were much the same. Four Southern Association clubs showed small increases, the other four small decreases. In the Texas League, all eight clubs were down. In Class A, the Central League reported a staggering decrease, as did the Western League, blaming flash floods and a windstorm that damaged the ballpark in Lincoln, Nebraska. Class B, C, and D leagues did better, but several league presidents and club owners agreed that stretches of rainy weather encouraged fans to stay home and listen to baseball on the radio or watch it on television.[9]

The Colonial League, embattled financially since its establishment in 1947, ceased operations on July 16, just eleven days after owners had voted to finish the season as scheduled. With all six teams located close to the burgeoning New York television market, the league, according to President John Scalzi Jr., "had never really experienced a successful season and there are no prospects in the foreseeable future of any attempt to revive it." Unusually bad weather added to the league's difficulties as did a strike by players on the Waterbury (Connecticut) club, who refused to board the rickety team bus for a night game in Kingston, New York. Rather than pay for a hotel, team owner Joseph Lombard had ordered the driver to return to Waterbury after the game in Kingston and then drive back to Kingston for another game the following night. Said the players, "We can't ride a bus all night and all day and still play baseball. Furthermore, the bus is too dangerous for use in such a long trip." Lombard fined each striking player $100, but he rescinded the fines later the same day, paid the players through July 12, and disbanded the club. The league followed suit four days later.[10]

The North Koreans surged across the 38th parallel. Seven infantry divisions, an armored brigade equipped with Soviet T-34 tanks, and other supporting units, at least 90,000 troops in all, achieved both strategic and tactical surprise. This was to be Kim Il Sung's war fought at his initiative, but Red Army troops had trained the Korean People's Army (KPA), and Soviets had designed the plan of attack. The Republic of Korea Army (ROKA) had about 32,500 soldiers stationed near the border, but they were underequipped and burdened by the corruption endemic to their country's government. Within three days after the invasion, President Syngman Rhee fled Seoul, the capital, and ROKA troops were in full retreat, many of them simply deserting.[11]

The United States responded to the invasion with alacrity. Secretary of State Acheson approached the UN Security Council before he called President Truman, at home in Missouri, with the news. Late Sunday afternoon, with the Soviet delegate boycotting the meeting, the Council unanimously passed a resolution condemning the North Korean attack. Truman returned to Washington, met with his senior advisers, and considered that the attack might be a challenge like Hitler's invasion of Poland in 1939. Truman had no desire to commit American ground troops, but he said, "There's no telling what they'll do, if we don't put up a fight right now." The president authorized General MacArthur to supply the South Koreans with equipment and ammunition. He told the Air Force to provide fighter aircraft to cover the evacuation of American civilians, and he instructed the Seventh Fleet to begin moving north from the Philippines.[12]

The situation deteriorated rapidly. Rhee called Washington on June 26, asking for more assistance, and MacArthur echoed his desperation. Truman responded by promising US naval and air support. He met with congressional leaders, who seemed to endorse decisions already taken. The president also repositioned the Seventh Fleet between Taiwan and mainland China to dissuade both Mao Tse-tung and Chiang Kai-shek from any thoughts of widening the conflict. On Tuesday, June 27, the Security Council passed a second resolution, endorsing US action and authorizing international military assistance to aid South Korea. MacArthur pressed on, asking that two American divisions in Japan be dispatched to Korea. The president agreed, and MacArthur later wrote that "I could not help being amazed at the manner in which this great decision was being made." Truman decided not to ask Congress for a declaration of war, reasoning that his authority as commander-in-chief permitted unilateral executive action. On Thursday, June 29, the president held a press conference at which he said, "We are not at war." He also agreed with a reporter that the United States was engaged in a police action under the United Nations.[13]

By the end of July, US air strikes had effectively destroyed the North Korean air force, leaving US aircraft flying for the UN free to support ground troops or bomb targets north of the front lines. On the ground, though, the fate of the UN's police action was far more dire. The first American troops arrived on July 1, but these units were understaffed, underequipped, and undertrained. They were rushed into positions in unfamiliar terrain, pelted by heavy rains, baked in temperatures over ninety degrees, and confronted by hardened North Korean forces who proved surprisingly effective as they moved south. The casualty rates on both sides were devastating as the UN forces retreated repeatedly, eventually to a position in the southeast bounded roughly by the Nakdong River on the north and the Sea of Japan on the east. But there resistance toughened. Artillery neutralized the T-34 tanks, more troops and supplies arrived at breakneck speed, and General Walton Walker, commander of the US Eighth Army, took advantage of cracked North Korean codes to protect and hold, albeit with difficulty, what became known as the Pusan Perimeter.[14]

MacArthur had first visited the front on June 29 ahead of the arrival of any American troops. Observing the rapid advance of North Korean forces, he conceived of an audacious counterattack, an amphibious landing on South Korea's northwest shore, close to the city of Inchon, only thirty miles from Seoul, and well behind North Korean lines. Washington officials at first balked at this plan, but MacArthur's force of personality carried the day. Both the Joint Chiefs of Staff (JCS) and Truman gave the go-ahead. The assault began on September 15 as US marines came ashore and overwhelmed a small garrison, taking Inchon and rushing on to Seoul. Simultaneously, US forces attacked outside the Pusan Perimeter and began to chase the North Koreans northward. Many were trapped and taken prisoner, but forty thousand escaped north of the parallel.[15]

This reversal of fortune, perhaps the greatest victory of MacArthur's career, brought to the forefront a basic question: was the purpose of the UN police action merely the restoration of the *status quo ante bellum*, or should UN forces press for the reunification of all Korea under one pro-Western government? Even before Inchon, the JCS had ordered MacArthur, in Truman's paraphrase, to "force the North Koreans behind the 38th parallel or to destroy their forces." Despite warnings that China might retaliate, the general "was to extend his operations north of the parallel and to make plans for the occupation of North Korea." Vague as this directive was, MacArthur planned to follow it, and Acheson told the Security Council on September 19 that the UN should seek to reunite all of Korea. A few days later, ROKA troops crossed the parallel, and in early October, a UN General Assembly resolution endorsed this new war aim.[16]

The *Daily Worker*, reflecting the views of the Communist Party of the United States, and two conservative newspapers, the *Wall Street Journal* and the *Chicago Tribune*, bemoaned America's intervention in Korea, but the *New York Times* praised Truman for a "momentous and courageous act."

Prominent figures across the political spectrum, including former Republican presidential candidate Thomas Dewey and Walter Reuther, head of the United Auto Workers, approved. General Dwight Eisenhower, serving as president of Columbia University, said, "We'll have a dozen Koreas soon if we don't take a firm stand." When Congress learned that the president had committed US troops albeit without consulting them, members of both houses stood and cheered. Soon, Congress approved an emergency defense appropriation of $10 billion, voted to approve a one-year extension of the military draft, and authorized Truman to call up the reserves.[17]

Public opinion polls also showed widespread support for Truman's decisions. *Newsweek* magazine did man-on-the-street interviews that indicated approval for the stand the country had taken. Said one man, "Truman was in a spot where he couldn't do anything else, but he did all right." Another added, "I think it's one of the few things the president's done that I approve of, and that seems to be the general feeling among people." Some young men viewed the war in idealistic terms and enlisted to be part of what one corporal, called to active duty after two years in the reserves, labeled "a great adventure." Another, whose brother had won the Congressional Medal of Honor during World War II, was thrilled to be recalled from the reserves and given his chance to earn glory. A third put his thoughts simply, saying, "They had a problem over there. We wanted to do something about it." Mobilization came quickly. Various units got deployment orders on July 2. Four National Guard divisions were activated on July 20, and the Defense Department asked Selective Service for fifty thousand conscripts in both September and October, seventy thousand in November, and forty thousand in December.[18]

Those who believed that American foreign policy had been wrong-headed since Yalta did not share in this patriotic fervor. At work in their thinking were three complementary ideas. They asserted that international communism was a subversive force that had infiltrated the federal government, especially the State Department. They held that the government's laxity in exposing and rooting out this infiltration had led to Mao's ascendancy. They saw containment not only as an insufficient response to Soviet expansion but also as a policy choice close to treason. These critics of the Truman administration in general and Acheson in particular damned the so-called "old China hands," experts who had warned that Chiang was corrupt and incompetent, as agents of his downfall. They pointed to the Soviet Union's development of its own atomic bomb ahead of schedule as evidence of treachery. They saw the conviction of Alger Hiss for lying under oath in January 1950 and the arrest of British atomic scientist Klaus Fuchs for substantial violations of the Official Secrets Act in February as further proof of their suspicions. And they evinced a certain grim glee when Senator Joseph McCarthy (R-WI) spoke to the Women's Republican Club of Wheeling, West Virginia, on February 9, claiming to possess a list of State Department employees known to be members of the Communist Party. Said Senator Robert Taft (R-OH), the intellectual leader of this group, McCarthy should "keep talking and if one case doesn't work out, he should proceed with another."[19]

No baseball games were postponed on Saturday, June 24, when news of the North Korean attack reached the United States, and none were postponed on Sunday either. Readers of the *Sporting News* did not see the word "Korea" in a war context until an August 2 advertisement urged Air Force trained specialists to reenlist. Yet, when major league owners met in Chicago on the day before the All-Star Game, they discussed the possibility that war might affect the balance of the 1950 season. Commissioner Happy Chandler assured the meeting that a wartime draft would take at least sixty days to begin operating. "If, by some mischance, we do get into another war," Chandler said, "I am quite sure it will not affect the current season." Owners speculated that a wartime draft might in any case take no more than eight or ten major leaguers in all.[20]

The Military Selective Service Act of 1948 required men ages 18 to 26 to register for the draft, but only twenty thousand men had been inducted in 1948 and less than half that in 1949. A survey taken in July 1950 revealed that the St. Louis Browns and the Phillies had the most players eligible for the draft, twelve each, and the A's the fewest, three. The Browns reported that only two players might be called, all the rest being exempt because of marital status, dependency, or previous military service. The Phillies said much the same thing. All their draft-age players were exempt either because they were married, former servicemen, or members of reserve units. Other teams got news of a different sort. Dodgers pitcher Ralph Branca and Cincinnati Reds pitcher Herm Wehmeier were both rejected for military service, Branca for an asthmatic condition and Wehmeier for ruptured cartilage in his left knee.[21]

The rosters of minor league clubs, especially those in the lower classifications, were full of young players, and they were the first to be affected when Selective Service increased the monthly draft calls. By early August, players in the Cotton States League, the Piedmont League, the Texas League, and the Western League had been called to active duty or at least summoned for physical examinations. The National Guard recalled the groundskeeper for the Riverside Rubes in the Sunset League, and the Sooner State League had a player, a co-manager, and an umpire called up by the Forty-Fifth Division in Oklahoma.[22]

Phillies owner Bob Carpenter had sought to protect two pitchers, Charlie Bicknell and Simmons, by having them join the Twenty-Eighth Infantry Division, part of the Pennsylvania Army National Guard, in 1949. Simmons had been the more valuable prospect. He had played three sports in high school and starred in American Legion baseball. After he graduated in 1947, the Phillies signed him for a $65,000 bonus. Simmons pitched and won the last game of the Phillies' season, but he struggled in 1948 and 1949 after his pitching coach forced him to change his delivery. Told in 1950 to return to his original pitching motion, Simmons excelled, winning his seventeenth game on September 2. "He [Carpenter] was trying to protect his investment," Bicknell recalled, but when war broke out, there were only two National Guard divisions that could be activated and go to training quickly, and the Twenty-Eighth was one of them. "So they activated our whole division," Bicknell said. Simmons added, "Of course, it's a tough break. I'd like to stick around, but I'll do what thousands of other fellows are doing, pitch in and help get the thing over." He left the team on September 10 and soon after injured the middle finger of his pitching hand unloading a truck. "A box pinched it," he said.[23]

Major league club officials speculated whether baseball would or could continue during a war. "Anything like complete mobilization of industry is bound to curb baseball along with other professional sports," said one. Another club president added, "The farm chains would be riddled. The majors might be able to keep going with former GIs they now have on hand, depending upon their age and state of health." Sports columnist John Carmichael noted that baseball had been very prosperous since World War II, "but how many club owners," he asked, "have kept the money they made?" Clubs were spending a lot on farm systems, bonuses, and ballpark maintenance, and "this, then," Carmichael wrote, "is the type of big business which the current war may stultify any time." But one American League spokesman took the other side, saying,

> It would not surprise me to have baseball continue through another war, because we have been given to understand that we did a good job of staying alive during the last one without hampering the effort. If and when "our case" comes up this time, we will be eager and willing to do anything that Washington might suggest as our part of the war.[24]

On August 1, Chandler revived the National Defense List with its rules that had protected players' rights during World War II. "Any player who enters military service for the Korean crisis will retain the status he held when entering the armed forces," Chandler said. George Trautman, president of the National Association, said he would place minor leaguers in the service on the "Government List" until the minors could pass new legislation guaranteeing players' rights at the 1950 winter meetings. At the end of August, the commissioner appointed a six-man committee to replace the National Defense List rules with revised regulations to be called the Armed Forces Service Rules. These new rules, due to be approved at the winter meetings, would recognize the existence of the players' pension plan and guarantee that any time spent by a player in the armed forces would count toward calculating his baseball service time for computing his pension benefits.[25]

The outbreak of war interrupted planning for a trio of baseball celebrations. In 1951, the National League would be marking its seventy-fifth anniversary while both the American League and the National Association would be fifty years old. According to Dan Daniel, a committee headed by an outside publicity director had developed a comprehensive plan that called for "moving the 1951 All-Star Game to Los Angeles or Montreal, or perhaps playing one All-Star Game in Philadelphia and another in California" with "Old-Timers' days and other extravaganzas to be held in all ball parks." On August 19, Chandler's secretary, Walter Mulbry, announced that those plans would be "held in abeyance." There was some back-and-forth discussion for a couple of days until American League president Harridge put his foot down, saying that he was opposed to any such festival. Chandler checked with Washington officials and "was told that, in view of our casualties in Korea, it would be best not to have any celebration in baseball."[26]

The American League pennant race remained a battle among four clubs well into September. The Tigers held onto first place until August 30 when the Yankees grabbed a one-game lead. The two teams jockeyed back-and-forth until September 16 when New York beat Detroit, 8–1, the seventh win without a loss for 21-year-old Whitey Ford, who had been called up from the minors on June 29. The Yankees finished three games ahead of the Tigers, aided in part by two other key acquisitions, relief pitcher Tom Ferrick, obtained from the Browns, and first baseman Johnny Hopp from the Pirates. The Red Sox batted a collective .302 and scored 1,027 runs, but their pitching and defense let them down. The Indians dropped to fourth place early in September and remained there, even while winning ninety-two games.[27]

On July 25, the Phillies swept a doubleheader from the Chicago Cubs, moving ahead of the Cardinals into first place. They won twelve games on a sixteen-game homestand, and on September 1, their lead stood at seven games. Simmons pitched only three games in early September before reporting for active duty, and two other starters lost time to injuries. To pick up the slack, manager Eddie Sawyer leaned on Roberts, who started nine of the club's final twenty-seven games, including games on consecutive days during two doubleheaders on September 27 and 28 against the New York Giants. The Phillies lost all four of these games. With Philadelphia idle the next day, the Dodgers played their third straight doubleheader on Friday, September 29, and won both games, cutting the Phillies' lead to two and setting the stage for a final two-game series between the two contenders. The Dodgers won Saturday's game to close within a game, but on Sunday, the Phillies avoided a playoff when Dick Sisler hit a three-run home run in the tenth inning to win the game and the pennant.[28]

4

The Whiz Kids Come Up Short, October–December 1950

The 1950 World Series pitted one team that had won just its second pennant against another that had won its seventeenth and its sixth in the last ten seasons. The National League champion Philadelphia Phillies were young. Their starting eight featured only one player, first baseman Eddie Waitkus, over thirty. Their pitching staff included only two occasional starters and one reliever, Jim Konstanty, over thirty. The best players on the New York Yankees, American League champions, included shortstop Phil Rizzuto, thirty-three; center fielder Joe DiMaggio, thirty-five; first baseman Johnny Mize, thirty-seven; and four starting pitchers over thirty.

Before the start of Game One on October 4, both teams and the game's umpires lined up along the foul lines in Philadelphia's Shibe Park, faced the crowd, took off their caps, and offered a silent prayer for peace, at the direction of Commissioner Happy Chandler, before the National Anthem was played. Curt Simmons was present but not eligible for the Series roster, and Robin Roberts had pitched three games over the season's final five days, so manager Eddie Sawyer picked Konstanty to start. "I was looking for someone different," he said, and it was a bold choice. Konstanty was strictly a relief pitcher, having not started even once during the Whiz Kids' historic season. He rose to the occasion, giving up only one run on a sacrifice fly through eight innings

Yankees manager Casey Stengel made a more conventional pitching choice, Vic Raschi, who gave up no runs and pitched a complete game as New York won, 1–0.[1]

The next three games were similarly close, but the Yankees won them all. In Game Two, Roberts and Allie Reynolds both pitched ten innings, but DiMaggio opened the tenth with a home run that proved decisive. The next day the Phillies took a 2–1 lead into the eighth inning, but New York scored one run in the eighth and one in the ninth to eke out a 3–2 win. Game Four proved to be the Phillies' last gasp. The Yankees scored two runs in the first as Bob Miller could get only one man out before giving way to Konstanty. He pitched seven and two-thirds innings but gave up three runs before Roberts came on to pitch the ninth. The Whiz Kids got two runs back on a dropped fly ball in the top half of the ninth, but it was not enough, and the Series was over.[2]

Following the Yankees' triumph, the club rewarded Stengel with a two-year contract with a base salary of $65,000, making him the game's highest-paid manager. "I can get as much as $75,000 a season, if I do a good job," the manager said. "When I came here," he explained, "I signed for two years, at something between thirty and forty grand. At the end of the [1949] season, I got a bonus which brought me up to fifty. The same thing happened this year." With two consecutive World Series titles in his pocket, Stengel was not satisfied. "A manager who stands pat with a winning club is open to indictment as a sucker," he said. "There is a situation around first base, and possibly another around third. It would seem that we also could stand some help in the outfield," he continued.[3]

Late in the season and in Game Four, Stengel had relied on young Whitey Ford. Over the season's last month, the lefthander had started and completed four games and relieved four times. He compiled a 4–1 record and a 2.84 earned run average. In Game Four, Ford came within one out of a complete game, but Stengel lifted him after the dropped fly ball and a single. "I've been in four leagues since I started playing for money," Ford said, "and I've got by in every one of them. So why shouldn't I do the same up here? It's the same game." A celebratory photograph taken after the Series showed Ford and his fiancée anticipating their wedding, but the caption in the *Sporting News* noted that "an uncle might stand in the way: Yes, the uncle's name is Sam." Ford did get drafted. After being inducted in November and completing basic training, he was stationed at Fort Monmouth, New Jersey, where he snagged a thirteen-day furlough, good enough for an April wedding and a short honeymoon.[4]

Two clubs, the Chicago White Sox and the Boston Red Sox, had changed managers during the season, and four others, the Brooklyn Dodgers, Cleveland Indians, Philadelphia Athletics, and St. Louis Cardinals, made changes after the last games had been played. Of these, the Athletics' announcement that Connie Mack would give up the club's managerial reins to coach Jimmie Dykes was most remarkable. Mack had begun managing in the major leagues in 1894, and in 1901 he became the A's first manager and co-owner of this new American League club. Mack's A's won nine pennants and five World Series, but since 1934 they had finished in the first division only twice. Mack and two of his sons also consolidated their control of the club by buying the shares held by another son, Mack's second wife, and the heirs of the Shibe family. Tellingly, though, they financed this transaction by obtaining a loan secured by a mortgage on Shibe Park.[5]

Three other clubs, the Washington Senators, the Pittsburgh Pirates, and the Dodgers underwent ownership changes. John Jachym sold his 40.4 percent interest in the Washington Senators to H. Gabriel Murphy, who in turn sold enough shares to club president Clark Griffith to give him controlling interest. Pirates president Frank McKinney sold his forty percent stake in the club to vice president John Galbreath and secretary-treasurer Tom Johnson with Galbreath assuming the presidency.[6]

The Dodgers made the biggest headlines right after the season when president Branch Rickey sold his shares in the club and resigned as general manager. Rickey had often locked horns with one of his co-owners, Walter O'Malley, who took issue with Rickey's compensation: salary, expense account, and 10 percent of team profits, plus his dividends as a stockholder. When the pair's third partner died in July 1950, O'Malley secured voting rights to his shares, and Rickey knew it was time to move on. The partnership arrangement said that anyone seeking to sell his shares had to give the others the right of first refusal. Rickey sought a million dollars, but O'Malley lowballed him by offering only $346,666.66. Galbreath connected his friend Rickey with William Zeckendorf, a New York real estate mogul. He did not balk at Rickey's asking price once Rickey promised him a $50,000 fee for his troubles. O'Malley then agreed to buy the stock, fuming all the while that Zeckendorf's offer was not genuine. No longer a co-owner, Rickey resigned as general manager, and two days later he signed a contract to become executive vice president and general manager of the Pirates.[7]

Former player and A's executive Ira Thomas approved of millionaire owners like Galbreath and O'Malley, noting that baseball had become a rich man's game. He explained that "baseball must have millionaires to continue," rich men willing to invest in the business of baseball. He warned, though, that, "I've seen yachting as many millionaires' main hobby. A lot of them, in time, had to get rid of their palatial craft because of the expense of keeping them up. Then I've seen millionaires sell off their horse racing stables because they couldn't afford them." Thomas feared that this pattern "could spread to millionaires who own baseball clubs and who might find them too expensive to operate as a hobby." Thomas pointed to five clubs owned by millionaires—the Boston Braves, the Red Sox, the Detroit Tigers, the Yankees, and the Phillies—each of which was stretched financially. "Only [Red Sox owner] Tom Yawkey could afford to pay Ted Williams $100,000 a season," Thomas said, adding that the Yankees, co-owned by two millionaires, had to pay big salaries to DiMaggio, Stengel, Rizzuto, and others. "The Phillies," he added, "won only because young and personable millionaire Bob Carpenter decided that he preferred running a baseball club to sitting behind a desk directing a part of his family's far flung DuPont interests."[8]

Club revenues depended heavily on ticket sales, and in 1950 only the Tigers, the Phillies, and the Chicago Cubs sold more tickets than in 1949. Overall, major league attendance fell more than 13 percent with the A's declining by more than half a million fans and the Dodgers and the Indians dropping by nearly half a million each. The minor leagues, after four years straight of record attendance, recorded a 19 percent decrease in total attendance. Only five leagues showed gains while seventeen suffered losses ranging from 150,000 to more than half a million. The Pacific Coast League endured the worst drop, from 3,834,692 in 1949 to 3,179,170 in 1950. An analysis by the *Sporting News* tried to correlate falling attendance with games televised, saying in part that "only one club that televised all games showed an increase in attendance," but even the Pirates, who televised no home games, saw their attendance fall by nearly three hundred thousand. Moreover, the Radio-Television Manufacturers' Association published a study by Jerry Jordan, a graduate student at the University of Pennsylvania, that blamed decreased attendance on a number of factors, including lots of bad weather and an overall decline in leisure spending. But even Jordan believed that "it is possible to put too much baseball on the air. Even the best things can be overdone."[9]

The decision to carry the war north of the 38th parallel was, according to historian James Patterson, "not taken in haste." Officials in Washington discussed the proposed change in policy with America's allies before giving General MacArthur his new orders. Warren Austin, US ambassador to the United Nations, presented a new resolution authorizing UN action beyond the parallel to the UN's Political Committee before Great Britain introduced it in the General Assembly. It passed on October 7 by a vote of 45–5 with seven abstentions. The resolution's two key clauses called for ensuring "conditions of stability throughout Korea" and "holding elections, under the auspices of the United Nations, for the establishment of a united, independent, and democratic government in the sovereign state of Korea."[10]

On the verge of what appeared to be a Cold War victory just weeks before the midterm elections, the Truman administration discounted the possibility that China might come to North Korea's aid. More than once, China's prime minister, Chou En-lai, had said that his government would stand with "the Korean people," but when K. M. Panikkar, India's ambassador to China, told the West that Chou had said that China would enter the war if American troops crossed the parallel, the American government dismissed this warning as propaganda. Truman later wrote that "Mr. Panikkar had in the past played the game of the Chinese Communists fairly regularly, so that his statement could not be taken as that of an impartial observer."[11]

But Chinese troops had been on the move for months. In April, China had redeployed its Fourth Field Army from south China to Manchuria, and in July other massive troop movements brought the total of Chinese forces near the Yalu River, the border between China and North Korea, to about 180,000 men.

Moreover, China staged "Resist American Invasion of Taiwan and Korea" week in July, and Chinese propaganda gradually replaced the term *fan tuei* (nonviolent opposition) with *k'ang yi* (active opposition).[12]

MacArthur decided to move north by dividing his forces in half. He sent the Eighth Army up the western half of North Korea, west of the Taebaek mountain range, and X Corps departed Inchon and Seoul and circled around the peninsula for amphibious landings at Wonsan and Iwon on the east coast. Thereafter, the two forces planned to pinch together and drive toward the Yalu. This plan worked at first. UN troops moved forward with remarkable speed, and by the end of October, a few ROKA advance units were near the Yalu. MacArthur told Truman to expect victory before Christmas.[13]

The apparent progress of the war notwithstanding, the president decided that he had to meet MacArthur face-to-face. As Truman later wrote, benignly, "We had never had any personal contacts at all, and I thought that he ought to know his Commander in Chief and that I ought to know the senior field commander in the Far East." Truman traveled from Washington to St. Louis to California and to Hawaii before meeting MacArthur at 6:30 a.m. on Wake Island in the North Pacific. The general greeted him with his shirt unbuttoned and wearing a cap that had, in Truman's words, "evidently seen a good deal of use."[14]

The president and the general met alone for about an hour. A second meeting included a much larger group, including several of MacArthur's aides and a broad contingent of administration officials. A third session focused on several short, small-group discussions. Before lunch, the whole conference was over. Truman boarded his plane first, bound for San Francisco where he spoke to the American people from the stage of the San Francisco Opera House. MacArthur hurried back to Tokyo, giving the impression that his duties there were more important than the president's.[15]

Since the Truman-MacArthur relationship deteriorated over the next few months, exactly what was said in these brief meetings was soon subject to debate and disagreement. Years later, though, it came to light that a door left ajar had allowed a secretary to listen in from the next room. The transcript of her shorthand notes, added to several other sets of notes taken by various administration officials, has given historians a good sense of what transpired.

Most importantly, it is clear that MacArthur reiterated his viewpoint that the war would soon be over and that the possibility of Chinese involvement was insignificant. "We are no longer fearful of their intervention," he said.[16]

Although the ground war continued to go well, MacArthur's assessment proved wrong. The Eighth Army took Pyongyang, the North Korean capital, on October 19, and X Corps made its landings shortly thereafter. But two weeks after the Wake Island meetings, ROKA soldiers began capturing Chinese soldiers who, under interrogation, said their numbers were vast. According to British historian Max Hastings, "between October 23 and 25 the intelligence staffs of MacArthur's armies failed to discern the slightest evidence of the movement of 130,000 soldiers and porters." The course of the war rapidly changed.[17]

As winter set in, Chinese troops attacked across the length of the front and blunted the advance of UN forces toward the Yalu. MacArthur was unmoved. "Having assured himself that the Chinese would not dare to intervene," Patterson wrote, "he refused to believe that they might prevail." In the words of another scholar, the general relied on his "personal infallibility theory of intelligence" in which he "created his own intelligence organization, interpreted its results, and acted upon his own analysis."[18]

Simultaneously, American troops began reporting to sick bay, suffering, according to the Marine Corps' official history of the war, "from what appeared to be shock. Some of them would come in crying; some of them were extremely nervous; and the doctors said it was simply the sudden shock of the terrific cold when they were not ready for it." In fact, the soldiers were confronting for the first time the ferocity of the Korean winter where temperatures plunged in some places to minus forty degrees.[19]

On the day after Thanksgiving, MacArthur's communiqué to his troops, on the eve of what he hoped would be the war's final offensive, closed with a prediction. "If successful," he wrote, "this [offensive] should for all practical purposes end the war, restore peace and unity to Korea, enable the prompt withdrawal of United Nations military forces, and permit the complete assumption by the Korean people and nation of full sovereignty and international equity. It is that for which we fight."[20]

This new offensive had hardly begun when the Chinese onslaught halted it. A pattern soon emerged. Carrying only a few pounds of equipment, Chinese troops moved quickly, held still when planes flew overhead, and often fought hand-to-hand with terrifying ferocity. The Chinese usually attacked at night, ambush-style, using hills and valleys to get behind UN lines and favoring small, isolated engagements to large, pitched battles. The attackers used bugles, flutes, drums, rattles, whistles, and shepherd pipes to disorient their adversaries, and they were relentless. Barely a week after the UN had launched its offensive, a retreat, soon dubbed "the big bug out," began. On December 5, UN forces abandoned Pyongyang, and by Christmas, they had fallen back below the parallel.[21]

Truman's biographer, David McCullough, called the last two months of 1950 "the most difficult period of his presidency." On November 1, two Puerto Rican nationalists fired gunshots at guards outside Blair House, the president's temporary residence while the White House was being renovated. A few days later, the Republican Party won significant victories in the off-year elections, shaving the Democratic Party's majority in both houses of Congress. GOP winners included Robert Taft, setting him up to be a presidential contender in 1952, and Richard Nixon, who had taken one of California's Senate seats. On November 30, the president suggested at a press conference that MacArthur might be authorized to retaliate against the Chinese by using atomic weapons, a gaffe that he later retracted.[22]

The Chinese advance shattered MacArthur's confidence, but he quickly decided that Washington, and not he himself, was to blame. He complained that he had not been given adequate support. He demanded that Chiang Kai-shek's army be unleashed to fight alongside UN forces and that the United States blockade Chinese ports and bomb industrial targets in Manchuria. "This group of Europhiles," he grumbled about the Truman administration, "just will not recognize that it is Asia which has been selected for the test of communist power and that if Asia falls, Europe would not have a chance."[23]

"The fighting that followed over the next few weeks," Patterson wrote, "was among the bloodiest in the annals of American military history." Stretched thin and undersupplied, UN forces had no choice but to retreat, and retreat sometimes became rout. Two brave episodes during this time became legendary. The first was the retreat from the Chosin Reservoir, during which the First Marine Division sustained over 4,000 casualties but inflicted an estimated 37,500. The second involved the Army's Seventh Infantry Division retreating over sixty miles of mountainous roads, including some six miles where the Chinese held high ground on both sides. The division took 5,000 casualties over the last three days of November.[24]

On December 15, the president went on television to declare a national emergency. He called for all-out mobilization that would increase the size of the armed forces to 3.5 million personnel. "Our homes, our nation, all the things we believe in are in great danger," he said. Fifty percent of Americans at home, according to polls, believed that World War III was imminent, while on the ground in Korea, fears mounted that another Chinese offensive involving a million soldiers might soon begin.[25]

In what was rapidly becoming an untenable situation—limited war vs. total war and president vs. general—fate intervened. Between November 24 and December 12, UN forces took thirteen thousand casualties, but one death proved especially significant. On the morning of December 23, the Eighth Army's General Walker was killed in an accident. According to journalist and historian David Halberstam, Walker and the soldier assigned as his driver "always pushed their jeep too hard on Korea's terrible, narrow, icy roads." The general, his driver, and two others were hurrying northbound on a road where southbound vehicles were stacked up. "Suddenly," Halberstam wrote, "a weapons carrier from a South Korean division swung into his [Walker's] lane, and there was no time to avoid an accident." The jeep slid off the icy road into a rice paddy and flipped over. All four occupants were thrown out. The other three survived, but Walker died of severe head injuries.[26]

The long-term stability of the players' pension plan was still a bit shaky when some players clamored to have the $800,000 Gillette paid to sponsor the 1950 World Series on television diverted from the pension plan to the players' pool, the money to be distributed to the teams playing in the Series and to the next three finishers in each league. Veteran catcher Birdie Tebbetts, an insurance executive in the off-season, disagreed. "Until the pension fund is unequivocally set up, the television money should go into that fund," he said, "and I, for one, would hate to see it diverted into any other channels." Wary of what might unfold in Korea and elsewhere, Chandler worried that Uncle Sam might call to arms as many as 75 percent of all major leaguers in 1951. Clubs would then be responsible for those players' contributions to the pension plan plus a portion of the premiums paid by their replacements. The commissioner discussed this problem with both leagues' player representatives in October, but he took no action because the players did not present a concrete proposal. He then asked three attorneys to consult with actuaries, and their report recommended that the television money not be diverted. The player representatives agreed with this assessment, and so did the owners.[27]

Players continued to get called to take pre-induction physicals. Braves catcher Del Crandall's local board classified him 1-A on August 14 before summoning him for a physical. On the same day, Cubs first baseman Preston Ward took his exam, and outfielder George Shuba left the International League's Montreal Royals to return home for his physical. White Sox righthander Howie Judson, who had served in the Navy during World War II, got a notice to take a physical, too, and manager Floyd Geiger left the Seminole Ironmen in the Sooner State League to report to the 120th Medical Company in Tulsa, Oklahoma. Tigers catcher Frank House, a bonus signee, was deferred by his local board because he was married, and his teammate, pitcher Art Houtteman, had his draft decision postponed pending examination of his medical records stemming from a near-fatal automobile accident in 1949. Selective Service reached beyond the player ranks, too, snagging Horace Billings, sports editor of the *Salisbury* (NC) *Evening Post*, Len Allen, a sports announcer in Ogden, Utah, and Bob Addie, sports columnist for the *Washington Times-Herald*.[28]

Rickey and the Pirates maneuvered around the military draft by selecting outfielder George Metkovich from the Oakland Oaks in the major league draft for $10,000. Metkovich had been the PCL's Most Valuable Player in 1950, but he was thirty years old, beyond the reach of Selective Service. Rickey explained his thinking by saying that "Some of the things that are going to be done with the Pirates don't fit into our plans for a championship team, but we are definitely going to have in mind a wartime ball club if the occasion arises." Oakland's owner, Brick Laws, was livid at what he called this "legalized raw deal, . . . legalized only because we are parties to the draft." He added, "I not only paid $25,000 for Metkovich, . . . but I also assumed the $10,000 salary the White Sox paid him." He continued, "If the Pirates wanted Metkovich, why didn't they call me and make a deal for his purchase ahead of the draft?" Pirates vice president Branch Rickey Jr. responded for his father, saying, "Laws knew he was going to lose Metkovich in the draft. Why didn't he try to sell him? . . . We merely proceeded according to baseball law."[29]

Late in the fall, DiMaggio and former major leaguer Lefty O Doul embarked upon a twenty-five-day trip to visit American troops in Korea and Japan. DiMaggio was the game's preeminent star, albeit at the tail end of his career, and O'Doul, once a fine player, was beloved as the sport's unofficial ambassador to Japan, visiting many times before and after World War II. The pair visited Korea first, stopping at hospitals to visit the wounded. "We were less than twelve miles from the front," DiMaggio said, "and could hear guns booming to the north." He added, "It looked like an all-out war to me. And the boys want the people in this country to know they're not just a police force." In Japan, the Americans visited more hospitals and took in several games, including the first two games of the Japan World Series. DiMaggio took part in a ten-day Home Run Derby but was outhit by several Japanese sluggers. "I couldn't find a Japanese bat that felt any good," he said.[30]

The widening war was much on executives' minds as they gathered in St Petersburg for the winter meetings. For the sixth time, the minors and the majors met in the same city, the minors' meetings commencing on December 4 and the majors a week later with a joint meeting wedged in between. Prior to the opening sessions, newspapers floated many trade rumors, but few deals ensued. John Drebinger of the *New York Times* explained that "No one will let go of an old player because no one is certain that by next summer that old hand may not be one of the key members of the club. No one wants to risk trading for a youngster because by tomorrow he may be on his way to a military training base."[31]

The minor leagues rejected a proposal to give Triple-A leagues special privileges in their relations with the majors, and they also voted down an increase in draft prices. A resolution to repeal the rule governing the signing of high school players passed with a committee appointed to draft a new rule. In addition, the minors were somewhat assuaged by the commissioner's decision to create a special committee to deal with the continuing problems posed by broadcasting and telecasting major league games into minor league territory.[32]

The only vote that surprised onlookers was the minors' decision to repeal the bonus rule. In 1949, the minors had voted on the rule twice, and repeal failed each time. In St. Petersburg, the vote was unanimous, fifty-seven leagues in favor of killing the rule and none opposed. Perhaps some minor league executives had decided to change their minds after Cincinnati Reds president Warren Giles announced that he had changed his. Giles had been the principal author of the bonus rule and its chief defender, but in a letter to Cardinals vice president William Walsingham Jr., he said that he now favored its complete repeal. He gave two reasons. First, as he wrote, "There is so much 'under the table' dealing and circumventing the rules that I believe clubs that are trying to keep the rules are getting the worst of it." And second, "With players already having been drafted and the fact that increased mobilization will make further inroads on the rosters of the ball clubs, I believe it is in the interest of the clubs and the players themselves that there should be as few restrictions as possible, keeping, of course, those restrictions which protect the players' rights and interest."[33]

When the majors convened, they, too, voted to repeal the high school rule and the bonus rule, and they handled some more mundane pieces of business as well. The American League approved a plan to set aside the two days after the close of the regular season to play any postponed games that would affect the pennant race. National League owners adopted a rule, later modified, to bar photographers from the playing field during a game, and they extended the contract of league president Ford Frick by four years while increasing his annual salary to $55,000. Together the two leagues approved a request to give the minors equal representation on a new playing rules committee, voted to hold the 1951 All-Star game in Detroit to help celebrate that city's 250th anniversary, and approved identical Armed Forces Service Rules.[34]

After the major leagues' morning sessions on December 11, owners met again that afternoon in Yankees co-owner Dan Topping's hotel suite to discuss renewing the commissioner's contract, as they had promised to do the year before. A new deal would require a three-fourths majority, that is, twelve votes from the sixteen clubs, but an unofficial tally revealed only nine clubs favoring renewal and seven opposed. Del Webb, Topping's partner, called for an official vote, and the result was an eight-to-eight tie. When Webb and Cubs owner Phil Wrigley told Chandler that his contract would not be renewed, the commissioner demanded another vote. This time, he got one more, but still three short of what he needed.[35]

Chandler's first reaction to this rebuff was to announce that he would resign immediately. The next morning, he changed his mind and said he would remain in the job until his term was up. When a rumor arose that the owners had considered buying out his contract for $100,000, Chandler fired back, "Gentlemen, among you, you don't have enough money to buy me off." And when the owners cast another vote, this time unanimous, in favor of selecting a new commissioner as soon as possible, Chandler said, "What kind of eminent person would take the job, in view of the way you are treating me?"[36]

Sportswriters were divided on how well Chandler had done his job and on why the owners had decided to oust him. Historian William Marshall concluded that "Chandler's downfall was not precipitated by one specific instance but instead was instigated by a minority . . . who either came to the conclusion that the commissioner had outlived his usefulness or held specific grievances against him." Chandler returned to his Cincinnati office and finished negotiations with Gillette and Mutual on a six-year, $6,000,000 contract to televise the All-Star game and the World Series with all the money earmarked for the pension plan.[37]

As the year ended, the editors at the *Sporting News* lauded major league and minor league club owners for exhibiting a "spirit of sacrifice" in the face of international uncertainty. "Many clubs and several leagues," read an editorial, "found themselves in desperate straits, but by patching here and making temporary repairs there, they displayed a determination to fight it out on the same line all next summer, come what may." The editors concluded that "the year 1951 looms as fraught with many uncertainties and misgivings and none realize it more than those in baseball. But the game's representatives at St. Petersburg demonstrated they were mentally, if not wholly physically, equipped to shoulder their obligations, ready and willing to answer any call made by the nation."[38]

5

Facing Manpower Shortages, January–March 1951

Club owners approached the start of the 1951 season with a good deal of trepidation. They began the year with a lame-duck commissioner and no clear path toward selecting his successor. The economics of their business remained tight as players continued to demand higher salaries. Most immediately, they faced an extended spring training bound to put an additional strain on their pocketbooks. But overriding all this was their concern about what might happen in Korea.

After major league owners voted in December not to renew Commissioner Happy Chandler's contract, they established a four-man search committee—Ellis Ryan of the Cleveland Indians, Del Webb from the New York Yankees, Phil Wrigley of the Chicago Cubs, and Boston Braves owner Lou Perini—to review applicants and nominees. These four cast a wide net for candidates, including businessmen, politicians, military leaders, judges, and baseball officials, but they found their task difficult. Edgar G. Brands reported in January that the job, as he saw it, would require a broad set of attributes. The new commissioner, he wrote, would have broad and deep authority over the game. He would need to be a business executive, a public relations man, a diplomat, and a fluent public speaker. In addition, he would have to have a prominent personality, know the rules and procedures of the game, and be willing to express his love for the National Pastime.[1]

The committee intended to submit its report at an owners' meeting in February, but that gathering was canceled. Instead, Chandler called a meeting for March 12 in Miami Beach, ostensibly to consider the committee's winnowed list of candidates but perhaps to save his job. According to William Marshall, "Chandlerlites hoped that the meeting would turn out to be a successful referendum on his own candidacy." Indeed, National League owners met the day before and "unanimously voted that at the Joint Meeting on March 12 the National League vote in favor of the proposition that the consideration of candidates for the election of a Commissioner be confined to the candidacy of A. B. Chandler."[2]

Convening at the oceanfront Shoremede Hotel, the owners first rejected by secret ballot a motion to hold an open vote on renewing Chandler's contract. Thereafter, Walter O'Malley of the Brooklyn Dodgers moved that Chandler be reelected to a second seven-year term, and Clark Griffith of the Washington Senators offered a second. Exactly as in December, nine owners voted for Chandler and seven against, but getting just nine votes again left him three short of the required three-fourths majority. The commissioner, who had left the room during the vote, returned and said, "Naturally, I regret this action, but I want to make it as easy as possible for baseball to elect a desirable successor and will cooperate to that end to the fullest extent." With Chandler fully out of the picture, Wrigley told the press that the screening committee would proceed. "Our job now," he said, "is to try to analyze the job, try to set out the requirements, and formulate a pattern which may be acceptable to all."[3]

In January, the *Sporting News* reported on significant decreases in attendance at night games in 1950. Figures compiled by the major leagues' service bureaus, that is, their publicity departments, revealed that "night ball, counted upon as a bonanza that would make everybody in the majors rich, is following the general trend—downward." In fact, night game attendance in 1950 had dropped by 14 percent, a decline that would have been even greater had not the Philadelphia Phillies registered an extraordinary 62 percent increase at their night games. The story noted that "those seeking greater remuneration in 1951 have a good argument when they point to night attendance as playing an important role in the finances of a club. . . . But they have said little or nothing to indicate they appreciate the fact that night crowds fell off in 1950 in the same proportion as the overall attendance."[4]

Financial data released at the annual meeting of the Indians' sixty-nine stockholders in January showed how tight the economics of running a major league club could be. The Cleveland club made a profit in 1950 with receipts of $3,887,000 against expenditures of $3,427,000. The team grossed $2,900,000 from ticket sales, $280,000 from selling concessions and scorecards, and $250,000 from the sale of radio and television rights. They paid out $550,000 in salaries to players and coaches, $356,000 in executive and staff compensation, $179,000 to operate their scouting system (plus $33,000 for working agreements), and $171,000 to rent Municipal Stadium. Stockholders seemed pleased with this balance sheet, but Ryan announced that the club would not pay a dividend. Thirty-eight percent of the club's profits went to satisfy its federal tax bill, and the remainder was used to help retire the loan taken when Ryan and his partners bought the club in 1949.[5]

Financial conditions like Cleveland's did not dissuade players from asking for higher salaries. Yankees general manager George Weiss said in January that clubs faced "a runaway salary situation, about which most of us can do nothing at this time." Conveniently ignoring the reserve clause that gave each club ultimate authority on players' salaries, Weiss complained that "you do not have any success in efforts to teach a winning ball club the elements of political economy and the laws of finance." A few weeks later, Weiss noted that reserve outfielder Cliff Mapes, who played 108 games in 1950, batted .247, and drove in sixty-one runs, had returned his contract unsigned because he did not like the increase the club offered. "We have won two straight world's championships and have been drawing over two million a season," Weiss said, "and out of these circumstances have grown salary demands which, if acceded to, would land us away over the $600,000 mark." Weiss added that Joe DiMaggio, about to play his thirteenth season in the majors, would be offered $100,000, the same salary as in 1949 and 1950. After the Yankees' star agreed to that amount during a telephone call, he said, "Am I satisfied with my contract? Sure, what's the use of squawking? I am happy with it. I would not have signed if I were not happy."[6]

The *Sporting News* asked editorially "where will the inflation in the game stop and what will be the consequences if it isn't halted," but a majority of 352 subscribers polled by the weekly disagreed that players' salaries were too high.

They also opposed, by a narrower margin, a club limit on salaries, as there was in the minors. But many of these readers decried the high salaries being paid some of the game's biggest stars. Solid majorities agreed that DiMaggio and Ted Williams of the Boston Red Sox [$125,000] did not merit the salaries their clubs were paying them, but that Stan Musial of the St. Louis Cardinals deserved his [$75,000]. Roger K. Baird of Aberdeen, South Dakota, doubted "if Ted Williams, Joe DiMaggio, and Stan Musial are worth the salaries mentioned, because no one can be quite that good," but William D. Ott from Columbia, South Carolina, disagreed. "I think that Williams, DiMaggio, and Musial are worth every cent they get and can get. Let us not forget that the years of a player's career are very limited," he wrote.[7]

Cincinnati Reds president Warren Giles offered a counterweight, arguing that newspaper stories about high salaries and bonuses paid to prospects often mentioned exaggerated figures that were harmful to the game. He suggested that fans as well as players got distorted ideas from the figures reported in the press. Agreeing with Giles, another club official said, "You would be astounded, if you saw the figures, what they actually are. But no club will give actual figures, even on players transferred to it, because there is an unwritten law that the salaries or payments involved are a private matter between the club and player." Giles concurred, adding that "a printed account of bonuses and salaries rarely shows the true picture, and in most cases, figures are greatly exaggerated. Most of the time they reflect the writer's idea and are not based on information officially announced." He admitted that "clubs are not entirely blameless, however, because rarely, if ever, does a club attempt to correct the situation, probably because these high figures tend to glamorize the player and arouse in the public a desire to see him." Indeed, later research revealed that while Musial likely earned $75,000 in 1951, the salaries for Williams and DiMaggio probably topped out at $90,000.[8]

A *Sporting News* headline proclaimed, "Training for '51 Season to Be Costliest in History." All clubs observed the March 1 date for the official start of spring training, but a few, including the Dodgers, invited some players to participate in voluntary workouts a week or so before. Dan Daniel explained that while some fans thought clubs made "vast profits" during the spring, in recent years the cost for some clubs had risen to $30,000, reaching "financial heights never before dreamed of . . . so that breaking even on training is virtually impossible." Some clubs were inviting as many as two hundred players to camp, Daniel wrote, and some were paying premium rates at hotels that would prefer vacationers who would stay longer. In addition, "complicating things for the ball clubs, financially, is the rule, now four years old, which forces them to pay each player $25 a week for tips, laundry and other incidental expenses through the training season."[9]

General Walker's successor, named at General MacArthur's request, was Lieutenant General Matthew Ridgway, vice chief of staff of the army. Halberstam's assessment was that Ridgway was quite remarkable, "the best the American army had" and the man President Truman and the Joint Chiefs of Staff would have chosen to prosecute the war if MacArthur had not already been stationed in Tokyo. Ridgway had a superb record. He had planned the airborne invasion of Sicily in 1943 and jumped with his division on D-Day in 1944. He had also been in line to lead an airborne assault against Japan if the war had not ended after American atomic weapons annihilated Hiroshima and Nagasaki.[10]

Ridgway was known as a "soldier's soldier," thriving at the front line and interacting with his troops in a way totally unlike MacArthur, all the while with a hand grenade and a medical kit strapped to his chest. He was an imposing man with a forceful personality, and he believed that the men under his command were the direct descendants of all the troops who had come before, going all the way back to the horrific winter at Valley Forge. A Spartan in behavior, "he worried," Halberstam wrote, "that America was in decline because of the country's ever greater materialism." A fierce anti-Communist, he nevertheless accepted that Korea would be a limited war.[11]

Ridgway was enjoying an after-dinner drink in Washington when he got the news that he would replace Walker. He told his wife the next morning, packed a few things, and flew to Tokyo and then to Seoul, arriving on December 26. The first thing he noticed, Halberstam wrote, was the cold. "It stuck to the bone," he remembered, and he was shocked by the conditions he found when he went to the front. The new commander saw low morale, bad food, and poor clothing. In addition, "All intelligence could show me was a big red goose egg out in front of us with '174,000' [the total number of enemy troops in the area] scrawled in the middle of it," he wrote.[12]

Ridgway had contemplated a rapid counteroffensive, but, as he later wrote, "I had discovered that our forces were simply not mentally and spiritually ready for the sort of action I had been planning. . . . This was a bewildered army, not sure of itself or its leaders, not sure what they were doing there, wondering when they would hear the whistle of that homebound transport." He visited every headquarters he could, sometimes down to the company level, and he demanded that troops get out of their warm jeeps and trucks and begin to patrol the hills, the cold be damned. "Nothing but your love of comfort binds you to the roads," he said. "Find the enemy and fix him in position. Find them! Fix them! Fight them! Finish them!"[13]

On New Year's Eve, the Chinese army, aided by reconstituted North Korean forces, began a new offensive, the first of three over the next six months designed to conquer all of Korea. The Chinese government announced that the offensive's goal was "to liberate Korea . . . crush the imperialist aggression . . . [and] drive warmonger MacArthur into the sea." Ridgway bought some time by ordering a controlled retreat to a line about seventy miles south of the parallel, even though this meant seeing Seoul change hands for the third time, which happened on January 4. The general also worked to stabilize his troops' defensive capabilities by bringing in more artillery and air power.[14]

As Ridgway attempted to hold the line after the longest retreat in American military history, some 275 miles, the Joint Chiefs in Washington sent MacArthur a new directive. The administration did not consider Korea a place to fight a major war, the order said, and the general would get no reinforcements. But, JCS continued, he must defend the line and stay on in Korea. "A successful resistance to Chinese-North Korean aggression at some position in Korea," the directive said, "would be of great importance to our national interest."[15]

MacArthur's "scorching reply," in British historian David Rees's words, was a counter-proposal with four parts, not exactly new: blockade China; destroy China's industrial capacity to wage war; ship Nationalist Chinese troops to Korea as reinforcements; and allow the Nationalists to pursue diversionary actions against the Chinese mainland. In other words, no limited war. Washington shot back, not only with a series of documents, including a personal letter from Truman, but also with a visit to Tokyo and Korea by Army Chief of Staff J. Lawton Collins, Air Force Chief of Staff Hoyt Vandenberg, and Walter Bedell Smith, head of the Central Intelligence Agency.[16]

This trio of officials learned that the overall situation in Korea was not as dire as the picture MacArthur had painted. As Rees wrote, they "saw for themselves that Ridgway was curing the bug out fever" and "that offensive preparations were under way." Moreover, they came to understand that Ridgway, "less than a month out of the Pentagon, must have known what Truman wanted in Korea, fully agreed with that policy, and had his own ideas on how to fight for it, which were soon to be spectacularly demonstrated."[17]

Ridgway had begun a series of offensive operations designed to turn the tide of the war once again. Some of these forays were focused on gathering intelligence, but others had another purpose. "I'm not interested in real estate," the general said, "just killing the enemy." Operation WOLFHOUND determined that there were no large enemy forces close to the front lines. Operations THUNDERBOLT and PUNCH resulted in over 4,200 Chinese dead versus seventy UN fatalities. Operation KILLER united seven US divisions across the front, retook Seoul on February 14, and pushed to within thirty miles of the parallel. Operation RIPPER followed, and by the end of March, UN troops had regained almost all the territory south of the parallel.[18]

More than any other factor, it was Ridgway's personality that made the difference. Brushing aside MacArthur's histrionics, he insisted on renewed commitments to training and discipline. Ignoring the confused international politics, soldiers under his command began to fight not for a cause but because they were ordered to do so. As a regimental commander told *Time* magazine, "the boys aren't up there fighting for democracy now. They're fighting because the platoon leader is leading them, and the platoon leader is fighting because of the command, and so on right to the top."[19]

Following MacArthur's December meetings with his superiors, Washington attempted to silence him, but he continued to give interviews to the Tokyo press corps, complaining that prosecuting the conflict in Korea as a limited war should be unthinkable. Truman and his advisers were losing their patience, but almost no one had the temerity to suggest the removal of such a legendary figure as MacArthur, especially after Inchon. The only one who had, in fact, advanced this bold idea was Ridgway himself before he had been dispatched to Korea. He asked Vandenberg why the Joint Chiefs simply did not *tell* MacArthur what to do. Vandenberg responded, "He wouldn't obey the orders. What can we do?" Ridgway's answer was straightforward. "You can relieve any commander who won't obey orders, can't you," he said.[20]

Chandler rejoiced in January when he signed the contract with Gillette and Mutual covering telecasts of the All-Star Game and the World Series, but as James R. Walker and Robert V. Bellamy Jr. pointed out, he had essentially frozen television rights fees for more than half a decade at 1950 prices when just 9 percent of American homes owned a television. Just a few weeks later, the Senators concluded that television could be a curse as well as a blessing. They reduced the number of home games they would allow to be televised from seventy-seven to twenty-one. Club president Griffith said, "I'm taking a cut in revenues from television, but I'm convinced it is the practical move. There is no substitute for fans in the park." Griffith noted that his club had drawn seventy thousand more fans when it finished eighth in 1949 than it had in 1950 when it finished fifth, and he blamed television for the slide in attendance. Besides, he added, "We can't sell our concessions to folks who see the games in their living rooms. And our surveys show that our fans spend nearly forty cents per capita on concessions when they come to our games."[21]

Weiss believed that major league baseball would benefit from television eventually, but he expressed sympathy for the plight of the minor leagues. "I regret greatly major league TV and radio in minor league areas," he said. "I am hopeful that soon the problems of the minors, as they trace to video and radio, will be solved through major league agreements." But some minor league owners decided they could not wait. In Kansas City, Parke Carroll, general manager of the American Association Blues, announced that his club would play Wednesday, Saturday, and Sunday home games in the afternoon to avoid conflicting with evening television. The Buffalo Bisons in the International League did much the same thing in addition to beginning night games earlier and reviving Ladies' Day, a feature abandoned more than a decade before. In the Pacific Coast League, six clubs had televised home games in 1950, but as of February only two, the Los Angeles Angels and the Seattle Rainiers, had deals in place for 1951.[22]

What was needed, the minors decided, was a coordinated radio and television policy across all leagues. To this end, the National Association appointed Matty Brescia, a public relations entrepreneur with experience in broadcasting, to a new position to do just that. Within a few weeks, the National Association of Broadcasters and the Radio-Television Manufacturers Association distributed to their members a package of ideas that listed thirty-one ways to promote baseball, radio, and television. "A proper working agreement between baseball executives and broadcasters," said William B. Ryan, president of the Broadcasters' Advertising Bureau, "will not only insure continued radio-baseball service to the public, but also convince club owners that a medium which has proved its ability to sell all kinds of service can also sell baseball games."[23]

Baseball's rules committee met in New York in February and Miami Beach in March, but it made no significant changes to the rule book adopted just a year before. The committee made a few grammatical changes and some small edits aimed at closing loopholes, eliminating contradictions, and clarifying uncertain wording. A proposal to allow a so-called courtesy runner to replace an injured player temporarily did not pass, and the new balk rule, requiring the pitcher, with one or more runners on base, to stop for one full second at the set position before delivering the pitch to the plate, was vigorously endorsed. National League president Ford Frick said that he would insist that his league's umpires enforce the rule, noting that pitchers in 1950 had adjusted to the mandated pause and that the number of balks had decreased as the season went on.[24]

On January 26, the Hall of Fame announced that the BBWAA had elected Mel Ott and Jimmie Foxx as the Hall's newest members. Some 266 ten-year members of the BBWAA voted with 170 votes (75 percent) required for election. Ott received 197 votes and Foxx 179. Paul Waner missed by eight votes and Harry Heilman by seventeen. This election brought membership in the Hall to sixty, with just twenty-three of them elected by the writers.[25]

A week later, the National League commenced a three-day celebration in New York to mark the seventy-fifth anniversary of its founding in 1876. Plans for an elaborate jubilee jointly feting both major leagues and the National Association had been shelved, but the league went ahead with a smaller program, calling it an anniversary. On February 2, the league hosted six hundred guests, including sixteen living members of the Hall of Fame and ninety-year-old Arlie Latham, whose major league career began in 1880, for a dinner at the Grand Central Hotel, formerly the Broadway Central Hotel, the site of the league's founding. The following day, Frick entertained his guests privately, and on Sunday, February 4, they were feted at the annual dinner of the BBWAA's New York chapter.[26]

At the writers' dinner, Chandler, the main speaker, addressed baseball's future given the war in Korea. "The situation in 1941 is completely paralleled by what we in the national pastime face right now," he said. "Now, as we are about to begin another championship season, the familiar dark clouds dim our horizon. We will play baseball as long as sixteen major league clubs can field nine men, or until Washington tells us to desist."[27]

The war was indeed on baseball's mind. In January, three minor leagues, the Southeastern League and the Alabama State League, both revived in 1946, and the Rio Grande League, having played only in 1949 and 1950, all suspended operations. Southeastern League president Stuart X. Stephenson blamed his league's demise on three factors, "barren territory," that is, loss of two clubs during the previous season; economics, with little chance to recoup 1950's losses; and war scare. "We will be back," he promised, but in fact neither his league nor either of the other two ever played again.[28]

In January, Secretary of Defense George Marshall testified before a Congressional committee. He responded to inquiries that some baseball players and other athletes might be receiving preferential treatment from Selective Service as they had during World War II. Marshall told the House Armed Services Committee, "I don't think there will be any repetition of that." He announced that baseball players and professional athletes with physical defects would not be deferred and classified 4-F but would be called for limited service. Assistant Secretary of Defense Anna Rosenberg later explained that athletes would be treated like everyone else. Both major league presidents quickly concurred with Marshall, and National Association president George Trautman said, "If the country's young baseball players can qualify for military service, that's where they should be. We will adapt our game to the needs of government during the present emergency."[29]

At a National League meeting in February, Cardinals owner Fred Saigh moved that the league buy 2,500 copies of each week's issue of the *Sporting News* at ten cents per copy and distribute them to servicemen and hospitals. The motion passed.[30]

Slowly, but seemingly inexorably, the number of minor leaguers and major leaguers lost to military service continued to grow. In January, the Chicago White Sox reported that seventeen players in their organization had been called to serve, and the Pittsburgh Pirates said they had lost twenty-four farmhands and two major leaguers, shortstop Danny O'Connell and pitcher Bill Macdonald. Other major leaguers called included Preston Ward, Cleveland outfielder Jim Lemon, and Dodgers pitcher Erv Palica, who hoped he would be assigned to kitchen duty because he was, in his wife's opinion, a "pretty good cook" at home. Minor leaguers summoned included Reds prospect Ed Bailey, Yankees prospect Bill Skowron, Dodgers prospect Dick Williams, and Pirates bonus player Paul Pettit. Ward's induction brought the number of National League players in the service to twenty-three, nearly matched by twenty-one from the American League. Only the Philadelphia A's and the Senators had not lost a player.[31]

Former catcher and manager Mickey Cochrane, who served in the Navy during World War II and ran the baseball program at the Great Lakes Naval Training Center near Chicago, passed a physical and prepared to be recommissioned as a lieutenant commander. George Sisler Jr., another veteran and a former Cardinals executive, reported to Fifth Army headquarters in Chicago to become an assistant special services officer.[32]

Private Al Aber, who had pitched one game for Cleveland in 1950 before being inducted into the Army and sent to Ft. Benning, Georgia, for basic training, contributed to the war effort in a unique way, teaching other soldiers how to throw a hand grenade. He explained, "The old way was to throw grenades with a sidearm, stiff-arm motion. Now they've decided a pitching motion is best. The lieutenant called on me to demonstrate. I just wound up and threw." Following basic training, during which Aber lost twelve pounds, the Army sent him to Military Police School at Camp Gordon, Georgia.[33]

Not all players summoned by Selective Service were called to serve. Red Sox pitcher Chuck Stobbs was rejected because of asthma, and Yankees prospect Mickey Mantle, a 19-year-old shortstop, got deferred because of acute osteomyelitis in his left ankle. The Army found Detroit Tigers pitcher Art Houtteman, who had been drafted in October, "not fully qualified for combat duty with an infantry division." He got to pitch for the camp baseball team. Marine private Spere Spiliotis, a Cardinals catching prospect drafted in August, was less fortunate. He was wounded in Korea, lost part of his left leg, and risked losing his right big toe because of frostbite.[34]

6

Truman Fires MacArthur, April–June 1951

As the minor leagues prepared for the start of the 1951 season, club owners realized that the era of post-World War II prosperity for their business was ending. Postwar attendance had grown to unprecedented heights. More than thirty-two million fans attended minor league games in 1946 and more than forty million in each of the next three years. In 1950, this happy trend ground to a halt. Total attendance fell by more than seven million. As the 1951 season began, two new leagues entered the fray, but ten established leagues went out of business. A year later, the National Association published *The Story of Minor League Baseball*, an official history. It offered this explanation: "The decline in the number of leagues is easily explained by the fact that hundreds of players were going into service and that there was a feeling of uncertainty across the nation concerning the imminence of all-out war."[1]

The start of the season provided no mitigation. When the Pacific Coast League opened its season on March 27, the four games in Los Angeles, Oakland, Sacramento, and San Diego drew a total of 27,811 fans, 13,363 fewer than on Opening Day in 1950, down 32 percent. The Southern Association, to give another example, drew 56,853 fans to its eight opening games, 3,251 below 1950's total, and its lowest total on Opening Day in five years. Both league presidents blamed cold weather for the poor starts, but after a month of play in the PCL, total attendance was still down 31 percent from 143,352 in 1950 to 98,921.[2]

The *Sporting News* took note of these disturbing numbers and faulted the minor leagues themselves. "Minor league club owners blame radio and television broadcasts of major league games," the editorial said, "but this reasoning falls flat in the face of the actual facts. . . . It is not the televising of ball games that cuts into minor league attendance, but television itself. . . . Television is moving ahead rapidly, improving all the time. . . . What is baseball doing to keep pace?" Very little, the editorial continued. "Most minor league clubs are in search of angels, meaning major league sponsors. Once they form affiliations with major league clubs, they sit back and take things for granted."[3]

Maybe it was time, the editors proposed, for the minors to revert to their former business model, to recruit retiring players to run minor league clubs and help develop talent independently of major league farm systems. "Baseball was never before as good an investment as it is today. . . . The opportunity . . . beckons to men who know baseball and are willing to work, who have faith in the game that provided them with a livelihood and will mean even bigger earnings to them if they have the good sense to cash in on their knowledge."[4]

The major leagues, on the other hand, approached the season with some optimism with several clubs particularly enthusiastic about a promising crop of rookies. The Pittsburgh Pirates were hoping that Bob Friend, a 20-year-old right-handed pitcher from West Lafayette, Indiana, could make the grade after just one year in the minors. The Brooklyn Dodgers put some faith in Rocky Bridges, a 23-year-old infielder who had already served five months in the army and received a medical discharge. The Cleveland Indians, New York Yankees, and St. Louis Cardinals were looking at a trio of right-handed pitchers, Bob Chakales, Tom Morgan, and Joe Presko, respectively.[5]

The Yankees were also counting on Mickey Mantle to be their next star. The youngster from Commerce, Oklahoma, had played only two seasons in the minors, but when he arrived at spring training, clubhouse manager Pete Sheehy assigned him uniform number 6, a not-so-subtle suggestion that he was supposed to follow Babe Ruth (#3), Lou Gehrig (#4), and Joe DiMaggio (#5) into the Yankees' pantheon. Mantle was already a prodigious switch-hitter, but his defense at shortstop left much to be desired. Shockwaves reverberated through the Yankees' camp when DiMaggio told three New York sportswriters that 1951 would be his last season, but this announcement gave manager

Casey Stengel an opening: move Mantle to right field where he could learn the outfield playing next to DiMaggio in center.[6]

The New York Giants had their eyes on an emerging phenom, too. Willie Mays had played with the Birmingham (Alabama) Black Barons in the Negro American League in 1948, two years before he graduated from high school and signed a contract with New York. In 1950, he hit .353 in eighty-one games with Trenton (New Jersey) in the Interstate League. The Giants assigned him to the Minneapolis Millers in the American Association for 1951. He hit .408 in the spring for the Millers and showed enough promise to prompt veteran sportswriter Halsey Hall to write, "You watch him run and throw and hit, and you are on his side in a minute."[7]

At least two major league club owners looked beyond the upcoming season and urged their partners to engage with the potential of the future. Chicago Cubs president Phil Wrigley asserted that "the entire map of Organized Ball should be reorganized, and progressive business methods should be adopted so that baseball can keep pace with the growth of our great nation." Looking particularly at Los Angeles where he owned the minor league Angels, Wrigley went on to say, "I don't believe it is fair for eleven [sic] cities in the United States to have what amounts to a perpetual monopoly on major league baseball." But he admitted that "the heads of Organized Baseball move slowly. Getting the major leagues to take action like this is a slow and tedious process."[8]

Boston Braves president Lou Perini echoed Wrigley's interest in the West Coast. Taking note of the Pacific Coast League's repeated pleas to become a third major league, he argued instead for expanding each existing league from eight teams to twelve. Perini said that he would look to Triple-A cities as candidates for expansion. "Let's start with Montreal," he said, "the French-Canadian city of a million people to our north." He added, "a jump to California would not be illogical, and that—I would guess—would include two northern teams (San Francisco and Oakland) and two southern teams (Los Angeles and Hollywood)." He went on to ask if Chicago might host a third club or Detroit a second or if Milwaukee, Baltimore, or Houston might prove suitable. "Within twenty-five years," he concluded, "California will have more people than any other state in the USA. Can the major leagues afford to stand still?"[9]

Yet Organized Baseball's present was rocky enough to dissuade too much focus on the future. Commissioner Happy Chandler had said that he would step down as soon as his successor was named, but that process had bogged down, and several owners expressed their impatience over his reluctance to leave. One highly placed official told the *Chicago Tribune* on March 31 that the owners would soon demand his resignation or even abolish the commissioner's office, a move that would leave the game's governance in the hands of a four-person Executive Council. Over the next few weeks, the two sides came to an agreement. Chandler's attorneys negotiated a separation that paid the departing commissioner his full salary and indemnified him against personal liability in any lawsuits involving his tenure in office. Chandler signed the agreement on June 21 and wrote in July 15 as his retirement date.[10]

The game's economics were uncertain, too. Dan Daniel reported in April that general overhead was at an all-time high, but that ticket prices remained static. "Even the most opulent owners," he wrote, "are not disposed to use red ink." The Yankees, he said, anticipated total operating expenses of two million dollars. "There are a few club owners," he wrote, "who believe that lifting admission prices is inevitable," but most "like to think that, amid all the inflationary turmoil, baseball has held the price line, as the greatest, cheapest popular show."[11]

In addition, Congressman Emanuel Celler (D-NY), chair of the House Judiciary Committee, told sportscaster Bob Wolff on May 15 that his subcommittee on monopoly power would soon begin an inquiry into baseball's antitrust status and particularly the reserve clause. "Many complaints have reached us regarding the reserve clause," he said, adding that "If the reserve clause is essential, so be it. If it is illegal, something must be done about it."[12]

On April 5, the Eighth Army launched yet another offensive, this one called Operation RUGGED. Its goal was to advance the UN position from phase line IDAHO, just south of the parallel, to a series of phase lines called, from south to north, KANSAS, UTAH, and WYOMING, just above the parallel. On the evening of April 11, while General Ridgway was at the front in a snowstorm supervising preparations for an assault on a Chinese stronghold, he learned that he had been appointed General MacArthur's successor. It was a stunning development.[13]

Official Washington had been consumed for weeks by a prolonged discussion, dubbed "the Great Debate," about the future of American foreign policy. The Truman administration had its supporters in Congress and the press, but MacArthur had his congressional allies, including Robert Taft. In brief, the administration regarded Western Europe as more important than the Far East, feared the possibility of a Soviet attack, and desired to reap the benefits of the Marshall Plan and strengthen NATO. Given these priorities, including stationing American troops on European soil, the conflict in Korea had to remain a limited war.[14]

Taft had long been part of the isolationist wing of the Republican Party. His biographer wrote that "he had opposed American military commitments to Europe in 1940 and 1941, tried to cut funding for the Marshall Plan, and voted against NATO." But in 1951, his position on Asia was less consistent. He told reporters that he would not have committed American troops to South Korea's defense when the invasion began and that he would have unleashed Chiang Kai-shek, as MacArthur had wanted. Yet, by allying himself with the general, he also associated himself with a group of senators and congressmen, labeled "Asia-firsters," who demanded an American military presence in Asia, and with crude red-baiting people such as Joe McCarthy and Richard Nixon.[15]

On March 20, two matters of import had collided. First, the Joint Chiefs told the general that the president planned to ask the UN to seek a negotiated settlement with China. MacArthur exploded. He released his own statement on March 24, proposing that he should meet with the Chinese and, if they refused to do so, threaten to invade. In Truman's words, "This was a most extraordinary statement for a military commander of the United Nations to issue on his own responsibility. It was an act . . . in open defiance of my orders as President and as Commander in Chief."[16]

On the same day, MacArthur sent a letter to Representative Joseph Martin (R-MA), the House minority leader, responding to a speech Martin had given in February in which he had called for victory in Korea. Without victory, he said, "this administration should be indicted for the murder of American boys." The general's letter, verbose and equally blunt, ended thusly: "There is no substitute for victory." On April 5, Martin read it aloud on the House floor.[17]

Truman now knew that he had to act. He later wrote that he had made up his mind before April 5, but he nevertheless used the next several days to consult with his closest advisers and with the Joint Chiefs. On Monday, April 9, he told a small group that he had decided back on March 24 to relieve MacArthur. The chairman of the Joint Chiefs prepared the orders with the intention that Secretary of the Army Frank Pace fly to Tokyo and deliver them to MacArthur in person. A news leak truncated this plan and led to a White House news conference at 1:00 a.m. on April 11. Truman's announcement noted the policy differences he had with the general, but it stressed the basic constitutional principle that no military commander could be allowed to challenge the president's authority as commander-in-chief.[18]

MacArthur left Tokyo quietly, but he returned home to a tumultuous welcome. The great American hero met huge crowds in Hawaii and San Francisco before reaching Washington. There he met with the Joint Chiefs and gave a thirty-four-minute speech to a joint session of Congress. He outlined his policy differences with the administration, paused for applause thirty times, and in his final paragraph included the memorable line, "Old soldiers never die; they just fade away." A parade along Pennsylvania Avenue followed, and the next day a ticker-tape parade in New York drew an enormous crowd. Over the next few days, the White House received over twenty-seven thousand letters and telegrams, most of them disapproving of the president's decision.[19]

When Ridgway replaced MacArthur, Lieutenant General James Van Fleet, a corps commander during World War II and more recently the leader of the Joint US Military Advisory Group fighting against Communists in the Greek civil war, replaced Ridgway as head of the Eighth Army. As Ridgway moved to Tokyo, "he took with him," as Hastings wrote, "the military skills he had already displayed in full measure in the peninsula and showed in addition all the discretion and political judgment that had so conspicuously eluded MacArthur."[20]

Van Fleet professed not to know what his goal was as commander of the Eighth Army, but his immediate task was to halt the Chinese spring offensive. This job began on April 22 and became the single greatest military effort of the war. National radio in both North Korea and China projected retaking

Seoul by May and conquering all of Korea, regardless of the consequences, and at first the seven hundred thousand troops under the command of Chinese General Peng Teh-huai met with success. But the defense the UN forces mounted held, aided in no small part by the heroics of the British Brigade, a multinational force from England, Belgium, and Northern Ireland, at the Battle of Gloucester Hill. By the end of the month, the offensive had ground to a halt, and Chinese forces had retreated.[21]

Back in Washington, the uproar surrounding MacArthur's dismissal morphed into hearings held jointly by the Senate's Foreign Relations and Armed Services Committees and lasting almost two months. Senator Richard Russell (D-GA) chaired the proceedings, and MacArthur was the first witness. He testified for three days. Without addressing the conduct that Truman regarded as insubordinate, he railed against the very concept of a limited war. "I do unquestionably state," he said, "that when men become locked in battle, that there should be no artifice under the name of politics, which should handicap your own men."[22]

Many witnesses supported the administration and rebutted MacArthur's point of view. Secretary of Defense Marshall testified that both he and General Eisenhower had often disagreed with their civilian superiors during World War II, but they had never voiced those disagreements in public. MacArthur's actions, he said, were "wholly unprecedented." General Omar Bradley, chairman of the Joint Chiefs, outlined the Truman policy and focused on the futility of fighting a land war against China. "This strategy," he said, "would involve us in the wrong war, at the wrong place, at the wrong time, and with the wrong enemy."[23]

Immediately after the Chinese retreat at the end of April, Van Fleet anticipated a second spring attack and ordered enhanced defensive preparations, including new minefields using napalm and petroleum, carefully focused artillery, and interlocking bands of machine guns. On the night of May 15–16, twelve Chinese divisions attacked, but they made little progress. Within four days, the offensive ended, and UN troops began a counterattack with great success. Chinese troops began surrendering in large numbers, and by the end of June, nearly all territory south of the parallel was under UN control.[24]

The Chinese armies had sustained perhaps seventy thousand casualties during the spring, but Van Fleet pressed his advantage only so far. Truman recalled that the National Security Council, meeting on May 2 and 3, had "distinguished between the political aim—a unified, independent, democratic Korea—and the military aim of repelling aggression and terminating the hostilities under an armistice agreement." But how might such an agreement be reached? Secret talks between East and West commenced in New York, and on June 23, Soviet Foreign Minister Jacob Malik indicated that the "problem of the armed conflict in Korea" could be settled and that "as a first step discussions should be started . . . for a cease-fire and an armistice providing for the mutual withdrawal of forces from the 38th Parallel." On June 30, Ridgway broadcast a message intended for the enemy that he was prepared to name a representative to discuss the cessation of hostilities.[25]

On the cusp of Opening Day, 209 members of the BBWAA cast ballots in the *Sporting News*'s annual poll, and 149 of them picked the Boston Red Sox to win the American League pennant. Despite Boston's frustrations over the preceding few seasons, they outpolled the Yankees, Cleveland, and the Detroit Tigers. In the National League, the writers picked the Giants to unseat the defending champion Philadelphia Phillies with Brooklyn finishing second, Philadelphia third, and the Braves fourth.[26]

Truman made his first public appearance after firing MacArthur nine days later when he threw out the ceremonial first pitch before the Washington Senators' home opener against the Yankees. A *Washington Post* sportswriter reported that the president's appearance drew "a cool greeting and two outbursts of boos." The Air Force Band played "Ruffles and Flourishes" followed by "Hail to the Chief" and drowned out the fans' displeasure. The president wore a special Rawlings glove, the "Harry S. Truman Presidential Model," on his right hand and tossed the ceremonial pitch left-handed. Yankees pitcher Allie Reynolds caught the ball and brought it to Truman for an autograph. A few boys booed again when the president left the ballpark at the end of the game.[27]

The surprise team in the early weeks of the American League pennant race were the Chicago White Sox. Picked to finish in fifth place, Chicago started slowly, but beginning in mid-May, they put together a fourteen-game winning streak, eleven of these victories coming on the road. The White Sox were sparked by an unusual reliance on stolen bases and by the results of a three-team trade that brought them their first player of color, outfielder Orestes Miñoso, called "Minnie." At the end of June, Chicago held on to first place, a half-game ahead of the Yankees and three games ahead of Boston.[28]

With DiMaggio hobbling through his final season, Stengel relied on starting pitching to keep his team in the race. His aging star batted only .278 through the end of June with just six home runs and twenty-seven runs batted in. Mantle, the heir apparent, did only a bit better, hitting .262 with six homers and forty-four runs batted in, and he was sent back to the minors in mid-July. But the Yankees had three outstanding starting pitchers—Eddie Lopat, Vic Raschi, and Reynolds, who doubled as a reliever—and they kept New York in the race.[29]

By the end of June, Brooklyn appeared to be in control of the National League pennant race. Owner Walter O'Malley had replaced manager Burt Shotton with Charlie Dressen, and the lineup seemed to feature a star at nearly every position. By the time O'Malley traded for Andy Pafko to play left field, a deal sportswriter Joe King called "earth-jarring," the Dodgers seemed well on their way to their third pennant in five years. Brooklyn's offense was so powerful that King wrote, "If the Dodgers don't finish first, a saliva test will be in order." The Dodgers took over first place on May 13, and by the end of June, they had a 5½-game lead over New York with the defending champion Phillies tied for fourth, nine games behind.[30]

The Giants had gotten off to a rocky start. After winning two of their first three games, they lost eleven straight and then won eleven of their next fourteen. But they did not get over the .500 mark until May 27, and they did not reach second place until June 12. Manager Leo Durocher, having watched Mays play in spring training, had lobbied owner Horace Stoneham to include the youngster on the Opening Day roster, but Stoneham resisted. Mays collected twelve hits in his first week in Minneapolis, and he was hitting .477 when Durocher got his way in mid-May. Mays doubted that he was good enough to hit major league pitching, and in fact, he went hitless in his first twelve at-bats before hitting a home run against Warren Spahn, the Braves' star left-hander.[31]

Off the field, Organized Baseball found itself entangled with the federal government in several ways. Celler's announcement that his subcommittee would hold hearings was not the first blow. Earlier, Attorney General J. Howard McGrath had ordered the FBI to investigate whether baseball's 1949 Rule 1(d) restraining radio broadcasts and telecasts of major league games in minor league territories was legal. McGrath anticipated that the investigation would take from thirty to sixty days and noted that an adverse finding might lead the Justice Department to go to court and bring an antitrust action against baseball.[32]

Rule 1(d) was being attacked from both sides. Four States Broadcasters, Inc., operators of radio station KFSB in Joplin, Missouri, sued the Joplin Miners in the Western Association for refusing to allow the station to broadcast Cardinals' games when the Miners were playing at home. Simultaneously, radio station WFIN-FM in Findlay, Ohio, sued the nearby Lima (Ohio) Phillies in the Ohio-Indiana League, the Philadelphia Phillies (Lima's parent club), and the Indians for refusing the station's proposal to broadcast Indians' games while the Lima club was playing at home.[33]

On the other side, four Michigan clubs in the Central League threatened legal action after Chandler ruled they were not entitled to compensation for alleged losses in attendance caused by Tigers' games being broadcast in their territories. In May, Judge Walter E. Bailey denied the Joplin station's request for a temporary injunction. Two days later, Judge Frank L. Kloeb similarly denied the Findlay station's request for temporary relief. Pending negotiations, the Central League clubs did not sue, but George Malnes, president of the Flint Arrows, said, "All we want to know is who we are to deal with in getting a slice of the $2,000,000 received by major league clubs for broadcast and TV rights."[34]

Nearly simultaneously, members of both houses of Congress introduced legislation to amend antitrust law to exempt baseball and other professional sports, thereby protecting the reserve clause. Senator Edwin C. Johnson (D-CO), who was also president of the Western League, introduced a bill in the Senate, and a trio of congressmen, including A. S. "Bud" Herlong (D-FL), former president of the Florida State League, did so in the House. These bills undergirded Celler's decision to hold hearings. He explained that if baseball needed the reserve clause to survive, "a law must be passed. . . . The matter cannot be allowed to drift as a result of the New York Appeals Court decision to remand the Danny Gardella case back to a lower court for review."[35]

The case to which Celler referred had originated after Chandler banned Gardella, an infielder with the Giants in 1944 and 1945, and others who had jumped from Organized Baseball to play in the outlaw Mexican League in 1946. Gardella sued, challenging both the ban and the reserve clause as antitrust violations. A federal district court judge dismissed the suit, reasoning that he did not have the authority to overturn the 1922 Supreme Court decision that Organized Baseball did not engage in interstate commerce and was not subject to federal antitrust regulation. But the US Court of Appeals for the Second Circuit reversed this ruling and allowed the suit to proceed. This terrified club owners, and one month before the trial was scheduled to begin, Gardella and Organized Baseball settled out of court.[36]

Baseball had been warned, and several other lawsuits underscored the point. Former major league pitcher Jim Prendergast sued in April 1951, arguing that the reserve clause had prevented him from selling his talents on the open market after Syracuse in the International League traded him down to Beaumont in the Texas League where his salary would have been reduced. Onetime Yankees farmhand George Earl Toolson sued in May after New York demoted him from Oakland in the PCL to Binghamton in the Eastern League. Minor league outfielder Walter Kowalski sued in June, complaining that Brooklyn had shuffled him downward in its farm system to protect him from the minor league draft.[37]

Major league baseball's sixteen clubs were located in just ten cities, but in three of them, Boston, Philadelphia, and St. Louis, one club resident therein was skating perpetually on thin financial ice. The St. Louis Browns' position was the most precarious of all. The club was certainly not a success on the field, and off the field, the Browns were a disaster, too. Their annual attendance bottomed out at 80,922 in 1935, and since 1936, when the heirs of the late Phil Ball sold the club, the Browns had changed hands twice more.

In January, co-owners Bill and Charley DeWitt dismissed a rumor that they were about to sell the club to a Milwaukee brewer, but in March, the club negotiated a $600,000 loan from a St. Louis bank, $465,000 to pay off club indebtedness and $135,000 earmarked as working capital. Yet within weeks, rumors circulated that the DeWitts were willing to sell and that Bill Veeck, who had previously owned the Indians, was willing to buy. The deal, announced in June, had the DeWitts selling their shares to a syndicate headed by Veeck with the expectation that he would pursue the purchase of all additional shares, giving him complete ownership of the club "instead of having to deal with some 1,400 scattered stockholders." Said Veeck, "I have come here to accept a challenge and the Browns are it."[38]

Most ballplayers called to serve in the armed forces found themselves beginning to play ball at forts and camps throughout the United States. But some were less fortunate. In April, the *Sporting News* reported that Edward Leneve, a private first class in the Marines and a former minor league catcher, was the first professional ballplayer killed in action in Korea. Leneve died on December 2, 1950, at the Chosin Reservoir, but he was not the first. James Pickett had signed a contract with the Dodgers organization in 1948 and was assigned to the Ponca City (Oklahoma) Dodgers in the KOM League. Pickett joined the Marines instead and was a private first class with the First Marine Division when he was killed on November 30, also at the Chosin Reservoir.[39]

Two more ballplayers were killed in Korea before the All-Star break. George Sulliman, a graduate of Yale who played varsity baseball with future president George H. W. Bush, played in the Cardinals' organization in 1948. He joined the Marine Corps Reserve, and his unit was activated in late 1950. Three weeks after arriving in Korea, he died on April 24, trying to clear a jammed machine gun during a furious battle. Leonard Glica, an infielder from Omaha, played in the Dodgers' organization from 1947 through 1950. He entered the Army on November 30, 1950, was assigned to the Twenty-First Infantry Regiment, Twenty-Fourth Infantry Division, and was killed in action on May 26, just four days after arriving in the war zone.[40]

7

Frick Replaces Chandler, July–September 1951

As the major league season reached the All-Star break, with the game set for Detroit on July 10, Commissioner Happy Chandler's staff was packing up his belongings, but there was no one ready to assume the duties of his office. Plans to fill the job expeditiously after the owners had closed the door on extending Chandler's contract in March had floundered. The list of potential candidates to succeed him, once down to as few as four, had ballooned after Chandler agreed to resign, but the committee in charge of the process did anything but hurry.[1]

Brooklyn Dodgers president Walter O'Malley expressed his frustration at this lack of progress, ticking off the imminent Congressional hearings and "litigation of various sorts going on in many places" as reasons "to obtain the leader who best can co-ordinate our efforts, and go out and hire the varied specialized talent we will require." O'Malley insisted that he had no candidate, but he added that "if [National League president] Ford Frick were nominated, there is a man whom I certainly would not be opposed to. He has done a great job for our league, and I am sure he could do as well for our sport."[2]

Meeting in Detroit, the screening committee agreed to submit a new list of those who met the qualifications for the job at an owners' meeting tentatively set for around August 1 in Washington. In fact, that meeting occurred in New York on August 7, at which time owners trimmed the committee's list of forty names to nine. Four of these nine had not yet been approached to assess their interest in the job, but the *Sporting News* reported that the other five were Frick, Cincinnati Reds president Warren Giles, and three generals, Dwight Eisenhower, Maxwell Taylor, and the recently retired Douglas MacArthur. Later, three of the other four were identified as Penn State University president Milton Eisenhower (the general's younger brother), Ohio governor Frank Lausche, and Air Force general Emmett "Rosie" O'Donnell.[3]

The committee promised an election on August 21 and prepared to present O'Donnell, commander of the Eighth Air Force, as its recommendation, but President Truman declined to release the general from his active-duty commitment. Thus, the list of finalists was revised to include five candidates, Milton Eisenhower, Frick, Giles, Lausche, and MacArthur. Finally, on September 20, at a nine-hour meeting that included fourteen ballots before a dinner break and two after, the owners elected Frick, with Giles immediately replacing him as head of the National League.[4]

Frick had already done his duty as league president, testifying over two days before the Celler subcommittee and taking pains to defend baseball's status quo. In his statement, he explained the reserve clause by saying, "Frankly, gentlemen, I don't see why all the furor about the reserve clause. Basically, it is a long-term contract which is nothing unusual where distinctive personal services are contracted for." When Congressman Patrick Hillings (R-CA) asked about the Pacific Coast League's request to become a third major league, Frick said that "the problem at the time, Mr. Congressman, was that the members of the Pacific Coast League themselves, after a discussion, after we had shown them balance sheets and costs of operations . . . decided that they were not ready for the major league[s]."[5]

Before Celler called the first witness, Dan Daniel predicted that "the committee is expected to go far deeper than the question of the reserve clause, which started the ball rolling. The public is going to learn a lot about the operations of leagues and clubs in both the majors and minors, it is understood, with the officials of O.B. [*sic*] volunteering some information that a reporter could not touch with a ten-foot pole."[6]

The subcommittee took testimony for eight days spread over three weeks. The key witnesses besides Frick, were Ty Cobb, National Association president George Trautman, and Chandler, by then the former commissioner free to speak his mind as a private citizen. From this perch, he declined "to pass on the character and conduct of all the fellows who own clubs, . . . [but] I think there are some owners in American baseball that the sport could do without." He also spoke in favor of expanding the major leagues, saying that "it's inconceivable to me that a country can grow in fifty years and still have just two leagues," but he also defended the reserve clause by declaring that "I think it is not too objectionable to anybody."[7]

Technically, the subcommittee met to consider three bills, each of them written to ensure that antitrust law "shall not apply to organized professional sports enterprises or to acts in the conduct of such enterprises." A committee staff member said, in fact, that "there's a wrong impression that we're trying to hurt the game, [but] I think our investigation will tend to clear up the whole matter for baseball." But the game's leaders were not convinced. They had also heard Celler say that "if baseball is going to be exempted from antitrust laws, it's going to have to change its thinking about a lot of things." Thus, when the chairman announced on August 10 that "it is our plan to resume these hearings in the fall after the World Series," Organized Baseball was not relieved.[8]

Traditionally, owners had held their financial cards close to their vests, but Bill Veeck, new owner of the St. Louis Browns, was hardly a traditionalist. A Marine injured during World War II, he had owned the minor league Milwaukee Brewers during the war and the Cleveland Indians from 1946 to 1949. Veeck rankled other owners not only by integrating the American League in July 1947, but also by staging an array of promotional and publicity stunts designed to attract fans regardless of how his team was playing. In addition, the Indians won the World Series in 1948 and drew home crowds that set an American league attendance record.[9]

As Veeck assumed control of the Browns, he explained how the deal to buy the club had developed. Four cities had approached Veeck to acquire the Browns and move them from St. Louis, but New York Yankees co-owner Del Webb encouraged him to keep the club in St. Louis. The DeWitt brothers, assisted by former Browns owner Donald Barnes, proved amenable to a sale, but finalizing the transaction was contingent upon Veeck's acquiring an additional 17 percent of the stock. That would give his syndicate 75 percent, enough to liquidate the existing corporation, pay off all minority stockholders, and form a new business. This Veeck did on July 3 when a board member sold him 8,572 shares, putting him over the top.[10]

The Browns were in last place on July 4, more than twenty games behind the first-place Chicago White Sox, and their prospects looked none too bright. Veeck promised fans that coming to Sportsman's Park, even to watch a losing team, would be fun, and he went right to work. During a twi-night doubleheader, he announced that drinks were on the house. The club gave out 6,041 soft drinks and 7,596 bottles of beer, and a fireworks show followed the final out. Veeck persuaded Satchel Paige, who had pitched for the Indians, to leave the Chicago American Giants in the Negro American League and return to the majors. He challenged the St. Louis Cardinals to a postseason charity game, and he signed Frank Saucier, the *Sporting News*'s 1950 Minor League Player of the Year, to a contract months after the outfielder had retired from baseball to manage his oil well that was producing 150 barrels a day.[11]

Veeck's most memorable stunt took place on August 19 during a doubleheader against the Detroit Tigers. The Browns were celebrating the fiftieth anniversary of the American League and the supposed fiftieth anniversary of Falstaff Beer, the team's radio sponsor. Veeck hired Eddie Gaedel, three feet seven inches tall, to participate in two stunts. Between games, staffers wheeled onto the field a giant papier-mâché birthday cake out of which Gaedel emerged wearing a St. Louis uniform and the number 1/8. Fans received free beer to mark the occasion. Easily topping this stunt came Gaedel's second appearance. When the Browns came to bat in the bottom of the first inning of the second game, the public address announcer told the crowd that Gaedel would bat in place of Saucier, the listed lead-off batter. As the Tigers protested, the Browns produced a signed contract, and the home plate umpire allowed the game to proceed. Gaedel crouched, making his strike zone impossibly small, and pitcher Bob Cain understandably walked him on four pitches. The following day, league president Will Harridge voided Gaedel's contract. But Veeck had outsmarted his colleagues again.[12]

A spate of games that stretched into the early morning hours moved some to suggest that the major leagues adjust their curfew rules. The American League rule was that no new inning could begin after midnight, but prior to the season, the National League dropped its rule that no inning could begin after 12:50 a.m. In addition, a Pennsylvania law required teams playing Sunday games in either league, including the second games of doubleheaders, not to begin a new inning after 7 p.m.[13]

On August 23, the Dodgers played seventeen innings against the Pirates in Pittsburgh with the game ending at 12:39 a.m. Two nights later, the Philadelphia Phillies played at Pittsburgh. This game lasted fifteen innings and ended at 12:12 a.m. On June 22, the Dodgers were back in Pittsburgh for a game scheduled to begin at 8 30 p.m. The lights failed, and the first pitch was not thrown until 10:44 p.m. The game took only nine innings, but it did not end until 1:56 a.m.[14]

Player representatives for the two leagues urged establishing reasonable curfews, but other players and some fans objected. In addition, how to conclude games cut short by curfew or bad weather remained an issue. In the American League, such games were finalized using the score at the end of the last complete inning, but in the National League, suspended games were resumed at the point of interruption whenever the two teams next met. The *Sporting News* suggested a uniform midnight curfew and pressed the American League to adopt the National League's rule on suspended games. In addition, the weekly editorialized "that the major league club owners take decisive action to keep the action on the field moving and to eliminate the useless delays that have added so much boredom to many a game."[15]

"The outbreak of the Korean War," historian Alonzo Hamby wrote, "instantly revived the fear of inflation." Prices had risen rapidly after the end of World War II as pent-up demand for consumer goods overwhelmed limited supply. This pressure abated after a while, but a wave of scare buying after the North Korean invasion worried economic officials in the administration. The president's approach was, Hamby wrote, to ask Congress "to enact a moderate economic program built around credit controls and government aid for the expansion of vital industries."[16]

Truman did not want to alarm the Soviet Union by proposing anything close to total mobilization, and he trusted economist Leon Keyserling's analysis that an expanding economy could meet both defense and consumer needs, that is, provide both "guns and butter," without inflation. The Defense Production Act, enacted in September 1950, had given the president the authority he wanted, but the Chinese attack forced the administration to change its approach.[17]

After the president declared a national emergency, effective December 16, he asked Congress to approve an excess profits tax, grant him special powers to improve the system for procuring military goods, and give him the authority to impose wage and price controls. Using these authorizations, Truman created the Office of Defense Mobilization under the direction of Charles E. Wilson, who left his job as president of General Electric. The ODM served as an umbrella "super-agency" overseeing the work of nineteen other agencies, including the Economic Stabilization Agency, charged with halting inflation, the Office of Price Stabilization, managing prices for consumer products, the Wage Stabilization Board (WSB), controlling compensation for hourly employees, and later, the Salary Stabilization Board (SSB), to control salaries.[18]

The first orders to freeze prices came in January 1951, and initial regulations on freezing wages followed shortly thereafter, albeit haphazardly, in part because Wilson, in Hamby's words, "surrounded himself with other businessmen and failed to appoint even a single liberal farm leader or labor union chief to a responsible policy-making position." Following a vigorous protest from James Patton, president of the National Farmers Union, labor union leaders agreed unanimously to withdraw their representatives from the wage board, and its work slowed.[19]

Regulations governing salary increases were still in draft form as baseball clubs were finalizing players' contracts for the upcoming season. Sportswriter J. Roy Stockton explained that players who had prolonged salary talks might have cost themselves money. "If the wage freeze follows the pattern of the World War II action," Stockton wrote, "the top salary on any ball club will be that club's ceiling and special permission will have to be obtained to boost a man's salary over that top." Indeed, the Wage Stabilization Board announced on April 2 that baseball pay would be subject to the same regulations imposed on other industries. "In effect," reported sportswriter Shirley Povich, "the WSB slapped ceilings on the wages of professional ballplayers in both the major and minor leagues with the ruling that the scale of pay must not exceed the top wage paid by each club in the season of 1950."[20]

This ruling snagged Cardinals star Stan Musial, who had just persuaded owner Fred Saigh to raise his salary from $50,000 to $75,000. Saigh had resisted giving Musial such a large raise at first, but once the contract was signed, the owner declared that he would petition the WSB on the player's behalf. Saigh claimed that Musial was getting a merit raise, allowed under the regulations, but a WSB official said that "the board will probably okay some sort of a raise for Musial, but $25,000 is way out of line with any industry, and baseball is no different from the others." In August, the SSB created a three-man panel to study baseball players' salaries. The panel, including University of Maryland president H. C. Byrd, sportswriter John Kieran, and Ty Cobb, met August 21–22 in New York, but issued no quick decision.[21]

On the other side of the world, the war continued. On July 2, Kim Il Sung and General Peng Teh-huai replied affirmatively to General Ridgway's message of June 30. Instead of acquiescing to Ridgway's suggestion to meet on a Danish hospital ship in Wonsan Harbor, they proposed that talks begin in Kaesong, a village about three miles south of the parallel. Ridgway agreed, and preliminary talks began on July 8. In Washington, the Joint Chiefs thought it might take about three weeks to reach a cease-fire agreement and another three to get an armistice, but it soon became clear to the negotiating team that the Communists would try to define the talks as a UN surrender and to extract from them as much of a propaganda victory as possible.[22]

Vice Admiral C. Turner Joy, who led the UN delegation and later wrote about his experiences, used a baseball analogy to explain how the two sides could differ on almost any issue, including setting an agenda. The UN side, he wrote, might seek to arrange a baseball game by offering a list of suggestions, such as where the game would be played, when it would be played, and who the umpires would be. The Communists, he continued, would counter with their own list of conclusions, such as the game should be played in Shanghai, the game should be played at night, and the umpires should be Chinese.[23]

The UN side soon realized, too, that Kaesong was not located in "no-man's land," but was firmly under Communist control. Various provocative incidents near the talks' location caused Ridgway to suspend negotiations on August 4 for nearly a week, and when they resumed, the two sides stared at each other for more than two hours without a word being spoken. By August 22, not one substantive issue had been settled, and North Korean General Nam Il, his side's chief negotiator, broke off the talks after accusing the UN forces of trying to murder members of his delegation with a napalm bomb.[24]

The UN Command had to decide how much military pressure to apply to advance the negotiations. By August, General Van Fleet had nearly six hundred thousand troops under his command, a fighting force that, in Rees's words, was "the hardest-hitting army the US had ever put into the field up to this time." Later in the month, he authorized a limited but substantial offensive to protect Seoul's water and electric power, to secure key roads running north from the capital, and to inflict as many casualties on the enemy as possible. Intense fighting lasted several weeks, during which American casualties were substantial. Units of the Second Infantry Division seized Heartbreak Ridge on September 5 and neighboring Bloody Ridge on October 13, thus ending the last major UN offensive operation of the war.[25]

The Pacific Coast League continued to bemoan its place in the baseball universe and to seek relief for its grievances. The Celler subcommittee had heard some testimony about the PCL's complaints, including the injustice of the major league draft, but no progress seemed forthcoming. The current rule exposed PCL players to the draft if they had played at least four years in Organized Baseball or spent any time in the majors. Each winter, major league clubs could draft such players for only $10,000 each, far below their market value, with the proviso that each PCL club could lose only one player per year.[26]

PCL owners were upset about several other things, too. They hated that major league clubs cannibalized the PCL audience by playing exhibition games in PCL territory before the PCL season began. They cringed at the fact that PCL fans could sometimes listen on the radio to as many as four major league games a day. But it was the draft that caused the most distress. All we want, PCL owners said, was the right to retain our own stars or sell them to the majors for reasonable prices. San Francisco Seals owner Paul Fagan even threatened to "lock up the park for good" if his league did not get relief from the draft.[27]

In late July, PCL owners met and devised a possible solution. They proposed that each PCL player be allowed to sign a new contract that would specifically exclude the draft proviso unless the player consented to attach a codicil opening himself to the draft. Should this new wrinkle not be approved, the owners came close to moving to sever their league's relationship with Organized Baseball and becoming an independent league. Fagan, not satisfied with the new contract proposal, urged independence, but Bob Cobb, vice president of the Hollywood Stars, argued that "to break away would be suicidal at this time."[28]

Oakland Oaks owner Brick Laws thought that most players would prefer not to expose themselves to the draft. He reminded everyone that PCL players did not receive a bonus when drafted, but players whose contracts PCL clubs sold received part of the purchase price. Yankees co-owner Webb said unofficially that he thought the majors would approve the PCL's proposal, but when the majors responded, they said that every PCL player would have to waive his draft rights for the proposal to be approved. After this rebuff, PCL owners voted unanimously to leave Organized Baseball in 1952. But still holding out hope of reconciliation, they announced that each PCL player would have to sign two contracts on a contingency basis, one to take effect if the league remained in Organized Baseball and a second to be activated if the league went independent.[29]

The American League pennant race remained a close affair between two teams into the season's final week, but the White Sox were not one of these two. They won only eleven of their thirty-two games in July and fell from contention. After play on September 16, the Yankees and the Indians were tied for first place, but Cleveland had played five more games. Thereafter, New York won ten of thirteen while the Indians lost six of nine, and the Yankees clinched their third straight pennant by winning a doubleheader against the Boston Red Sox on September 28.[30]

Allie Reynolds pitched a no-hitter, his second of the season, in the first game of that doubleheader and wound up with seventeen wins. Eddie Lopat and Vic

Raschi won twenty-one games each, but the key to the team's pitching success was the steadying presence of veteran Johnny Sain, acquired from the Boston Braves on August 29. He pitched in seven games down the stretch, winning two and saving one. Rookie Gil McDougald was the only Yankee to bat over .300. Catcher Yogi Berra hit .294 with twenty-seven home runs and eighty-eight runs batted in, and he won the league's Most Valuable Player award.[31]

Joe DiMaggio finished his final season by playing 116 games. He hit .263 with twelve home runs and seventy-one runs batted in. New York recalled Mickey Mantle from Kansas City on August 20, installed him in right field, and gave him uniform number 7. He played in twenty-seven games, batted .284 with six home runs and twenty runs batted in, and moved to center field for the season's last weekend.

The Dodgers came out of the All-Star break by winning thirteen of nineteen games during the rest of July and six of their first nine in August. On August 11, they won the opening game of a doubleheader against the Braves, the first game ever televised in color, and stretched their lead over the second-place New York Giants to 13½ games. Brooklyn and New York had been fierce rivals, both on and off the field, going back to before 1898 when the New York legislature forced the city of Brooklyn into an amalgam called Greater New York that also included Manhattan, Queens, Staten Island, and the Bronx.[32]

Over the years, the Giants had consistently outshone the Dodgers. During the first four decades of the twentieth century, the New York club had finished first in the National League thirteen times and won four World Series. The Brooklynites had finished first only twice and lost the Series both times. The Giants had finished sixth, seventh, or eighth just three times while the Dodgers had finished near the league's bottom twenty times, including a run of five straight sixth-place finishes. The Giants were known as a classy organization whose games attracted leaders from the worlds of politics and entertainment while the Dodgers played so ineptly at times that they earned a pejorative nickname, the "Daffiness Boys." The rivalry was palpable, dividing neighborhoods and even families in Greater New York. Perhaps most famous was an incident that occurred in 1934. When reporters asked Giants manager Bill Terry in January if he feared Brooklyn, he quipped, "Is Brooklyn still in the league?" Yet, on that season's final weekend, Brooklyn defeated New York twice, thereby denying them the pennant.[33]

The Dodgers' rise to respectability began in 1939 when new manager Leo Durocher led them to a third-place finish. Over the next eleven years, they won three pennants and finished second four times. Meanwhile, the Giants tumbled, often finishing in the second division. Yet, in July 1948, Durocher, under pressure from club president Branch Rickey, did the unthinkable. He resigned and immediately became manager of the Giants, who had simultaneously fired Mel Ott. And it was Durocher in charge as the Giants began to stalk the Dodgers in August 1951.[34]

On August 9, the Dodgers swept a doubleheader from the Giants, earning their twelfth win over their rivals against only three losses. But the two teams' clubhouses adjoined each other, and the Dodgers went out of their way while showering to berate their ex-manager and serenade the Giants with a loud and boisterous version of the "Beer Barrel Polka," including the impromptu lyric, "Roll out the barrels, we've got the Giants on the run." On the other side of the wall, the Giants bristled. As team captain Alvin Dark later recalled, "Human beings can only take so much, and we had a belly-full. . . . You just can't treat human beings like they treated us and get away with it."[35]

The Giants' assault began quickly. The Dodgers lost the nightcap of their doubleheader against Boston on August 11, and the lead dropped to thirteen games. The next day the Giants took two games from the Phillies and started a sixteen-game winning streak that included three games against Brooklyn. By August 27, the Dodgers' lead was down to five games. The next day, Brooklyn won, and New York lost, but any celebrating proved premature. After play on September 20, the Dodgers were 92–52 with ten games to play while the Giants were 89–58, 4½ games behind, with seven to play. But New York won all seven of its remaining games while Brooklyn won only four of its last ten, and the two teams wound up in a tie, necessitating the second playoff in National League history.[36]

Everything had jelled for New York during the final third of the season. Willie Mays sparkled defensively in center field and, in Durocher's words, "transformed the whole lineup." Left fielder Whitey Lockman and first baseman Monte Irvin switched positions and prospered. Bobby Thomson moved from center field to third base and hit .357 from July 20 on. On the mound, Sal Maglie and Larry Jansen each wound up with twenty-three wins, and the relief staff, led by George Spencer and Dave Koslo, did its job well. From August 11 through September 30, the Dodgers' record was 26–22, but the Giants' was 37–7.[37]

As exciting as this season was, attendance fell off in both major leagues. Total American League attendance dropped more than 250,000, while the National League's mark was down nearly 1.1 million. In the American League, the Yankees showed a decrease but still drew the most fans, 1,950,107, and the Browns showed an increase but still drew the fewest, 293,790, just a bit over four thousand per home date. In the National League, Brooklyn drew the most fans, 1,282,628, and Boston the fewest, 487,475. Only three teams in each league saw attendance rise. The White Sox saw the greatest increase, more than half a million, and the Braves absorbed the greatest decrease, down 456,916.[38]

During these summer months, three more minor league ballplayers died in Korea. Bill Crago from East Gary, Indiana, was killed in action on July 26 and was posthumously awarded the Silver Star. He had played the outfield with Marion in the Ohio State League in 1947 and with the Fitzgerald Pioneers in the Georgia State League from 1948 through 1950 before entering the Army. John Lazar from Kewanee, Illinois, played in the Browns' farm system in 1947 and 1948 before joining the Army in 1949. After being discharged, he played ball again in 1950, but the Army recalled him to active duty after the season. Lazar was killed by a sniper on September 7 and was posthumously awarded several military honors. Infielder Marcel Poelker, born in St. Louis, played in the minors from 1947 through 1950 after which he was inducted into the Army. Poelker advanced to the rank of sergeant and was killed on September 25 during the Battle of Heartbreak Ridge.[39]

St. Louis Cardinals outfielder Enos Slaughter posed in his batting stance to help il-lustrate the strike zone as defined in the 1950 rule book. Sporting News

New York Yankees pitcher Whitey Ford and his fiancée, Joan Foran, celebrated after the Yankees won the 1950 World Series. The couple got married in April 1951 when Ford secured a thirteen-day furlough from his military obligation. National Baseball Hall of Fame and Museum, Cooperstown, NY

Lefty O'Doul (left), manager of the San Francisco Seals in the Pacific Coast League, and Joe DiMaggio of the New York Yankees arrived at Kimpo Air Force Base near Seoul on November 10, 1950, and saw a poster that read "Welcome to Korea, Joe DiMaggio and 'Lefty' O'Doul." Signal Corps Photo #FEC-50-21578, Photographs of American Military Activities, National Archives and Records Administration

Lieutenant General Matthew Ridgway, Major General Doyle Hickey, and General Douglas MacArthur sat in a jeep at a command post in Korea, approximately fifteen miles north of the 38th parallel, on April 3, 1951. Photographs of American Military Activities, National Archives and Records Administration

President Harry Truman prepared to throw out the ceremonial first pitch before the Washington Senators' opening game against the New York Yankees on April 20, 1951. Standing to the president's right (right to left) were his wife Bess, Vice President Alben Barkley, and Barkley's wife Jane. To the president's left (left to right) were Senators manager Bucky Harris, Senators owner Clark Griffith, and Yankees manager Casey Stengel. Abbie Row, National Park Service, Harry S. Truman Library

After Lieutenant General Matthew Ridgway was named commander-in-chief of all UN forces in Korea, he met with Syngman Rhee, president of the Republic of South Korea. National Archives and Records Administration, Alamy

Emanuel Celler served in the U.S. House of Representatives from 1923 to 1972 and chaired the Judiciary Committee. In 1951 his subcommittee on study of monopoly power held hearings to examine the antitrust exclusion granted to Organized Baseball by the Supreme Court's decision in Federal Baseball Club of Baltimore v. National League of Professional Baseball Clubs (1922). William C. Greene, 1951. New York World-Telegram and the Sun Photograph Collection, Library of Congress, Prints and Photographs Division

In Game Two of the 1951 World Series, New York Yankees right fielder Mickey Mantle wrenched his knee when he stepped on a drain trying to avoid colliding with center fielder Joe DiMaggio. National Baseball Hall of Fame and Museum, Cooperstown, NY

Negotiations to end the war moved to this tent in Panmunjom in October 1951. US Air Force photo, National Museum of the United States Air Force

Colonel James Murray Jr., USMC, and Colonel Chang Chun San of the North Korean Communist Army initialed maps showing the north and south boundaries of the demarcation zone during the Panmunjom cease-fire talks in October 1951. General Photographic Files, General Records of the Department of the Navy, National Archives and Records Administration

By November 1951, more than 120,000 Communist prisoners-of-war were being held in a camp on Koje-do, an island off Korea's southeast coast. In this view are buildings, tents, and prisoners lined up for inspection. Sydney Morning Herald, Alamy

The Marines notified New York Yankees infielder Jerry Coleman in January 1952 that he would be recalled to active duty. After playing in a doubleheader on April 30, he reported for eight weeks of flight training. National Baseball Hall of Fame and Museum, Cooperstown, NY

On May 13, 1952, minor leaguer Ron Necciai pitched a no-hitter for the Class D Bristol (Virginia) Twins. He walked one batter, hit one, and struck out twenty-seven in the nine-inning game. National Baseball Hall of Fame and Museum, Cooperstown, NY

In Game Five of the 1952 World Series, New York Yankees pitcher Johnny Sain hit a ground ball to second baseman Jackie Robinson. His throw to first base was late, but the umpire called Sain out. National Baseball Hall of Fame and Museum, Cooperstown, NY

With the bases loaded and two out in the seventh inning of Game Seven of the 1952 World Series, New York Yankees second baseman Billy Martin dashed into the infield to snare a popup hit by Jackie Robinson of the Brooklyn Dodgers and record the third out, preserving New York's 4-2 lead. National Baseball Hall of Fame and Museum, Cooperstown, NY

New York Yankees second baseman Bobby Brown, a medical doctor, was drafted in July 1952. National Baseball Hall of Fame and Museum, Cooperstown, NY

St. Louis Cardinals owner Fred Saigh (left) *spoke with Anheuser-Busch president August "Gussie" Busch Jr. three weeks before they announced that Saigh was selling the Cardinals to the brewery on February 20, 1953.* Edward Burkhardt/St. Louis Post-Dispatch/POLARIS

Boston Braves officials supervised the destruction of game tickets for the 1953 season. No longer needed since the club was moving to Milwaukee, tickets were dumped onto the ground near Braves Field and incinerated. Boston Public Library, Leslie Jones Collection

President Dwight Eisenhower returned to Washington from the Augusta National Golf Club in Georgia and threw out the ceremonial first pitch at the Senators' delayed opening game against the New York Yankees on April 13, 1953. Pictured here in the front row are (left to right), House Majority Leader Charles Halleck (R-IN), Senate Minority Leader Lyndon Johnson (D-TX), Senator Homer Ferguson (R-MI), Speaker of the House Joseph Martin (R-MA), Eisenhower, Senators manager Bucky Harris, and Yankees manager Casey Stengel. Eisenhower Presidential Library and Museum

Lieutenant General W. K. Harrison Jr. (left table) and North Korean General Nam Il (right table) signed the armistice documents on July 23, 1953. US Air Force photo, National Museum of the United States Air Force

8

"The Giants Win the Pennant!" October–December 1951

When the Brooklyn Dodgers finished in a first-place tie with the St. Louis Cardinals in 1946, the Dodgers won the coin toss, and manager Leo Durocher chose to play the first game in the best-of-three playoff in St. Louis, with the second game and the third, if necessary, in Brooklyn. The Cardinals won the first two games and went on to defeat the Boston Red Sox in the World Series. Come 1951, Brooklyn again won the coin toss, and manager Charlie Dressen elected to play the first playoff game at Ebbets Field and the remaining one or two at the Giants' home, the Polo Grounds.[1]

In the opening game on Monday afternoon, October 1, Dressen sent Ralph Branca to the mound to oppose the Giants' Jim Hearn. Brooklyn's Andy Pafko hit a home run in the second inning, but the Giants got two runs in the fourth on a Bobby Thomson home run and one in the eighth on Monte Irvin's homer to win, 3–1. The next day, Brooklyn's offense came to life, getting thirteen hits, including four homers, and bested New York, 10–0.

In Game Three, the Dodgers' Don Newcombe, who had won twenty games during the season, faced off against Sal Maglie, winner of twenty-three. Brooklyn scored a run in the first, and that lead stood up until the bottom of the seventh when Irvin doubled and scored on Thomson's sacrifice fly. In the top of the eighth, the Dodgers scored three times, the first run coming home on a wild pitch and the next two on singles by Pafko and Billy Cox. Brooklyn led, 4–1.

Newcombe retired the Giants in order in the bottom of the eighth, and Larry Jansen, in relief of Maglie, did the same to Brooklyn in the top of the ninth. Alvin Dark opened the bottom of the ninth with a single, and Don Mueller followed with another single to put runners on first and third. After Irvin fouled out, Whitey Lockman doubled to left. Dark scored, and Mueller broke his ankle sliding safely into third.

Here Dressen made two key decisions. First, he removed Newcombe and replaced him with Branca, even though Branca had lost six of his last seven decisions and would be pitching with only one day's rest. Second, with pinch-runner Clint Hartung on third and Lockman, the tying run, on second, Dressen opted to pitch to Thomson instead of walking him and facing Willie Mays, whose offensive production had fallen off in the second half of the season.[2]

The next at-bat stood for a long time as the most famous at-bat in major league history. Branca threw a fastball down the middle, and Thomson took it for a called strike. Branca's intention on the next pitch was to throw another fastball, up and in, just outside the strike zone. This the right-hander did, but Thomson turned on the pitch and hit a line drive that sailed into the lower deck of the left-field stands. "The Giants win the pennant!" screamed Giants' radio announcer Russ Hodges repeatedly, and indeed they had, completing a marvelous comeback crowned by Thomson's "Shot Heard Round the World" and stabbing the Dodgers and their fans, causing an emotional wound from which some never recovered.[3]

The Giants were ecstatic, of course, but there was still a World Series to play against the New York Yankees with Game One set for just two days later. The Series went six games. The Giants won Games One and Three, but the Yankees took Game Two and bounced back to win the last three. The Yankees outscored the Giants, 29–18, and benefited from three complete games, two by Eddie Lopat and one by Allie Reynolds. Most significantly, in Game Two, Joe DiMaggio, playing center field, nearly collided with right fielder Mickey Mantle in pursuit of a Mays fly ball. Mantle stepped on a drain, wrenched his knee, and came out of the game. Mantle did not play again in the Series, and DiMaggio announced his retirement on December 11.[4]

As the Giants had prepared for the Series, they took advantage of a scouting report on the Yankees prepared by former major league infielder Andy High. High worked for the Dodgers, who, after they lost, turned over his written observations to their arch-rivals. Had Brooklyn won the playoff, High's work would have been augmented by an even more detailed analysis by Allan Roth, work the Dodgers did not share with the Giants. The "demon statistician," as one sportswriter called Roth, had charted every pitch to every batter in twenty late-season Yankees games and had compiled a book of more than four hundred pitches thrown to each Yankee batter along with similar analyses on each pitcher. "High sat next to me," Roth said, "and we compared notes as we went along. . . . In general, my figures agree with High's report." But Roth's data collection, abruptly halted when Thomson hit his Game Three home run, was more detailed. It included pitch sequences and how each batter performed against various counts.[5]

On October 15, the Monday after the World Series ended, the Celler subcommittee began its second brace of hearings on Organized Baseball. Before the first witnesses appeared, sportswriter Jack Walsh explained that the subcommittee's lines of inquiry would continue to focus on the reserve clause and what might be needed to make it reasonable, and "how far such safeguards as the draft, waiver rules, player limits, salary minimums, and arbitration set-ups should go in order to be fair to players, club owners, and fans." Walsh also predicted that "there is an excellent chance that the question may still be far from satisfactorily answered at the conclusion of the probe."[6]

Over eight days, subcommittee members heard testimony from twenty-five witnesses and received written statements from four others unable to attend. Those who testified in person included, among others, several present and former players, a former umpire, owners and other club officials, sportswriters, American League president Will Harridge, and, making a return appearance, Ford Frick, barely a month into his new job as commissioner of baseball[7]

Every witness offered some criticism of how Organized Baseball operated. Some argued for tinkering with the reserve clause or abolishing farm systems or expanding major league baseball to the West Coast or modifying the sport's antitrust status, but no one wanted Congress to write a broad code of conduct delimiting the way the business of baseball might function. After the last witness had finished speaking, the *Sporting News* editorialized that "the game fared well under a thorough grilling. And regardless of whether any legislation results, baseball cannot help but be the gainer from the better understanding of its problems which the hearings brought to the fans."[8]

The subcommittee's inquiries included requiring Organized Baseball to release more financial data than it had ever done previously. Documents showed that the sixteen major league clubs had total revenues in 1950 of $32 million and expenses of $25.5 million resulting in an operating income of $6.5 million. American League clubs took in $16.3 million and spent $12.6 million, leaving an operating income of $3.7 million, while in the National League, revenue totaled $15.7 million against expenses of $12.9 million, leaving an operating income of $2.8 million. Each league then reduced its operating income by subtracting the cost of minor league player contracts, farm systems, and income taxes, leaving the American League with a consolidated net income of $623,000 and the National League with $53,000.[9]

Frick was already knee-deep in baseball's problems. Soon after he took office, he confronted a list of nine proposals major league players wanted owners to consider at the forthcoming winter meetings. Since 1946, players on each club had selected a player representative to speak for their interests, and it was this group, led by the two league player representatives, Ralph Kiner of the Pittsburgh Pirates and the Detroit Tigers' Fred Hutchinson, who had introduced six of these ideas during the All-Star break and added three more during the World Series.[10]

The players' list was hardly revolutionary: extending to a player with eight years' service the same right not to be sent to the minors without his consent that a player with ten years' service had; giving each player on a major league roster two tickets to each World Series game; paying players called to special fall training camps; banning night games during spring training; prohibiting doubleheaders during spring training; banning night games on getaway days; avoiding scheduling doubleheaders after night games; returning to the 12:50 a.m. curfew on night games; and banning all major leaguers from playing winter ball. Plus, Kiner added, "the one last thing we would like to have is a background for the hitters in all parks, especially in Wrigley Field, Chicago."[11]

The players did not expect Frick to respond, and he did not. He did move the commissioner's office from Cincinnati to New York, and he hoped that the same "horse sense" he had used as National League president would hold him in good stead in his new post. "I'm still going to be the same Ford Frick," he told sportswriter Fred Lieb, "tackling problems as they come along—and solving them one way or another." But serving as commissioner carried an extra burden when the two leagues, operating independently, disagreed on a proposal that would affect them both. In such a case, Frick said in December, he would support the status quo. "In ordinary circumstances," he explained, "I am not going to cast my tie-breaking vote for new legislation. That, in my opinion, would not be right."[12]

Frick did go out on a limb in October when he endorsed Warren Giles's suggestion that the entire structure of Organized Baseball be reorganized. As Giles moved into his new job, National League president, he reminded Lieb that he had been calling for minor league realignment since 1939. "Some cities that are natural rivals are in different leagues; they should be grouped together. Other cities have outgrown their leagues, and some good-sized cities are out of Organized Ball because there is no place for them to go," he said. "In such a realignment," he continued, "I see a chance for cities which now feel they properly belong in the big leagues. . . . I now am talking not only of the large [Pacific] Coast league cities of Los Angeles, San Francisco, and Seattle, but of other cities such as Montreal, Baltimore, Buffalo, Milwaukee, and Houston, which believe they are ripe for major league ball."[13]

Responding to Giles's prompt, Frick endorsed a change in baseball regulations that would, according to Lieb, "enable cities to move up the ladder to higher classifications, as do players, when they qualify." He added,

I would put it all in the book so that fast-growing cities would know there is a future for them in baseball, just as there is a future for the player who outgrows his minor league status. I am not only talking for some of the great cities which today hunger for major league baseball, but for cities in minor leagues of lower classification which feel they are entitled to a better grade of baseball.

At the same time, though, he cautioned that "this isn't only something for the commissioner to work out. It requires a lot of serious thought by everyone concerned, the majors, the minors, the commissioner's office."[14]

On September 6, General Ridgway had suggested that the peace talks be moved to a more suitable location than Kaesong, the village that remained in Communist hands. A month later, the Communists proposed a small hamlet called Panmunjom as a new site, and after more than a dozen meetings, the two sides agreed. The Communists erected tents in which negotiations would continue, and the UN side supplied electricity, heat, and four giant balloons to mark the boundaries of this neutral zone.[15]

The military pressure exerted by General Van Fleet's campaign to take the area around Heartbreak Ridge and Bloody Ridge drove the Communists back to the bargaining table. Talks resumed on October 25, but negotiations on every question moved slowly. Each morning on which talks were scheduled began with the Communist delegation arriving in a black Chrysler Imperial that had been captured in Seoul in the early days of the war. The UN delegation arrived by helicopter. Delivering the opening statement alternated from one session to the next, but each speaker had to proceed sentence by sentence and then await translation. If the North Korean delegate spoke first, his every sentence would be translated first into Chinese and then into English. When the American delegate spoke, his remarks would be translated into Korean and then Chinese. Nothing happened quickly.[16]

A plenary session sent to a sub-delegation the most important item on the agenda, namely, where to draw the demarcation line that would separate the combatants and establish a demilitarized zone as a basic condition for a cessation of hostilities. As far back as July, the Communists had insisted on using the parallel as the dividing line, but Van Fleet's forces had advanced north of the parallel, and the UN side rejected this idea. The Communists then backed off and offered to accept a demarcation line based on the firing line, if only the two sides could agree where that line was.[17]

On November 5, the UN negotiators proposed that the demarcation line should be the "actual line of contact at the time of the signing of the armistice."

This meant, of course, that fighting could continue, and Van Fleet would have been prepared to do just that. Understandably, the Communists refused to accept this proposal, and a week later, Ridgway ordered Van Fleet to stop all offensive actions and to defend what became known as the MLR, the Main Line of Resistance. UN forces would henceforth no longer initiate any attack involving more than a battalion without permission from higher up. Van Fleet's troops would be limited to strengthening the MLR, establishing an outpost line a couple of miles ahead of the main position, and defending against any enemy incursions.[18]

On November 17, the UN side offered a startling new proposal designed to break the deadlock and bring the war to an end, an outcome that the American government earnestly wanted. The UN side said that the current contact line could become the final demarcation line if an armistice was signed within thirty days after the Communists agreed to the proposal. This was a stunning idea, intended to show that the United States and the United Nations had no interest in any further territorial gains. It would stabilize the front for a month and create a de facto cease-fire.[19]

Once again, a plenary session referred this proposal to a sub-delegation. Its members agreed to some modifications on November 23, and a new plenary session ratified the amended proposal on November 27. But what happened next exposed the folly of the UN initiative. According to Hastings, "for thirty days they [the Communist negotiators] talked empty nothings at Panmunjom. And while they talked, immune from major UN military action, on the mountains their armies dug." Working from "this breathing space," in Rees's words, the Chinese and North Koreans created a "vast fourteen-mile-deep defensive network which protected the communist armies for the rest of the war."[20]

The Communists' defensive position, trenches and tunnels that shielded 855,000 troops and made them almost impregnable to artillery, set the stage for the rest of the war. China and North Korea understood that Americans were growing weary of this so-called police action. The Communists knew that they would not be able to achieve their primary objective, a military takeover of South Korea, but they also knew that the United Nations was not willing to expand the war in search of victory. They also realized that, as Admiral Joy later wrote, "because the fighting slackened, we lacked the essential military pressure with which to enforce a reasonable attitude toward the negotiations."[21]

The first snow in Korea fell on the night of November 23, and two days later, it snowed all day. Another cold winter on the peninsula had begun, and peace was elusive as ever. For when the thirty-day cease-fire expired, there was no armistice to sign.[22]

On October 15, a contingent of seventeen major and minor league players led by Lefty O'Doul, until recently the manager of the Pacific Coast League's San Francisco Seals, left San Francisco by airplane, bound for Hawaii and then Japan where they were scheduled to play a series of goodwill games against Japanese major leaguers. Airplane trouble delayed the start of the first game in Honolulu until 10:30 p.m., but a crowd of some fifteen thousand stayed late to watch the Hawaiian All-Stars, made up of professional ballplayers in the service, defeat O'Doul's squad, 8–6. The next day, nearly a million Japanese welcomed the players, including Joe DiMaggio, upon their arrival in Tokyo, after which the team met with Ridgway. In their first two games, the Americans beat the Yomiuri Giants, 7–0, before fifty thousand fans at Korakuen Stadium, and the Mainichi Orions, 11–0, with a crowd just as large as the day before.[23]

Over the next few weeks, O'Doul's team traveled around the country, playing Japanese major league teams and all-star aggregates. They won thirteen games, lost one, and tied two, almost always before standing-room-only crowds. During a break in the tour, five players, including Dominic DiMaggio and young Billy Martin, visited US troops on the front lines in Korea. As the tour ended, O'Doul commented on the quality of play his team had witnessed. "Don't underestimate Japanese baseball," he said. "We had a pretty well-balanced aggregation of American players on this trip. . . . In every game the Japanese played fine baseball and did not appear to be outclassed by any means."[24]

The minor league players on O'Doul's team returned to the United States knowing full well that their part of the baseball business was in crisis. The minors had set an all-time attendance record in 1949, selling nearly forty-two million tickets, but that number declined in 1950 to 34.7 million, and it dropped further in 1951 to 27.6 million. Eight fewer leagues operated in 1951 than in 1950, but taking their absence into account still resulted in a fifteen percent drop in the overall gate. Only four leagues had registered increases in total attendance in 1951, the Gulf Coast League and the Provincial League, both of which expanded from six clubs to eight; the Kitty League, which replaced a weak team in Cairo, Illinois, with a stronger one in Paducah, Kentucky; and the Southwest International League, whose ten clubs averaged 2,653 more fans per club than they had in 1950 when they played in two leagues, the Arizona-Texas League and the Sunset League.[25]

Losses in the other forty-six leagues ranged from 14,500 in the Georgia-State League to 890,700 in the Pacific Coast League, down 14 percent from 1950. Despite the general decline in attendance, twelve leagues had one club each whose attendance surpassed their league's best mark in 1950, and one club, the San Angelo Colts in the Longhorn League, set an all-time league record, 115,818, up from 97,936 in 1950. The worst attendance in all the minors belonged to the Granite Falls Graniteers in the Western Carolina League. Their total attendance was 11,500 as they endured losing streaks of twenty-six and thirty-three games and compiled the worst record in all Organized Baseball, 14–96.[26]

Sportswriter Cliff Kachline blamed the minors' woes on "tighter economic conditions" and the continuing problems caused by broadcasting major league games in minor league territory. Matters were made worse when major league club owners called a special meeting on October 8 and, under pressure from the Department of Justice, repealed Rule 1(d) entirely. This rule had attempted to standardize some limits on major league broadcasts, but its abolition threw control of radio and television back into the hands of individual club owners. Thus, two national radio networks that had plans to broadcast major league games in 1952 over 450 stations were suddenly forced to make new deals with the sixteen clubs.[27]

Polled by the *Sporting News* in the fall, minor league club owners testified to an uneasy relationship, at best, with major league broadcasts. Some seemed satisfied if local radio stations broadcasting major league games would read announcements about the minor league team's home games. Others blamed declining attendance on bad weather, but L. D. Norris, owner of the Topeka

Owls in the Western Association, expressed the frustration undoubtedly felt by others in his situation. Norris said that local stations cooperated in promoting his club, but that one station, KJAY, broadcast all St. Louis Cardinals games and some Liberty Network games, day and night, and another station, KTOP, carried all the broadcasts of the Mutual Broadcasting System. "I would not object to major league broadcasts," he said, "if they were confined to daytime broadcasting of games. But many stations, independently owned, such as KJAY, couldn't operate without the revenue obtained from baseball games."[28]

Those major league players seeking to augment their incomes by barnstorming in California after the conclusion of the World Series also had to deal with the effects of televised baseball. Jackie Robinson's barnstorming team drew nearly fifteen thousand fans when they played a team led by Cleveland Indians pitcher Bob Lemon in Los Angeles, but other barnstorming aggregations did less well in big cities and made money only when they played in smaller cities. Promoter Kent Parker blamed the World Series telecasts for the sparce crowds. "Most of these localities saw major league baseball at its best shortly before the barnstormers arrived," he said, "and that is why the barnstormers drew larger crowds in smaller cities, where TV was unavailable, or at least limited on baseball telecasts."[29]

In late September, Leslie O'Connor, who had been Commissioner Kenesaw Landis's assistant throughout his tenure and was now legal counsel for the PCL, restated what Organized Baseball had to do to keep the PCL from becoming independent. The league, he said, wanted three things: first, "lifting of the rule that forces them to be subject to the draft"; second, "granting the same territorial rights which the major leagues enjoy; namely, that no big league club could invade Coast league territory without the unanimous consent of the Coast league"; and third, "a status whereby the Coast league can contract directly with the major leagues instead of being a one-fiftieth party to an agreement [as a member of the National Association]."[30]

Over the next few weeks, major league club owners, acting through the Major-Minor League Committee, showed some willingness to compromise. At first, an idea emerged that the price for drafting a PCL player might be increased from $10,000 to $15,000 and that the length of time before a PCL player would be eligible for the draft might be extended from four years to five.

But shortly thereafter, perhaps at Frick's suggestion, the committee proposed that the minor league classification system be expanded to include a new Open classification above Triple AAA but still below the majors.[31]

To qualify for this new tier, a league had to meet four criteria that only the PCL could meet: no salary limit; an average annual total attendance of at least two million for the five preceding years; total ballpark seating capacity of at least a hundred twenty thousand; and approval from at least six clubs in an eight-team league. A league opting for the Open Classification would operate under special rules, including allowing individual players in the league to waive the right to be drafted and having the draft price raised to $15,000.[32]

When the National Association held its winter meetings in Columbus, Ohio, in early December, its member leagues approved the creation of the Open Classification. They also heard Frick introduce a multistep process by which a minor league could advance to major-league status. Any league seeking to do so would have to have an aggregate population of fifteen million in eight cities, potential seating capacity of at least twenty-five thousand in each ballpark and average total paid attendance of 3.5 million over the preceding three years. In addition, a league seeking promotion must agree to play a schedule of at least 154 games; adopt the major-league minimum salary agreement with no maximum salary limits; accept the existing uniform players' contract; and join the existing players' pension plan or adopt a comparable plan. This was a process, to be sure, but it was one whose standards not even the PCL could meet.[33]

When the major leagues held their joint meeting in New York a few days later, they quickly approved Frick's proposal. They also approved the players' agenda that had been reduced to three items: banning night games on getaway days; banning doubleheaders on the day after night games; and establishing a bureau within the office of the commissioner to handle certain player-management disputes and pension fund questions. They took no action on the rules governing radio or television broadcasts, including a resolution passed by the minors asking the majors to split half their broadcasting profits with the minors. They also passed a new high school rule, effective in 1953, that allowed clubs to sign high school players prior to graduation with the stipulation that these signees could not play professionally until the day following graduation of the class in which they had entered high school.[34]

Two other contentious proposals failed to pass. Pirates vice president and general manager Branch Rickey introduced a resolution that would have eliminated the right of major league clubs to recall players from the minors with just twenty-four-hours' notice and bar the recall of optioned players until the minor league season was over. The Braves and the two Philadelphia clubs proposed that the active playing roster be cut from twenty-five to twenty-three between mid-May and September 1.[35]

Dodgers vice president Buzzie Bavasi argued against both proposals, especially if both were to pass. "If both went through," he said, "we would be in tough shape. No club could afford one injury of any consequence and be able to present the quality of baseball which is now so pleasing to the fans." Both leagues voted against Rickey's proposal, defeating it, but the National League supported the roster reduction while the American League opposed it. Frick then polled the owners and found them divided, eight against eight. Acting on his intention not to cast a tie-breaking vote that would initiate a rules change, he voted no. Voting in favor "would have been contrary to the policy I have adopted," he said.[36]

In the last months of the year, professional ballplayers continued to leave the game for military service, even though most were not sent overseas. Red Sox pitcher Leo Kiely was drafted in October, but he was disqualified from combat because of a childhood injury and assigned to Camp Kilmer, New Jersey. Pirates pitcher Vernon Law, on the verge of being drafted, enlisted in the Army and was sent to Ft. Eustis, Virginia.[37]

The Cardinals reported that ninety-five players in their organization had been called to serve. Besides Spere Spiliotis, wounded earlier, this total included one other wounded player and one killed in a stateside accident. Jack Cohan, a righthanded pitching prospect, had been drafted in the spring. He joined the Eighth Cavalry Regiment as an automatic rifleman in August and was wounded on October 9 during his unit's advance to high ground west of Heartbreak Ridge. Cohan was hit twice in his left leg, and his main artery was severed in two places. After he was evacuated to a field hospital, his leg was amputated.[38]

Pitcher Ray Jankowski had pitched in the minors in 1948 and 1949, but he missed the 1950 season because of injury. He was inducted into the Army in March 1951 and was stationed at Fort Huachuca, Arizona, when he was struck by a bulldozer on November 2 and died several hours later. A month before, Bill Sweiger was killed in action. Born in Baltimore, he played minor league ball briefly in 1943 before being drafted. He served in the Army until 1946 and then returned to the minors. He was recalled to active duty after the 1950 season and joined the Fifth Cavalry Regiment of the First Cavalry Division. On October 4, his unit was pinned down by machine gun fire, and he charged the enemy's position, losing his life. He was awarded the Silver Star.[39]

9

Salaries, Ticket Prices, and Integration, January–March 1952

Bobby Thomson's epic home run not only decided the 1951 National League pennant and sent the New York Giants to the World Series for the first time since 1937. It also carved out a hallowed place in baseball's pantheon of great moments. On the day after the game, wrote historian Jules Tygiel, the *New York Daily News* evoked Ralph Waldo Emerson's poem, "Concord Hymn," and dubbed Thomson's feat "The Shot Heard 'Round the Baseball World." The *New York Times*, Tygiel noted, used the same imagery and called Thomson's line drive "the home run heard around the world." Shortly thereafter, baseball fans merged the two phrases into "the shot heard 'round the world," an everlasting description of one of the most famous home runs in major league history.[1]

Tygiel also pointed out that using the words "the world" signified the preeminent place of baseball in the cultural life of the postwar United States. Although major league games were played only in one quadrant of the nation, the sport felt close and intimate, the players "less remote and more accessible," Tygiel added. "The game seemed, both figuratively and literally, closer to the fans than later editions." In addition, the rosters of the Giants and the Brooklyn Dodgers, both racially integrated, included a mix of various ethnicities that, while threatening to some, reflected the dynamism of Cold War urban America.[2]

Then, too, it was throughout the wider world that many Americans experienced the Giants' triumph and the Dodgers' heartbreak. Only 34,320 fans braved the uncertain weather on that October day, leaving one-third of the seats at the Polo Grounds empty. Others watched the game on television, and many more listened to the radio, locally on the Giants' and Dodgers' radio stations, nationally on the Mutual Radio network, and internationally on Armed Forces Radio available to service personnel in Europe and Asia, including Korea.[3]

Yet, as baseball looked ahead to the 1952 season, continued apprehension over these changes in how fans were experiencing the game they loved, along with other problems, gripped the sport's magnates. Owners worried about the loss of more players to the armed services, the precipitous decline of the minor leagues, lawsuits attacking the reserve clause, exorbitant bonus payments to untried players, and the imminence of the report from the Celler subcommittee.[4]

In the wake of Joe DiMaggio's retirement, players on the New York Yankees hoped that part of his 1951 salary, $100,000, would be divided among them. The club had the highest payroll in the majors, some $600,000, but it had already saved $40,000 the year before, when Tommy Henrich retired. Yankees players argued that they had won a third straight World Series in 1951 and that even though attendance had fallen by 130,000 to just under two million, the club had earned enough revenue through television to compensate for the drop in ticket sales.[5]

Pittsburgh Pirates slugger Ralph Kiner sought a raise too. He had led the National League in home runs in each of the previous five seasons, and he was coming off a two-year contract that had paid him $65,000 annually. The size of Kiner's paycheck, however, would be restrained by the Salary Stabilization Board's freeze on salaries unless the three-man committee appointed in August to review ballplayers' particular situations recommended an alternative approach.[6]

The board announced its decision on January 17 after numerous players had already returned signed contracts to their clubs. The new directive specified that there would be no ceiling on any individual player's salary but that "a major league club's total payroll for players, manager, and coaches, for 1952, must not exceed that for 1951, or for any year between 1946 and 1950," although a club could add 10 percent to any of these preceding years to cover increases in the cost of living.[7]

Where this left the St. Louis Cardinals' Stan Musial and the raise he had been promised but denied in 1951 was uncertain. Owner Fred Saigh, when asked if Musial would get his money retroactively, admitted that he was puzzled. "I'd say," he commented, "that it's not so much a problem of how much was promised Musial as it is a problem of how much already has been paid to others." The Cardinals' largest payroll during the five years used by the salary board was 1950. Add 10 percent, Saigh said, and then subtract the total of what every other player had been paid, and the balance would be the raise Musial would receive.[8]

Brooklyn owner Walter O'Malley complained that the timing of the salary board's announcement "produces an asinine result" for his club, and he filed an objection. He said that more than two-thirds of the players on the Dodgers roster had already returned their signed contracts and that he would now either have to recall these signed agreements for reconsideration—"and I know of no rule of law that would permit us to recall contracts executed in good faith under the old ruling," he groused—or else sign his remaining players for salaries lower than what they had earned in 1951.[9]

The Philadelphia A's grumbled too. General manager Arthur Ehlers said that "they ought to change the regulations. . . . In our case, it looks as if 1951 was the high year—meaning that we'll have to stand pat. That is, if we want to give someone a $2,000 raise, say, we'd have to cut four other players $500 apiece. You can see where a scheme like that might lead."[10]

The *Sporting News* agreed with these criticisms. "It is difficult to understand," the weekly editorialized,

> why the [salary board's] decision was delayed for nearly a year. . . . The delay left both clubs and players in an awkward position and allowed little time in which to make satisfactory adjustments. . . . No one questions the authority of the wage board, and baseball has no intention of challenging any of its decisions. However, the game is entitled to a working formula that will reward merit and that takes into consideration all the unusual circumstances in time for practical application.[11]

O'Malley got a hearing on his grievance before John Kieran, who represented the government. The St. Louis Browns, planning to increase salaries as part of a rebuilding program, joined O'Malley, and four lawyers, including National

League attorney Louis Carroll, represented the plaintiffs. Carroll argued that baseball salaries were not inflationary. He noted that the total payroll for the National League in 1951 was only 2.6 percent over 1950 and 4.7 percent over 1949. He also admitted, though, that the Cardinals said they would be able to pay Musial his full 1951 salary without violating the January regulation. Kieran took a sympathetic view but cautioned that he could do no more than make a recommendation.[12]

Kieran's report to the salary board urged "a sympathetic and flexible" approach. He suggested that bonuses paid to new players be excluded from the board's controls, but he agreed with the wage board's policy. Editorially, the *Sporting News* "hoped that the board itself will adopt an equally understanding attitude." Kiner, meanwhile, got his raise, signing a contract for a reported $75,000 that the Pirates managed to fit within the January regulation.[13]

Wage and salary controls went hand in hand with price controls to combat inflation, and yet the government ruled in January that six major league clubs could raise specific ticket prices and that minor league clubs could increase the price of all tickets by 8 percent. The Office of Price Stabilization explained that the six clubs, the Chicago Cubs, Chicago White Sox, Cleveland Indians, Detroit Tigers, the A's, and the Philadelphia Phillies had not raised prices in recent years. They could do so now, the government said, to catch up with raises in salaries and cover increases in travel expenses and ballpark maintenance.[14]

The Cubs, who had not raised ticket prices since 1919, "pondered long and hard" before deciding to increase the price of a box seat from $2.00 to $2.50 while holding the line on all others. The White Sox kept their 1951 prices intact because of "the loyalty of the fans," but the Tigers raised the price of a reserved seat to $1.75, up a quarter, and hoped thereby to balance their books. "We will receive 21 cents of the increase," said club secretary Harry Sisson, "and the other four cents will go to the government in taxes." The other three clubs also raised some prices but not others. Most minor leagues made no adjustments. They had already set league-wide ticket prices for the coming season and could not alter them except at special league meetings.[15]

Well before the start of the season, the minor leagues reported a critical shortage of talent. Minor league clubs had authority to list up to 9,141 players under their control, but the number available to play was only 5,775, a deficit that included 1,590 players in the service. Faced with this shortfall, eight leagues gave up the battle and went out of business, including the Central League. Playing on and off since 1903, the Central blamed its demise on the military draft and radio broadcasts of Tigers' games into its cities. One 1951 game in Flint, Michigan, had drawn only two paid admissions. "If we could get the sponsor of the Tigers broadcasts to chip in with $10,000 a team each season, we'd be riding high," league president T. J. Halligan said.[16]

Anticipating its first season in the new Open classification, the Pacific Coast League announced that, starting in 1953, its clubs would move toward independence by terminating all working agreements with the majors and no longer accepting players optioned from the majors. Some PCL clubs also expanded their scouting staffs and extended their own farm systems. The league also reported that most of the players who signed their 1952 contracts and returned them early had waived their right to be drafted by the majors.[17]

Cubs business manager James Gallagher argued that the minors' plight was tied to the universality of farm systems, a method of business operation, he said, that had outlived its usefulness and should be eliminated. Farm systems gave major league clubs nearly complete control of minor league rosters, but they were no longer worth the money, he said. "In the last six years," according to Gallagher, "the sixteen clubs of the major leagues spent $25,000,000 for players," but "the number of topflight white players moved up into the majors has been tremendously disappointing."[18]

Moreover, Gallagher added, the majors' control of so many players dissuaded many rich Americans from investing in the minors. "I know quite a few wealthy men . . . who would like to get behind local minor league operations. . . . But they say, 'Do you think I would stand with hat in hand before a major league general manager and beg for a couple of players? Nothing doing.'" Earl Mann, owner of the Atlanta Crackers in the Southern Association, agreed. "It might be a good idea to kill the farm system," he said, "and give each major league club control over only forty men."[19]

During the thirty-day cease-fire at the end of 1951, two fresh US National Guard divisions began arriving in Korea, replacing the First Cavalry and

Twenty-Fourth Infantry divisions. General Van Fleet commanded seventeen divisions at the front with two more in reserve while the Chinese moved in reinforcements that within months brought the total number of Communist troops to more than one million. The war continued albeit in short bursts—patrols, raids, artillery duels. In Hastings's words, "the UN armies alternately baked and froze, fought fierce little local actions, whiled away the weeks in their foxholes and bunkers—in the name of a cause whose meaning and purpose had long been forgotten by those 'at the sharp end,' if they had ever understood it."[20]

Against this dispiriting framework, the truce talks at Panmunjom plodded on. Both sides lobbed proposals and counterproposals, each of them designed not so much to solve problems as to score ideological debating points. The antagonists disagreed about what nations might be part of a neutral supervisory commission, whether more airfields might be constructed after a cease-fire, and how monthly troop rotations might be restricted. These were all difficult questions to resolve, but the negotiators eventually wrangled them into a rough-hewn agreement, leaving the toughest question, the disagreement over the repatriation of prisoners of war, unresolved.[21]

At issue, first, was how many prisoners of war there were, and second, whether they should be subject to voluntary or forced repatriation. Each side presented numbers that the other questioned or even rejected. In March 1951, for example, the Communists had claimed to hold 65,000 UN prisoners, but the list they produced in December included only 11,559 names. Similarly, the UN command had once reported holding 176,000 prisoners but now delivered a list of only 132,000 while also claiming that 62,000 of these desired not to return to North Korea, an assertion the Communists rejected.[22]

Article 118 of the 1949 Geneva Convention stated that "prisoners of war shall be released and repatriated without delay," and each side used this ambiguous language to support its position on how prisoners should be returned. The United States, in favor of total repatriation when the fate of over a million German POWs held in the USSR after World War II was at stake, now argued for voluntary release while the North Koreans and Chinese insisted on total, that is, forced repatriation. Sub-delegations tried to find compromise language that would appease each side. But no such language existed. The intransigence surrounding these two issues persisted and was almost solely responsible for prolonging the war for another year and a half.[23]

How prisoners were being treated by both sides also fell short of the standards set by the Geneva Convention. "We do not know about the Geneva Convention," a Communist officer told a British soldier when he was captured. Indeed, postwar analysis revealed that of 7,140 Americans taken prisoner during the war, 2,701 died in captivity. As terrifying to some was the Chinese use of interrogation and indoctrination techniques that later became known as "brainwashing" or "Manchurian candidate" syndrome. UN forces, though, were also guilty of prisoner abuse. According to Hastings, "many American officers and men . . . admitted knowledge of, or participation in, the shooting of Communist prisoners when it was inconvenient to keep them alive."[24]

The furor that had erupted in the United States after General MacArthur's dismissal abated after a short while, but Americans, fresh off winning World War II, found military stalemate in Korea not to their liking. The Truman administration bore the brunt of their frustration. Burdened additionally by charges of cronyism and corruption and saddled by the accusations lobbed by Joe McCarthy and his friends, the president saw his popularity plummet. Gallup polls tracked Truman's job performance ratings from a high of 87 percent immediately after he took office to a low of 22 percent in February 1952. It hardly mattered that the president's advisers, vexed by the stalled peace talks, considered widening the war. The American people had had enough.[25]

In 1952 Truman, who had entered the White House in 1945 and had been elected on his own in 1948, was eligible for reelection. The Twenty-Second Amendment, limiting how long a president could serve in office, had been ratified in February 1951, but Section 1 of the amendment granted Truman, the incumbent when Congress proposed the amendment, an exemption. Still, he had decided immediately after his inauguration in 1949 that he would not run again. He committed his decision to writing in a memo dated April 16, 1950, and he so informed his staff in April 1951, swearing them to secrecy, a bond they kept without breach.[26]

Truman's choice for his successor was Chief Justice Fred Vinson, experienced in all three branches of government, but he declined. The president then approached General Eisenhower, serving in Paris as Supreme Commander of NATO, but Ike, as he was called, expressed his long-held support for Republican Party principles. After Illinois governor Adlai Stevenson dithered when Truman invited him to run, the president allowed his own name to be placed on the ballot in the New Hampshire primary. Senator Estes Kefauver of Tennessee, a man Truman did not like, defeated him decisively. On March 29, the president announced his decision not to run again.[27]

When Gallagher railed against farm systems, he also praised Negro League clubs as independent sources of major league talent. "Many Negro players have come up, players of class," he said. "But we could have dipped into that reservoir thirty years ago. It was a supply of players with which we had no connection whatever, insofar as development is concerned." Gallagher added, "Compare the caliber of the rich bonus boys of Caucasian parentage with Jackie Robinson, Roy Campanella, Larry Doby, Luke Easter, and other Negro players seen in the majors in recent years, and our ridiculous farm system of operation and our crazy waste of money are emphasized more strongly than ever."[28]

Indeed, as the 1952 season approached, Organized Baseball was beginning its seventh season of integrated play, albeit still to a limited extent. The Dodgers had broken the so-called color line by signing Robinson to a minor league contract for 1946 and promoting him to the majors in 1947. Similarly, the Indians integrated the American League in July 1947, followed two weeks later by the Browns. The Giants put two Black players on the field in July 1949, the Boston Braves integrated in April 1950, and the White Sox followed in 1951. Afro Cuban Orestes Miñoso, called "Minnie," joined their lineup on May 1, and Sam Hairston, an African American, played his first major league game on July 21.[29]

Sportswriter Roger Birtwell analyzed the impact Black players were having on their clubs' success. In 1951, he noted, five clubs in the majors fielded Black players throughout the season, and all five finished in their league's first division. In the National League, Campanella won the Most Valuable Player award, New York's Monte Irvin finished third in the voting, and Robinson sixth. The Giants' Willie Mays won the NL Rookie of the Year award, and Miñoso finished second in the American League. Since 1947, Birtwell wrote, only one all-white National League team, the 1950 Phillies, had made the World Series.[30]

Ty Cobb criticized present-day baseball, too, but his perspective differed from Gallagher's. In a rambling, two-part article in *Life* magazine called "The Greatest Player of All Time Says: They Don't Play Baseball Any More," Cobb fired volleys at players, base running, managers, and the "many joke teams" in the majors, singling out the Browns. While anointing Musial and the Yankees' Phil Rizzuto for playing the game right, he was less than kind to Robinson, Ted Williams, and DiMaggio, who, he said, "was perhaps the outstanding example of how modern baseball players neglected to train and keep themselves in condition." He continued, "To an old timer like me, today's ballplayers seem like a particularly fragile lot."[31]

In January, American League president Will Harridge announced that, starting in 1953, its games would be officiated by four umpires. Umpire-in-chief Tom Connolly, who had umpired in the majors from 1898 through 1931, noted that the league staff numbered fifteen, including a pair whose first season in the majors was 1951. "We thoroughly scouted the minors last year for a sixteenth umpire," he explained, "but none came to light. Rather than accept a man with questionable ability, we'll wait until the right one comes along."[32]

On January 17, the Tigers announced the death of owner Walter Briggs Sr. at age 74. With a fortune made in manufacturing and real estate, Briggs, who bought 25 percent of the Detroit club in 1919 and assumed complete control after the 1934 World Series, committed himself to giving his city the finest team in the country and the finest ballpark. The Tigers won two World Series during his tenure, and he spent lavishly improving Briggs Stadium each year, including installing baseball's first underground sprinkler system. Walter Briggs Jr., called Spike, succeeded his father as club president.[33]

Prior to the start of spring training, the Braves, desperate to boost fan interest, invited several sportswriters to fly around the country at club expense and meet eighteen new Braves players either in their hometowns or winter residences. Beginning on January 21, a Pan-American B-23, dubbed the "Boston Braves Rookie Rocket," stopped first in Newark, New Jersey, and then flew on to Philadelphia; Miami; Havana, Cuba; San Juan, Puerto Rico; Los Angeles; Spokane, Washington; Denver; Milwaukee; St. Louis; and Columbus,

Ohio, before returning to Boston on February 8. Five newspapermen and one radio broadcaster plus their families made the trip, "a magic carpet flight of 11,000 miles," according to one writer.[34]

The Red Sox, Boston's other team, were jolted on January 9 when the Marine Corps notified Williams that he would be recalled from the reserves to active duty in the spring. Pursuant to the Universal Military Training and Service Act, the new draft law enacted in June 1951, Marines activated early in the Korean War were supposed to serve between sixteen and seventeen months, but a few months later, the Marines decided that those who had begun active duty prior to July 1951 would be released by June 1952, creating a manpower deficit. Then in December 1951, the Defense Department, needing replacements throughout the armed services, ordered the Marines to recall to active service an additional fourteen thousand reservists, including pilots.[35]

Williams had enlisted in the Marines reluctantly in 1942 and became a fighter pilot. He missed all of the following three seasons and returned home in 1946. He could have resigned his commission at any time, but he did not, instead remaining in the Marine Corps reserves and accepting promotions to first lieutenant in 1949 and to captain in October 1951. "They told me . . . that unless we got into another war, I wouldn't be called back," he wrote years later, "and I certainly didn't believe that what was going on in Korea would have them call back a thirty-two-year-old pilot."[36]

"I'm no different from the next fellow," he said publicly when he received his notice. "If Uncle Sam wants me, I'm ready." Years later, though, he took a more jaundiced view. "I'll tell you why they called a lot of us back. They wanted an appropriation from the government for airplanes and they needed pilots to fly them. So they recalled 1,100 pilots who hadn't flown for eleven [sic] years."[37]

A day after Williams received his notice, two other World War II veterans, Yankees second baseman Jerry Coleman and Cincinnati Reds outfielder Lloyd Merriman, got theirs. Unlike Williams, Coleman had seen combat as a Marine pilot of an SBD-Dauntless dive bomber and flown fifty-seven missions in the Pacific. Discharged in January 1946, he had remained in the reserves, returned to the minors, and made the major leagues in 1949. In October 1951, a major from the Alameda (California) Air Naval Air Station notified him that his recall to active duty was imminent. "Do me a favor," Coleman said. "Take me right now in October 1951 and let me out in March of 1953, and I'll miss a year." But the Marines' call did not come until January.[38]

Merriman had graduated from high school in Clovis, California, in 1941 and enrolled that fall at Stanford where he played on the freshman football team. At the end of the academic year, he enlisted in the Navy and was transferred to the Marines. He played football in the service and did not complete flight training until July 1945, just before Japan surrendered. "You had a choice when World War II ended," he explained. "You could go into the inactive reserves and go home immediately. Or you could go to China and finish out your tour. I myself didn't want to go to China."[39]

Back at Stanford, he played varsity football in the fall of 1946 and baseball in the spring. The Chicago Bears in the National Football League and the Los Angeles Dons in the All-America Football Conference drafted him, but he decided his future was in baseball, and he signed with Cincinnati for a $12,500 bonus in the summer of 1947. Merriman made the majors in 1949. He found himself overmatched by major league pitching, but the Reds, not a contending team, needed him. He batted .230 in 1949, .258 in 1950, injuring his wrist in a collision with the center-field wall, and .242 in 1951. After he got his recall notice, he took his physical in March and anticipated a return to active duty in April.[40]

Several other major leaguers, including Mays, received notices that Uncle Sam would soon want them. Selective Service had instructed Mays to report to his draft board in Fairfield, Alabama, right after the 1951 World Series. Mays went reluctantly, thinking he deserved a hardship deferral since he was supporting his mother and nine half-siblings. He passed his physical and then deliberately failed an aptitude test. His draft board demanded a second test, and with a proctor looking over his shoulder, Mays passed. His request for a deferral was then denied, the top Selective Service official in Alabama saying that Mays "owes perhaps a greater obligation to his country than other boys because of his promise in the sports world."[41]

Selective Service made Braves pitcher Chet Nichols, 11–8 in 1951, available for the draft after he passed his pre-induction physical in Providence, Rhode

Island. Brooklyn pitcher Don Newcombe was inducted into the army on February 26, and Red Sox rookie first baseman Norm Zauchin followed a day later, eleven days after getting married. The Yankees reported that 119 members of their organization were in the service, including major league pitchers Whitey Ford, who became a father in March, Dave Madison, and Bob Calderone.[42]

Players already in the service experienced the vagaries of military life. Browns infielder Red Friend, inducted into the Army in December 1950, got married and later injured his hand playing baseball for Brooke Army Medical Center in San Antonio. Bob Turley, who enlisted in the Army late in 1951 after pitching and losing one game for the Browns, slipped on the ice while on furlough at home in East St. Louis, Illinois, and broke his leg. Cubs catcher Carl Sawatski, drafted in early 1951, left Camp Chaffee in Arkansas, where he was playing baseball, for Tokyo where he would work as a physical therapist for soldiers in Omiya Hospital.[43]

Former minor league catcher and player-manager Fred Tschudin, employed by the Air Force as a civilian flight instructor, was killed on March 14 when a plane carrying him and a flight student crashed and burned near Kinston, North Carolina. A native of St. Louis, Tschudin had played three seasons in the minors before joining the Navy in 1943. Upon his discharge, he played ball from 1946 through 1951 and managed the Douglas (Georgia) Trojans in the 1950 Georgia State League and the Tifton (Georgia) Blue Sox in the 1951 Georgia-Florida League.[44]

10

Steelworkers on Strike, April–June 1952

Just as the 1952 season was about to begin, a *Sporting News* editorial examined the state of the game. The weekly's essay, "Heavy Responsibility on All in Game," began ominously, declaring that "Organized Baseball, for one reason or another, has been in a state of crisis for the last 30 years" and that "the so-called police action in Korea . . . is an increasingly heavy drain on personnel of all ranks."[1]

The editorial noted that Joe DiMaggio, one of the game's great stars, had retired, and another, Ted Williams, would soon be back in the Marines. Bob Feller, Ralph Kiner, and Stan Musial would be playing in 1952, "but from both circuits, the boys who really packed the parks have been graduated in alarming numbers." Since "this naturally means a shrunken income for most clubs," *TSN* urged owners "to stop the insane competition for bonus youngsters" and to curtail "training expenses, which probably set a new high in the conditioning period just concluded."[2]

The essay went on, asking clubs to consider what they might do to counter news coverage surrounding the upcoming presidential race that "will attract more attention than the pennant races" or what they could do "about recapturing the interest of millions of youngsters who have been distracted by diversions ranging from hot-rod cars to cowboy shooting irons." The editorial concluded with an uncertain prediction, saying, "Baseball will carry on. It must carry on. But it needs the help of all the good, wise people in its far-flung ranks."[3]

Adding heft to this sense of crisis were two baseball questions pending before the federal government. The first was whether the Salary Stabilization Board would amend its January rules to allow club owners some leeway to compensate star players and pay bonuses. The second was whether the Celler subcommittee would recommend legislation to deal with the reserve clause.

The salary board did clarify its rules, but not until May. While the regulation setting a ceiling for each club's aggregate salary remained in effect, the board granted clubs some flexibility. Bonuses paid to players signing their first professional contract would be excluded from the ceiling and so would money paid for participation in postseason games, that is, the World Series. Moreover, the board said clubs could appeal limits on certain individual salaries because of such factors as "the relatively short duration of professional careers, . . . wide differences in actual compensation depending upon ability, popularity and drawing power, . . . [and] the rapid advancement to highly-rewarded stardom of a limited number of players on the basis of outstanding performance."[4]

When the Celler subcommittee released its report, also in May, Organized Baseball breathed a collective sigh of relief. What had begun with a threatened bang ended with a whimper. Open to considering five possible legal paths, including outlawing the reserve clause entirely, the subcommittee recommended that Congress take no legislative action at all. In its report—232 pages long—the subcommittee concluded that "Legislation is not necessary until the reasonableness of the reserve rules has been tested by the courts."[5]

Along with its report, the subcommittee also published the testimony and accompanying exhibits from the 1951 hearings. Students of the game learned for the first time how the business of baseball operated, including the extraordinary fact that from 1920 through 1950, thirteen of the sixteen major league clubs, led by the New York Yankees and the St. Louis Cardinals, had positive net income. Despite the Great Depression and the dislocations of World War II, only three clubs, the Philadelphia Phillies, the Boston Braves, and the Boston Red Sox, had finished that thirty-one-year period in the red.[6]

Shortly after major league teams began spring training—ten in Florida and three each in Arizona and California—Yankees general manager George Weiss hummed his own glum tune, criticizing clubs that concluded their exhibition seasons with long barnstorming trips from their spring training sites to the cities where they would open the regular season. Spring training, he said, should be designed to get players into shape, not to raise extra revenue from playing meaningless games in faraway places.[7]

Weiss admitted that his club had been as guilty in this respect as any other. When Larry MacPhail was in charge of the Yankees, they had journeyed more than once to Latin America, and in 1951, the club not only trained in Phoenix, instead of Florida, but also took a trip to California. "It has been written," he said, "that we took a fortune out of California. . . . Well, that, obviously, is buncombe. We did draw well. But the hotel and traveling expenses were staggering."[8]

In 1952, the Yankees broke camp in St. Petersburg on April 3 and made "the shortest northward jump in the history of the club," stopping for games in Atlanta and Columbus, Georgia; Charlotte, North Carolina; Norfolk, Virginia; and Baltimore, before reaching New York and concluding exhibition play with three games against the Brooklyn Dodgers. The club's 1953 spring schedule had already been set, Weiss said, but he promised adjustments in 1954.[9]

As teams played out their exhibition schedules, it was clear that Ty Cobb's criticism of present-day baseball had hit a nerve. "Cobb's crazy," said Musial, whom Cobb ranked ahead of DiMaggio. "There never was a day when I was as good a ballplayer as Joe DiMaggio at his best. . . . He was the best, the very best, I ever saw in my life." Kiner—and his mother—also took issue with Cobb's jabs at the slugger's physical condition. "Why do old-time ballplayers always live in the past?" Kiner complained. "I have a size 32 waist, and I defy any athlete in baseball to show me a smaller waist." Beatrice Kiner added, "They tell me this is an age of specialization, isn't it? Ralph specializes in home runs."[10]

Washington Senators president Clark Griffith, Cobb's contemporary, weighed in as well. "Those old fellows who get out of the game should keep their mouths shut," the former pitcher and manager wrote in a letter to *Life*. He added, "The ballplayers of today are just as good as they were in Cobb's day or mine." Weeks later, on an NBC television-radio simulcast, Griffith went on, saying, "Cobb is out of order when he criticizes Ted Williams for not being able to hit to left field. Cobb [a left-handed batter] couldn't hit to right field on a bet. . . . He was a late hitter."[11]

Red Sox shortstop Vern Stephens was one of many current players who piled on. He asked, "Did Cobb ever have to play a twi-night doubleheader? Did Cobb ever have to play a doubleheader the day after a night game?" Pittsburgh Pirates manager Bill Meyer took a gentler approach. "You can't compare the two eras," he said. "Too many things have happened. The big players come along, and . . . the manager sits back and waits for the home run to come."[12]

Both league presidents avoided the Cobb controversy, but both announced several rules changes designed to "tie up some loose ends, speed up play, and minimize controversies on the field." The American League adopted the National's regulation that suspended games would be resumed from the point of suspension. The NL reciprocated, agreeing that there should be a curfew of 12:50 a.m., after which no new inning could start. Both leagues agreed that a night game could be scheduled on "getaway day," the final day of a series, but only with the prior approval of the visiting team. NL president Warren Giles abolished the rule that a huddle at the mound could include only three players, while Will Harridge said an AL huddle could include any number of players.[13]

Kiner had his own suggestion for a rules change. Bemoaning the 137 walks he drew in 1951, 13 of them intentional, the slugger said, "The time has come, I believe, to put a curb on deliberate bases on balls." His idea was that a player intentionally walked should get two bases, not one. "Look at it this way," he added. "When they walk you, it is true rules makers are kind enough not to give you a time at bat. . . . But what about the right to hit the ball a batter is deprived of—his right to hit the ball 137 times in a campaign by walks?" He compared his record with Musial's, saying that "Stan got on ninety-eight times on passes. . . . He had therefore thirty-nine times more to swing at good pitches than I did. . . . Why shouldn't a batter get credit if a pitcher is afraid to pitch to him?"[14]

The minor leagues prepared for their season, too, with forty-three leagues answering the call, down from fifty in 1951. One league in Class A, three in Class C, and four in Class D had gone out of business. One new league, the Arizona-Texas League, began play with six teams, the Western International League moved up from Class B to Class A, and the Pacific Coast League commenced its first season in the new Open classification. Several minor league teams moved during the season, and five teams in the lower minors disbanded.[15]

The minors were slowly getting used to the idea of integrated baseball. Jackie Robinson had, of course, integrated the International League in 1946, and the American Association and the PCL had broken their color lines in 1948. A few other leagues followed suit, but not until 1951 did integration come to leagues situated in Jim Crow territory. The next year, 1952, according to journalist Bruce Adelson, would be "the first year of widespread integration throughout baseball. By the end of May, 104 nonwhite players were scattered across the minor leagues, from California to Florida." Some club owners in the Florida International League went the extra mile, making sure that their clubs had at least two African American players "so these pioneers would not have to face Jim Crow alone."[16]

From the spring of 1951 forward, UN forces held most Communist prisoners on Koje-do, a small island, a fishing community, off the south coast of Korea near Pusan. Conditions there included overcrowding, insufficient medical care, and, according to Hastings, "an unbroken swell of boredom," all this in a population split into two camps, Communists and those who claimed to be South Korean civilians forced into the North Korean army. The situation deteriorated rapidly after Communist infiltrators allowed themselves to be captured to take control of the various POW compounds within the large camp.[17]

Violence, at first sporadic, grew more serious as inmates, soon quite well organized and disciplined, tested the will of their guards and evolved into a potent resistance albeit with makeshift weapons. They demanded better food, writing paper, and an improved daily routine. They went on strike and seized the psychological high ground from their captors. In February 1952, when UN officials entered one compound attempting to identify prisoners who wanted to be repatriated to North Korea and China, fifteen hundred dissidents launched an attack using implements they had fashioned in secret: steel pickets, spiked clubs, blackjacks. One American was killed along with seventy-five prisoners. A month later, more violence led to a dozen North Korean deaths.[18]

In March, Communist negotiators at Panmunjom attempted to break the deadlock by proposing that prisoner exchanges should be based on the lists exchanged in December. In other words, if the UN side agreed to drop its demand for those prisoners the Communists said had been "sent home" or "released at the front," the Communists would agree to drop their demand to repatriate those the UN said wished to remain in the South. The UN side seemed receptive to this approach, but in April, one of the chief Chinese negotiators demanded that new prisoner lists be made. When the UN completed this new screening and announced that only seventy thousand of the one hundred thirty-two thousand prisoners it held wanted to return, the Communist side reacted with unprecedented acrimony.[19]

Rear Admiral Ruthven Libby, one of the UN negotiators, despaired that "we have passed the point of no return," but the UN side made one more attempt to break the deadlock by co-mingling the prisoner question with other smaller outstanding issues. The North Koreans agreed to make some concessions but not on the prisoner issue, and it remained the biggest problem standing in the way of an armistice. "On this principle," Rees wrote, "the United Nations could not and would not yield."[20]

Violence at the POW camp on Koje-do continued into the spring. In April, American medics entered one of the compounds to remove a wounded man, but prisoners attacked the detail and held them hostage. Brigadier General Francis Dodd, Koje-do's commandant, ordered a hundred unarmed ROKA soldiers to retrieve the wounded man and the medics, but the resistance they encountered required covering fire from other guards on the perimeter. Other incidents, sporadic but intense, led to even more dead and wounded.[21]

Communist negotiators knew exactly what was happening on Koje-do; they had, in fact, planned the uprisings. Several months later, UN authorities in Tokyo discovered to what extent the disturbances at the prison represented a second front in a stalled war. The North Korean army regarded their imprisoned soldiers as combatants. The army and the Korean Communist Party had an overt presence within the camp. Radio receivers smuggled inside put the prisoners in touch with Pyongyang, and civilian agents living on the island passed messages in and out.[22]

May 7 proved to be a day to remember. On that Wednesday, UN negotiators announced that the POW issue remained unresolved and intractable. General Mark Clark arrived in Tokyo to replace General Ridgway, whose next assignment was in Europe. On Koje-do, Dodd entered Compound 76, where 6,400 of the most hardened prisoners were held, to listen to their grievances. At 3:15 in the afternoon, someone blew a whistle, and onrushing North Koreans seized the commandant. According to Rees, their demands included "permission to form a vast Communist POW organization, complete with inter-compound telephones, office equipment down to mimeograph machines, and a couple of trucks."[23]

Three days of negotiations followed during which Dodd asserted that his life was at stake. On the evening of May 10, Brigadier General Charles Colson, acting commandant, signed a statement that there would be no more forced repatriation screenings or inhumane treatment of prisoners. The North Koreans released Dodd, but shortly thereafter, Clark repudiated Colson's statement, and both Dodd and Colson were demoted to colonel. On June 10, US paratroopers smashed the resistance in Compound 76. Thirty-one prisoners and one American died in this action after which Chinese prisoners and Communist South Koreans were removed from Koje-do and sent to different facilities.[24]

Mobilizing the American economy to support the war effort proved to be more difficult than it had been during World War II. The nation's basic industry was steel, and the steel industry's contract with the United Steelworkers of America (USWA) had expired on December 31. Union officials bore a grudge, believing that the National War Labor Board had controlled wage increases during World War II more emphatically, that it had reined in corporate profits. The USWA was determined that the Wage Stabilization Board should act differently.[25]

Negotiations had begun in October. The Truman administration hoped that a new contract could be reached without government intervention or an increase in steel prices, but the talks made little progress. Loath to invoke the Taft-Hartley Act that would have provided for an eighty-day "cooling off period" during which negotiations would continue without fear of a strike, President Truman turned over the case to the Wage Stabilization Board on December 22 and got the union to agree not to strike until the board made its report.[26]

A special panel held hearings and recommended higher pay and enhanced fringe benefits, a package that would cost the industry about twenty-six cents per hour per worker. The administration accepted the recommendation, but the Office of Price Stabilization indicated that it would not approve a hike in the price of steel. The steel companies balked, arguing that the wage package would require a substantial price increase.[27]

A 1951 amendment to the Defense Production Act would have allowed the industry to raise prices by two to three dollars a ton, but steel company officials said they could not accept the WSB proposal without a price increase of ten to twelve dollars per ton. Concurrently, the union said its members would accept nothing less than what the WSB had proposed. Early in April, management offered the union a contract proposal well short of the wage board's recommendation, and the administration told the industry that it could raise the price of steel by $4.50 a ton. But neither side accepted this deal, and the union announced its intention to strike on April 9.[28]

Truman was stuck. He thought the steel companies were being greedy and unreasonable, but he knew that maintaining steel production was paramount. A Taft-Hartley injunction was off the table since the dispute had already dragged on for more than eighty days. So, on the evening of April 8, the president said on national television that the government was seizing the nation's steel mills "to keep them operating." Not doing so, he said, "would bring defense production to a halt and throw our domestic economy into chaos" and threaten American troops in Korea.[29]

Truman thought he had no choice. Steel production could not be interrupted. Moreover, the president's advisers told him that granting the industry the price hike it wanted would push the cost of living up 5 percent and cost the average American family at least $300 per year in an election year. But the reaction to the seizure was vituperative across the political spectrum. Truman was a man, some said, who had dragged the nation into an ill-advised war and who now seemed bent on dictatorship, willing to create a garrison state. Conservative business leaders and politicians added that the president was all too keen on capitulating to organized labor.[30]

The steel industry sued. A federal district court judge ruled the seizure "illegal and without authority of law." The administration won a stay of the judge's ruling and asked the Supreme Court to take the case immediately. Truman then asked Congress to grant him authority to act as he already had, but Congress took no action. The mills continued to operate, but on June 2, the Court decided, six-to-three, that the president had acted unconstitutionally. Congress again declined to do anything, and Truman refused to invoke Taft-Hartley. That set the stage for a strike that lasted fifty-three days.[31]

Although defense production did not stop, the auto industry and manufacturers of home appliances took an economic hit. Bargaining dragged on until July 24 when Truman himself intervened in the negotiations and wrangled a settlement. The steelworkers union won a raise of 21.5 cents per hour plus enhanced fringe benefits. Steel companies were allowed to raise prices by $5.20 a ton. "The price of the settlement might be far greater than the cost of the strike itself," wrote one commentator, but inflation did not jump, and the economy remained stable.[32]

Despite having won the World Series three times in a row, Casey Stengel's Yankees did not travel on that meandering path north as the favorite to add to their laurels. Members of the BBWAA participating in *TSN*'s annual poll picked the Cleveland Indians to win the AL pennant and the Dodgers to replace the New York Giants at the head of the National League.[33]

Of the 216 writers voting in the poll, more than half, 114, picked Cleveland to unseat New York while 91 thought the Yankees' dominance would continue. "The choice of the Indians," sportswriter Carl Felker wrote, "reflects the scribes' high opinion of the abilities of Manager Al Lopez, as well as the Cleveland pitching, rated by many observers as the best in the majors."[34]

"Contributing to the overwhelming choice of the Dodgers," Felker added, "was the recognition that the defending champion Giants had suffered serious losses through the deal that sent sparkplug Eddie Stanky to the Cardinals, the injury of Monte Irvin which may sideline him for most, if not all, of the season, and the induction of Willie Mays next month."[35]

The sportswriters, in fact, picked the Giants to finish third behind the Phillies, a club seeking to bounce back from fifth place in 1951 and regain the glory they had snared in 1950. Philadelphia hoped its chances would be bolstered by the emergence of rookie pitcher Steve Ridzik and the return of Curt Simmons from active National Guard duty in Germany. Sergeant

Simmons arrived at Washington National Airport on April 7 on an Air Force Stratocaster, ready to pitch. A month before, he had written teammate Robin Roberts that he was "taking light workouts indoors over here" and that "it shouldn't take me too long to get into condition after I return to the states."[36]

Tuesday, April 15, Opening Day, saw three games played in each league. President Truman attended the Senators' home opener against the Red Sox and watched Boston win, 3–0. As was the custom, the president threw out the ceremonial first pitch, two, in fact, both of which he tossed left-handed. The first ball, destined for the Hall of Fame, had been sent to Griffith by a fan in Sacramento, California, who said he had used it in an Adrian College game in 1895. Red Sox catcher Sam White caught the second ball and kept it as a souvenir.[37]

The PCL opened its season before the majors did and got off to a good start. Four Opening Day games attracted 35,568 paid admissions, and league president Pants Rowland predicted a fine season. By the end of the month, though, bad weather had wiped out four Sunday doubleheaders, and total attendance was down 81,405 from 1951. Ticket sales improved in June. The league cut its total attendance deficit to 24,329, up in four cities but down in four others. Sportswriter Joe King reported that the league's unabated drive for independence "reflects the urge . . . in those newer, fastest-growing parts of the nation, where the people want the best, and are willing to pay for it, if only they can find the means to go about it."[38]

King also reported that the Texas League had decided to flex its muscles by voting to allow exhibition games in its territory between two major league clubs only if one of them agreed to play an additional game against a Texas League club. That is, if the Giants and the Indians wanted to play in Dallas on their way back from spring training in Arizona, one of them would have to play the Dallas Eagles on the day before or after.[39]

The most spectacular performance in minor league history occurred in May. It did not happen in the high minors like the PCL, nor in Crowley, Louisiana, when two umpires in the Evangeline League used baseball bats to kill a cottonwood moccasin in the outfield. Rather, it was in Bristol, Virginia, where pitcher Ron Necciai of the Bristol Twins in the Class D Appalachian League struck out twenty-seven batters in a nine-inning game.[40]

Necciai, born in 1932 in Gallatin, Pennsylvania, was in his third season of professional ball. He had struggled in 1950 and 1951, and in 1952, he developed an ulcer in spring training. After receiving treatment, Necciai started the Twins' home opener, allowing just two hits and striking out twenty. Six days later, he gave up six hits and struck out nineteen. Three days after that, he appeared in relief, striking out eleven in four innings, and on May 13, he made history. He faced thirty-one batters. He hit one, and one walked. Two reached base on errors, one of them on a third strike the catcher could not handle. The other twenty-six batters struck out as the Twins won, 7–0.[41]

Fans of baseball on the radio learned on May 15 that the Liberty Broadcasting System had suspended operations effective immediately, victimized, said President Gordon McLendon by "baseball's dictatorial monopoly." Liberty had filed a $12 million suit against Organized Baseball officials and thirteen major league clubs in February, alleging that existing broadcast agreements excluding Liberty from broadcasting directly from ballparks represented a conspiracy in restraint of trade. On April 14, a federal district court judge denied Liberty's request for a temporary injunction, declaring that "clubs have a right to restrict the rights of persons attending their games and also have the right to profit by their games either directly or indirectly." In admitting defeat. McLendon said his company could not come back into baseball unless it won its suit.[42]

The Giants started quickly in the National League. After sweeping a three-game series from the Dodgers in late May, they were 26–8 and had a lead of 2½ games. But Mays left for the Army the next day, and after that, New York came back to earth. The Dodgers went 39–16 in May and June and took hold of first place on June 1. By the end of the month, they were 3½ games ahead of the Giants and 10½ games ahead of the third-place Chicago Cubs.[43]

In quest of a fourth straight pennant, Stengel had to juggle his lineup. Mickey Mantle had not yet recovered from his World Series injury. The Yankees traded young Jackie Jensen to Washington for Irv Noren, who played center field for a while. Stengel had to adjust his infield too. He installed Billy Martin at second base and made Gil McDougald his fulltime third baseman. New York struggled. They were 18–17 at the end of May before winning ten of their first eleven games in June to move into first place. At month's end, having lost yet another player, pitcher Tom Morgan, to the Army, they were 3½ games ahead of the Red Sox and the Chicago White Sox.[44]

Jerry Coleman played his last games for the Yankees on April 30, going four-for-nine in a doubleheader against the St. Louis Browns. Between games, the Yankees staged a going-away ceremony and gave Coleman a plaque and a tea set presented by pitcher Allie Reynolds. Co-owner Dan Topping gave Coleman a check for $5,000, and his teammates promised him a full World Series share. He departed for California that night to spend a couple of days with his family before reporting to Los Alamitos Naval Air Station for eight weeks of flight training. Coleman, who hadn't flown a plane in six years, later wrote, "I was doing my duty for my country—that's it."[45]

Ted Williams played his final game before reporting to the Marines on April 30, hitting a home run in his last at-bat as the Red Sox defeated the Detroit Tigers, 5–3. Boston mayor John Hines declared the day "Ted Williams Day," and Williams received several gifts including a set of cuff links from Filene's department store and a Cadillac from the club. Williams was thirty-three years old, and some doubted that he would return to the majors after his tour of duty. "How can I tell what will happen in the next seventeen months?" he said. Williams met up with two buddies, also recalled pilots, and reported to Willow Grove Naval Air Station in Pennsylvania on May 2. They got their refresher course in the same planes they flew during World War II and moved on to Cherry Point, North Carolina, at the end of the month to learn how to fly new jets.[46]

There, Williams reunited with Bob Kennedy, yet another ballplayer who had served in the Marines during World War II and had, in fact, trained Williams to be a pilot. Kennedy had made his major league debut in 1939 with the White Sox, missed three seasons during the war, and was traded in 1948 to Cleveland. Early in 1952, he thought that he would not be recalled because he was married and the father of four with another baby on the way, but the Marines reversed course and ordered him to report for active duty on May 29. The Indians gave him a send-off on May 21, including a $6,000 check to be used as a down payment on a $21,000 house. A week later, he began training in Jacksonville, Florida, and then went on to Cherry Point.[47]

Tigers catcher Frank House, who had received a $75,000 signing bonus in 1949, was inducted into the Army on April 17. Dodgers pitcher Don Newcombe, whose military service was put on hold because of a kidney ailment, was ruled fit for active duty on May 28. Tom Morgan was inducted into the Army on June 27.[48]

Two more professional ballplayers in the service died during these spring months. James Hudgens grew up in Little Rock, Arkansas. After playing freshman baseball at the University of Arizona in 1948, he played in the minors that summer before enlisting in the Navy for three years. On April 21, while his ship, the USS *St. Paul*, was engaged with the enemy off the east coast of North Korea, an eight-inch gun turret exploded. Thinking that the loaded gun had already fired, the gun captain ordered his crew to ram another shell into the breech, and the gun blew up. Thirty men, including Hudgens, were killed.[49]

James Ferguson, a native of Seattle, played Class D baseball in 1950 and was called to military service on January 18, 1951. He arrived in Korea in October and was assigned to the 160th Infantry Regiment in the Fortieth Infantry Division. On June 17, 1952, just three weeks before he was to be sent home, Ferguson was part of a patrol that was ambushed by North Korean forces. He was first listed as missing in action and declared dead on January 27, 1954.[50]

11

"We Want Ike,"
July–September 1952

As the major league season approached the All-Star break, the debate over offering first-year professionals huge bonuses flared up again. While the 1946 bonus rule was in effect, the number of players signing for $60,000 or more had dwindled to just a few, but in 1951, after the rule was repealed, clubs gave large bonuses to four players. The New York Yankees signed infielder Andy Carey for $65,000 and pitcher Ed Cereghino for $60,000. The Philadelphia Phillies signed shortstop Ted Kazanski for $100,000, and the Cleveland Indians signed pitcher Billy Joe Davidson for a sum perhaps as large as $150,000.[1]

The Boston Red Sox blew these numbers out of the water in 1952. Owner Tom Yawkey signed seventeen bonus players for a total of about $700,000. Included in this bunch were pitcher Ed Urness ($80,000), catcher Jerry Zimmerman ($80,000), pitcher Frank Baumann ($85,000), and outfielder Marty Kecugh ($100,000). Roughly half of this large crop reached the major leagues.[2]

The Red Sox were not alone. The Yankees signed first baseman Marv Throneberry for $85,000, the Detroit Tigers gave shortstop Harvey Kuenn $65,000, the Indians signed infielder Billy Moran and pitcher Herb Score for $60,000 each, and the Phillies gave $50,000 to pitcher Seth Morehead. Even the Brooklyn Dodgers, reluctant to sign any bonus players under the 1946 rule, signed first baseman Jim Gentile for $50,000.[3]

Sportswriter Hugo Autz reported that the Red Sox had arranged a "time payment" plan with many of their signees, spreading their bonuses over three or five years. In addition, as Baumann negotiated with the club, he was advised by Jim Fox, a certified public accountant, and Michael Aubuchon, an attorney experienced in writing contracts for boxers. The resulting deal covered five years with the player getting $8,000 in each of the first two years, his father getting $9,000 in each of these years, and the player getting $17,000 in the third, fourth, and fifth years.[4]

On July 7, the day before the All-Star Game, Commissioner Ford Frick announced the creation of a three-man committee composed of the two league presidents and the head of the minor leagues to review this "wild and crazy spending" and present recommendations at the 1952 winter meetings. Phillies owner Bob Carpenter said he wanted baseball to consider a draft of new talent, like professional football, and Pittsburgh Pirates general manager Branch Rickey agreed, saying he had favored such a draft for some time.[5]

Yankees general manager George Weiss admitted that his club had been paying bonuses, but, he said, "those bonuses have gone to players in whom we had the greatest confidence, and to get them we were forced to compete against other clubs." He added that he liked the old bonus rule, "but it was not enforced." With a new rule, he said, Frick "will see that it is not honored merely in the breach."[6]

The committee, including several added members, met in Pittsburgh to discuss various proposals. One idea for a universal draft, as it was called, would not have directly curbed paying bonuses, but it would have made all players in a club's minor league organization subject to a draft after one year's service. Chicago White Sox general manager Frank Lane approved of this approach, saying that baseball must act to "save us from our own financial indiscretions." After scheduling a second meeting for August 25, Rickey said, "We talked over many ideas at our first session, and we plan to take our time and come up with the best possible solution to the problem."[7]

By the end of September, the committee had narrowed its list of suggestions to two: either a universal first-year draft or a modified form of the previous bonus rule with some teeth in it. Rickey said, "In our judgment either will work." One club official, when asked what those teeth might include, suggested that every first-year player signing a contract and his parents would also have to sign a sworn statement attesting to the contract's terms and allow Organized Baseball to examine his income tax returns.[8]

Dick Burnett, owner of the Dallas Eagles in the Texas League, was more concerned with the state of the minor leagues than he was with major league clubs paying bonuses. Burnett believed that the majors' control of so many players in their farm systems was strangling the minors. His radical idea was that the majors should "withdraw completely from minor league ball so that we can put the game back on a basis of local ownership." Mourning the days when minor league clubs were independent and owned their own players, he argued that major league control "prevents the fans from acquiring any genuine affection toward the players. Instead of being 'our boys,' they're Brooklyn's boys or Chicago's boys."[9]

Burnett proposed eliminating farm systems entirely and returning ownership of minor league players' contracts to minor league clubs. He wanted the majors to surrender ownership of farm teams and working agreements entirely. He wanted each major league club to control no more than forty players, to be able to draft only from Class AAA, and to purchase any other players they might want with 25 percent of the purchase price going to the player.[10]

Frick expressed some sympathy for Burnett's ideas, and the *Sporting News* wondered if farm systems were worth the expense since major league teams, instead of dipping into the minors, so often made trades to fill roster gaps. A committee Frick charged with reviewing all Organized Baseball's administrative rules promised to give Burnett's ideas some consideration, but the longtime minor league owner did not relent. He argued that a neglected rule already limited major league clubs to control of no more than forty players and that if the rule were enforced, farm systems would end.[11]

Hinting that he might take legal action to press his point, Burnett declared that "minor league baseball is at the crossroads. . . . Operating costs continue to soar upward. Attendance records and gate receipts continue to move in the opposite direction. Discouragement of some owners borders on fatalistic pessimism." But Cleveland general manager Hank Greenberg fired back, claiming that many minor league operations were not profitable, and that

Burnett's plan was not feasible. The Indians, he said, had moved their team in the Eastern League from Wilkes-Barre, Pennsylvania, to Scranton after the 1951 season "because of lack of cooperation and support from the press and the city officials and because of a financial loss."[12]

Associated with the criticism that farm systems were not worth the money major league clubs were pouring into them was a growing disapproval of how teams were using the waiver system to get around the June 15 trade deadline, an administrative rule designed to fix a team's roster for the balance of the season. Before each year's deadline, teams could trade players within the same league but not to clubs in the other league. After the deadline, teams could move a player to another team in the same league only if all the other teams in that league waived their chance to acquire him. But once a team got waivers on a player from the other teams in its own league, it could sell the player to any team in the other league without restriction.[13]

In August, the *Sporting News* noted that Robert Burnes, sports editor of the *St. Louis Globe-Democrat*, had identified "a half-dozen transfers which had the form of legality, but the odor of sharp practice," deals in which players had moved from one league to another to bolster the rosters of teams contending for the pennant. The Yankees had used this gambit several times, and Cleveland had just strengthened its lineup by obtaining outfielder Wally Westlake from the Cincinnati Reds and infielder George Strickland from the Pirates. Greenberg said he had acted legally, but he admitted that this rule needed reform. "The way it is now," he said, "there might just as well be no deadline at all."[14]

Five teams tried to improve their performance in another way, by replacing their managers in the middle of the season. The Boston Braves, in seventh place, fired Tommy Holmes on May 30 and replaced him with Charlie Grimm, manager of their top farm team. The St. Louis Browns, also in seventh place, canned Rogers Hornsby and promoted coach Marty Marion on June 8. The sixth-place Phillies fired Eddie Sawyer on June 27 and hired Steve O'Neill as his successor. The last-place Tigers dismissed Red Rolfe on July 4 and picked Fred Hutchinson as his replacement, and the seventh-place Reds hired Hornsby on July 29 to replace Luke Sewell. Only one of these moves paid off.

O'Neill helped elevate the Phillies to a fourth-place finish, but the Reds ended the season in sixth place, the Braves and the Browns in seventh, and the Tigers in eighth.[15]

Following the release of General Dodd by Communist prisoners on Koje-do, Admiral Joy made his farewell appearance at Panmunjom. He lambasted the Communists, charging them with "a constant succession of delays, fraudulent arguments, and artificial attitudes," and he reiterated the UN's position that the Communists' "inhuman proposition" of forced repatriation was a proposal upon which "no amount of argument and invective will move us." Joy, who was leaving Korea to become superintendent of the US Naval Academy, was replaced by Major General William Harrison.[16]

In July, Communist negotiators announced that an armistice could be arranged if the UN would agree to forcibly repatriate all Chinese POWs. The UN side did not respond directly, but five days later came the results of its full screening of all Communist prisoners. Harrison said that the UN held 112,000 North Koreans and pro-Communist South Korean civilians, 76,000 of whom desired repatriation, and 20,000 Chinese soldiers, 6,400 of whom wanted to go home. In addition, the general said, the UN was beginning to release 38,000 anti-Communist South Korean civilian internees.[17]

Harrison suggested that if the Communists were willing to add these 38,000 to the nearly 83,000 who wanted repatriation, they could claim that 121,000 Communists had been released. The Communists rejected this idea, and discussions again ground to a halt. In August, a typhoon blew down the tents in which the negotiation sessions had been held, and the UN agreed to allow the Communist side to erect a wooden building as a replacement. Late in September, Harrison offered three alternative proposals for dealing with non-repatriates, but these drew no quick response.[18]

With President Truman out of the race for the Democratic nomination for president, the party turned to Adlai Stevenson. As McCullough wrote, Stevenson was everything Truman was not, "a graduate of Princeton, well born, a prosperous lawyer, eloquent, witty, urbane—and divorced." But Truman liked him, admiring him both for his midwestern background and his political philosophy. Moreover, several of the president's aides thought that Stevenson might be one candidate who could revitalize the Democratic Party.[19]

Stevenson was young, only fifty-one. He was the governor of a large industrial state, and he was a new face in a party beset by woes. Yet, when the president had invited him to Blair House in January and offered him the nomination, Stevenson said no. He intended to run for reelection in Illinois, he said, and privately, according to McCullough, he wondered if the Democratic Party, winners of five straight presidential elections, might have been in power too long. Besides, he told his friend and adviser George Ball that if the Republican Party were to nominate Dwight Eisenhower, the war hero general was sure to win.[20]

Selecting Eisenhower was exactly what the Republicans did. A year before the election, the leading candidate for the nomination had been Robert Taft, who had reached for the top spot on the ticket before. The Ohioan announced his candidacy in November 1951, but Taft had detractors within his own party. Early polling showed him to be the favorite among Republican senators and party regulars, but not among the GOP rank and file. And there seemed little prospect that he could attract independents or Democrats willing to stray.[21]

Eisenhower slowly emerged as Taft's rival, reluctant though Ike was to redefine himself as a mere politician. Some Republican financiers, including New York investment banker Clifford Roberts, cofounder and chairman of the Augusta National Golf Club, had organized Citizens for Eisenhower in the summer of 1951. Ike resisted their entreaties, saying he was still on active duty with NATO. Over time, his attitude softened a bit. He told friends that while he did not wish to become president, he would respond to a genuine draft, a display of positive public opinion. His friends knew, though, that they could not rouse such a display unless their man first became a declared candidate.[22]

In January 1952, Eisenhower allowed his name to be entered in the New Hampshire Republican primary, and he eased his way into active candidacy. The final determinant came in early February when Ike viewed a film of a midnight political rally at Madison Square Garden. The crowd, carefully managed, chanted "We want Ike" in unison and carried placards printed with "We Like Ike," the simple sentence that would become his campaign slogan. After seeing the film, Eisenhower told the filmmaker, "Tell Bill Robinson [a prominent Republican] that I am going to run."[23]

Taft believed he could count on the party's professionals, but Republican voters started opting for Ike. In New Hampshire, Eisenhower took 50 percent of the vote against three opponents—Taft, former Minnesota governor Harold Stassen, and General MacArthur—and won all fourteen delegates. A week later, after he nearly outpolled Stassen in Minnesota, Eisenhower made plans to resign his commission and return to the United States.[24]

Taft voters struck back. On April 1, Taft won primaries in Illinois and Wisconsin where Ike was not on the ballot and in Nebraska where he was. Eisenhower came home and opened his campaign on June 4, delivering a speech in Abilene, Kansas, his boyhood home. Speaking outside after a torrential rain, in a stadium only half full, he looked tired, fumbled his lines, and lost his place. Whatever momentum he had seemed lost.[25]

Approaching the party's convention in Chicago, with 604 votes needed to secure the nomination, Taft claimed 525 committed delegates and Ike seemed to have about 500. On the first ballot, Taft got only 500 votes, and Ike got 595, just nine short until Warren Burger, leading the Minnesota delegation, switched his state's votes to Eisenhower. Watching the proceeding on television in a Blackstone Hotel suite, Ike remarked, "That was an awfully close call, wasn't it?"[26]

Eisenhower's selection of Richard Nixon to be his running mate was no surprise. Nixon had worked behind the scenes with his California delegation to affect a shift from favorite son Earl Warren to Ike on a second ballot if that became necessary. Senator Henry Cabot Lodge, an early Eisenhower supporter, had recruited Nixon months before as a counter to Taft and dangled the vice presidency in front of him.[27]

In choosing Nixon, the Republicans were getting a Navy veteran who had been elected to the House of Representatives in 1946 and 1948 and to the Senate in 1950. He had been a member of the House Un-American Activities Committee when Whittaker Chambers accused Alger Hiss of being a Communist spy, and he had won election to the Senate by defeating Helen Gahagan Douglas, a staunch progressive. Nixon branded Douglas as "pink" and earned, for some of his campaign tactics, a durable nickname, "Tricky Dick."[28]

The Democratic convention was also held in Chicago. In the weeks since Truman's withdrawal, Stevenson had continued to dither, and the president had grown increasingly impatient. Truman considered supporting his own vice president, Alben Barkley, who was seventy-four, and then Averill Harriman, who had never run for public office—anything to stop Kefauver, who on the eve of the convention, had nearly half the delegate votes needed to win the nomination.[29]

On July 24, the same day as the steel strike settlement, Stevenson telephoned the president and asked if Truman would be embarrassed if Stevenson's name were placed in nomination. "I have been trying to get you to say that since January," was the reply. Still, on the next day, it took three ballots to get the job done. The party's leaders then huddled and picked John Sparkman, a segregationist senator from Alabama, as Stevenson's running mate.[30]

As the campaign began, it became apparent that Stevenson's politics were not much different from Eisenhower's. The governor was a Cold Warrior. He was ambivalent about the Taft-Hartley Act, and he opposed "socialized medicine," a derogatory term for federally funded health insurance that Truman had proposed. He had denounced Joe McCarthy but supported dismissing teachers who were Communists. Moreover, like Sparkman, Stevenson believed that civil rights was a question best left to the states. But he ran a dignified campaign during which he promised to "talk sense to the American people."[31]

The Eisenhower campaign threatened to derail shortly after it got started when a newspaper reported that Nixon was the beneficiary of a private fund of some $16,000, contributions raised from a bevy of California millionaires. This news looked like corruption, but as historian Jean Edward Smith wrote, "There was nothing illegal about the fund; no votes were bought, no favors were given, and the money went largely for office expenses not covered by Nixon's senatorial allowance." In addition, "the fund was administered by a third party, and Nixon did not know the names of the donors."[32]

Nixon overreacted, blaming "the Communists in government" for trying to smear him. But Ike's staff unanimously urged their boss to dump his running mate. Eisenhower composed a telegram asking Nixon for a full accounting of the fund, but through several back channels, he indicated his preference that Nixon withdraw. That did not happen, to Ike's dismay. Instead, during a telephone conversation that Smith called "frosty," Eisenhower told Nixon, "I think you ought to go on a nationwide television program and tell them everything there is to tell, everything you can remember since the day you entered public life. Tell them about any money you have ever received." Ike, in essence, was letting Nixon take the heat, and he gave no indication that a television address would save Nixon's place on the ticket.[33]

The Republican National Committee bought thirty minutes of national television time, and Nixon gave an address that Eisenhower biographer Stephen E. Ambrose characterized as "one of the great classics of American folklore." It came to be known as "the Checkers speech" because Nixon referred in it to his family's dog, Checkers, a gift, and "regardless of what they say about it, we're going to keep it." Eisenhower steamed as the speech proceeded, but the public reaction was overwhelmingly in Nixon's favor, and Ike was forced to keep him.[34]

On July 15, representatives from each league's schedule committee met in New York to discuss various clubs' dissatisfaction with the 1952 schedule, designed by retired bank executive Clement Schwener, and to suggest changes for the future. The National League even produced a draft of an alternative schedule for 1953, drawn up by Harry Simmons, secretary of the International League, but the American League found it wanting.[35]

Schwener had been devising major league schedules for decades, but both leagues, according to Dan Daniel, thought that "he had failed to move along with the trend toward night ball," and "failed to produce schedules with sufficient elasticity to make possible the insertion of a liberal dosage of after-dark play." The schedule for 1952 had each team making four or five trips to every other city, sometimes just for one game. Schwener defended his work. "Each schedule is carefully made," he said, and he noted that some of the one-game visits were the result of clubs altering his draft by moving a single game to another date to create a doubleheader.[36]

The Yankees had a particular beef. After September 1, they were set to play every remaining game on the road except for one three-game series in the middle of the month. Manager Casey Stengel objected to this arrangement and added his criticism of slow games leading to long doubleheaders. "We play baseball all day, or we play it all night, go to bed at all hours, then have to be up early for a doubleheader," he hollered. "Is it any wonder that strong men get weak, and weaker men get exhausted?"[37]

Just before the All-Star break, National Association head George Trautman visited San Francisco for the first time in fifteen years and weighed in on the state of the minors. He hoped that all forty-three leagues that had begun play would complete the season, but he noted that the most prosperous leagues were those farthest removed from major league television and radio broadcasts. "Attendance in some of the minor leagues has been spotty," he said, "but overall I consider the situation good." Trautman also offered his solution to the bonus problem, suggesting that all first-year players should spend one season in Class B, Class C, or Class D, after which "they'd be subject to sale or draft by the majors and higher minors."[38]

Trautman added that he did not approve of the aspirations of San Francisco and Los Angeles to get major league franchises. "In my opinion," he said, "the major league issue has been stressed to the detriment of baseball on this coast." He added, "The baseball traditions of San Francisco and Los Angeles are wrapped up in the Coast league. Were either of them to move up to the majors, it would mean the abandonment of friendly cities not yet ready for the jump. In my book that would not be right."[39]

All minor leagues did complete the season, but total attendance in the Pacific Coast League continued to decline, even though the schedule grew from 168 games to 180. Even before the season was over, some PCL owners thought their league should reconsider its decision not to accept players optioned from the majors. Hollywood's Bob Cobb argued that "if the Coast league bans acceptance of optioned players from the major leagues next year, our league would degenerate into an old men's home or a Class B league for youngsters." Others, including San Francisco's Paul Fagan, disagreed, saying that if the PCL really wanted to break away from the majors, there would be no time better to do so.[40]

After Willie Mays was inducted into the Army at Camp Kilmer in New Jersey, he was sent to Fort Eustis in Newport News, Virginia, for basic training. Assigned to the Transportation Replacement Training Center, Mays became a physical education instructor, but his real job was to play on the fort's baseball team. According to his biographer, Mays was excused from virtually all other responsibilities. One day, he saw one of his pupils catching fly balls with his glove held face up below his waist. Skeptical at first, Mays tried this novel technique and liked it, and thus was born his famous basket catch.[41]

Mickey Mantle, not in the service, was being harassed by some who thought he should be. Selective Service doctors had examined the young Yankee three times since December 1950 and disqualified him each time because of osteomyelitis. Yet in July, after a new regulation removed osteomyelitis as a disqualification for military service if it had been treated successfully for two years, his draft board reviewed his case again. This time, the board delayed a decision indefinitely, citing uncertainty about the new regulation and Mantle's new status as sole support of his widowed mother and four other children.[42]

Mantle became New York's everyday center fielder and helped lead the Yankees' offense to the American League pennant. He batted .311 with twenty-three home runs and eighty-seven runs batted in, while catcher Yogi Berra hit thirty homers with ninety-eight RBIs. New York's pitching staff required juggling. Fourteen different pitchers started at least one game. Allie Reynolds led the staff with twenty wins, and he led the league with 160 strikeouts and a 2.06 earned run average. Vic Raschi won sixteen games, and Johnny Sain won eleven.

The Yankees slowed down in August, going only 17–13, and the Indians jumped back into the race, even seizing first place by one percentage point on August 22. But New York regrouped and won the pennant by two games. Ferris Fain of the Philadelphia A's led the league in batting average (.327), while Cleveland's Larry Doby led in home runs (32) and his teammate, Al Rosen, in runs batted in (105). Philadelphia's Bobby Shantz, a diminutive lefthander, won twenty-four games and was named the league's Most Valuable Player.[43]

After June 1, the Dodgers were never overtaken in the National League pennant race. The New York Giants got as close as four games in late July and three games in mid-September, but Brooklyn clinched the pennant on September 23 by winning the first game of a twi-night doubleheader against the Phillies. The Dodgers' offense was their strength. They led the league in runs, home runs, walks, slugging percentage, and stolen bases. Jackie Robinson and Duke Snider batted over .300 while Gil Hodges led the club with thirty-two home runs and 102 runs batted in.

With Don Newcombe in the army, Brooklyn also used fourteen different starting pitchers, but it was Joe Black, a 28-year-old rookie, who pitched out of the bullpen and led the team with fifteen wins. St. Louis Cardinal Stan Musial hit .336 and won his sixth batting title. Hank Sauer of the Chicago Cubs and the Pirates' Ralph Kiner tied for the league lead in home runs with thirty-seven, and Sauer, the league's MVP, took the RBI crown with 121. League leaders on the pitching side included the Phillies' Robin Roberts with twenty-eight wins, Warren Spahn of the Braves with 183 strikeouts, and the Giants' Hoyt Wilhelm, a 30-year-old rookie knuckleballer, with a 2.43 earned run average.[44]

Three more minor league players and one former major leaguer gave their lives to the war effort during these months. Walter Koehler pitched three years in the minors before entering the Army after the 1951 season. Trained as a medic, he arrived in Korea on Easter Sunday, 1952. On July 28, his unit came under enemy fire, and Koehler dashed forward to assist a wounded comrade. He was mortally wounded by a fragmentation grenade. Koehler was at first reported missing in action, but his death was confirmed in October.[45]

John Hrasch was an All-American shortstop at Ohio University in 1950. He played minor league ball that season before being inducted into the Army in May 1951. On August 18, 1952, he and another soldier were killed in an automobile accident at Camp Pickett in Virginia. Charlie Wilcox was a minor league infielder from St. Francisville, Louisiana. He played in the minors from 1948 through 1951 and entered the Army in 1952. While serving with the Thirty-Eighth Infantry Regiment in the Second Infantry Division, he was killed in action on September 18.[46]

Infielder Bob Neighbors played seven games for the Browns in 1939. He entered the Army Air Force in May 1942, trained as a pilot and served in Italy and the Pacific. After the war, Neighbors remained in the Air Force. When the Korean War broke out, he joined the Thirteenth Bomb Squadron of the Third Bombardment Wing and flew a Douglas B-26B Invader, an attack bomber. On August 8, he and his crew, First Lieutenant William Holcom and Staff Sergeant Grady Weeks, volunteered for an extra mission. They hit their first target successfully, but enroute to their second target, they were hit by enemy fire. Radio contact was lost, and the crew was presumed to have bailed out. All three were listed as missing in action and declared dead on December 31, 1953.[47]

12

Four Straight for the Yankees, October–December 1952

The World Series began on Wednesday, October 1. The New York Yankees were seeking their fourth straight championship and fifteenth overall. The Brooklyn Dodgers were still seeking their first. They had lost to the Boston Red Sox in 1916, the Cleveland Indians in 1920, and the Yankees in 1941, 1947 and 1949.

Brooklyn's offense was powerful. It featured a group of players that would later be immortalized as the "Boys of Summer": Gil Hodges at first base, Jackie Robinson at second, Pee Wee Reese at short, Billy Cox at third, Duke Snider and Carl Furillo in the outfield, and Roy Campanella behind the plate. But the Dodgers' pitching, without Don Newcombe, was suspect, so manager Charlie Dressen elected to start Joe Black, a relief pitcher, in three Series games and to use only six pitchers in all. The Yankees had lost one more player to the service, third baseman Bobby Brown, a doctor who had finished his internship and was drafted in July. Casey Stengel had used ninety-five different batting orders during the season, but in the Series, he was able to rely on veteran starting pitchers.[1]

The teams split the first two games at Ebbets Field and the next two at Yankee Stadium before Brooklyn won Game Five, 6–5 in eleven innings, when Snider doubled home Cox. Back in Brooklyn, the Dodgers had two chances to close out their rivals but failed each time. The key play came in the bottom of the seventh inning in Game Seven and the Yankees ahead, 4–2. With two out and the bases loaded, Robinson hit a high popup, blown by the wind to somewhere between the mound and first base. Pitcher Bob Kuzava hardly moved, and first baseman Joe Collins appeared to lose the ball in the sun. At the last moment, as two runners were crossing the plate in an effort to tie the score, second baseman Billy Martin dashed in and made a knee-level catch to end the inning and save the game.[2]

The Yankees' triumph—and the American League's sixth in a row—earned Stengel a new two-year contract that, with bonuses, might pay him as much as $200,000. He was making more than any of his players and also accumulating money from the team's profit-sharing plan. As for Dressen, despite losing a playoff in 1951 and a Series, he signed his third one-year contract to manage the Dodgers in 1953 for $35,000, a $10,000 raise.[3]

Watching the Series as a Pittsburgh Pirates executive, Branch Rickey could not forget his struggles against the Yankees. Speaking to broadcast journalist Edward R. Murrow, Rickey accused the Yankees' starting pitchers of "utter disregard of the balk rule." In Game Six alone, he claimed that Vic Raschi had committed twenty-six balks, including ten in the first inning. "If these pitchers refuse to obey the one-second stop rule with men on bases, and the umpires don't call it, then it's time the rules committee threw out the balk rule." Moreover, he added, "the long years of non-enforcement of the balk rule have led clubs to de-emphasize the value of the stolen base and have made the training and acquiring of skills in 'breaks' and 'leads' almost a completely lost art."[4]

A week later, Rickey doubled down on his criticism, saying that baseball's rules committee should resign in protest "for they have been almost completely disregarded." Speaking editorially, the *Sporting News* agreed, saying that "the incongruous fact is that the official rules of the game include a regulation as clear and as simple as any other in the book, yet a regulation which is invoked no more frequently than if it never had been written."[5]

American League president Will Harridge disagreed with Rickey. "As we watched the [World Series] games, there was never an indication from the players or the umpires that the balk rule was being violated," he said. Ben Chapman, former manager of the Philadelphia Phillies and before that a skilled base stealer, did not see eye-to-eye with Rickey either. The text of the rule aside, he reasoned that league presidents and umpires had settled on a commonsense arrangement that was working satisfactorily. "After all," he asked, "how long is a second?"[6]

Umpiring in the Series came in for other criticism, too, after a photograph taken during Game Five showed an obvious error. Batting for the Yankees, Johnny Sain hit a ground ball to Robinson at second, who threw to first baseman Hodges. Umpire Art Passarella called Sain out, but the photograph showed Sain's foot on the base while the ball had not yet reached Hodges's glove. Commissioner Ford Frick said later that "It looks like Passarella called a wrong play, but if he did, he's only human. . . . What's all the shouting about? Players make mistakes, too. . . . But once an umpire makes a wrong call, he is crucified."[7]

Frick nixed a suggestion that cameras be used to check on some umpires' decisions. A veteran umpire raised the idea, saying that a camera would not be practical for most plays but could be used for close plays at first base. "With quick processing," one sportswriter wrote, "the umpire could determine through the negative, shortly after the decision, whether it was right or wrong."[8]

Harridge, though, admitted later that umpiring in his league had been substandard throughout the season, and he planned to assemble the umpiring staff in his Chicago office in November to voice his concern. According to Dan Daniel, "Harridge is expected to read the riot act, and to quote incident after incident, naming names, in his demand for a better job in 1953." The *Sporting News* suggested that the umpiring profession was suffering from a manpower shortage, with some young potential umpires being snatched by Selective Service and others dissuaded by poor training, low salaries, and unsatisfactory "working and living conditions, especially in the matter of umpires' rooms at the parks."[9]

One man who had his sights set on becoming a major league umpire was 37-year-old Emmett Ashford, the first African American umpire in Organized Baseball. Ashford had begun calling municipal games in Los Angeles in 1941. After three years in the Navy, he moved up to college baseball and worked often with former American League umpire Bill Stewart. Ashford got his big break in 1951 when the president of the Southwest International League offered him a two-week trial that turned into a contract. In 1952 he moved to the Arizona-Texas League. "I know that the road to the big leagues will be a hard one," he told sportswriter Hugh Keyes, "but most of my biggest obstacles are behind me now."[10]

The committee considering a new bonus rule to control the signing of first-year players worked throughout the World Series. By the time the Yankees defeated the Dodgers, the group had agreed to propose a new rule at the winter meetings, scheduled for Phoenix in early December. The proposal would require that both the player signing for a bonus and the signing club's top official execute sworn statements attesting to the contract's terms; that an official whose club violated the rule be fined and suspended for a year; that a bonus player remain on a club's twenty-five-man roster for two years; that the only way a club could dispose of a bonus player would be to ask unconditional waivers; and that the threshold for invoking the rule be $5,000 for the majors and high minors and $2,500 for the low minors.[11]

Major league clubs were not only concerned about spending recklessly on bonus players. They also took note that total attendance fell nearly 9 percent from 1951. American League attendance dropped 6 percent while National League attendance declined more than 12 percent. In the AL, three clubs saw a gain in attendance, and five, including the Yankees, registered a decline, falling from nearly 2 million in 1951 to 1.6 million. In the National League, attendance for two clubs rose, while the other six saw attendance fall. The Dodgers led the league with 1.1 million paid, but this was down from 1.3 million the year before. The Boston Braves drew only 281,278, worst in either league by far.[12]

Meeting in late October, Pacific Coast League owners declined to repeal or even relax their no-option rule. Instead, they passed additional legislation making it even more difficult to sell players back and forth between their league and the majors. Rickey continued to insist that the no-option rule would ruin the PCL. "By 1954," he asserted, "the Coast league won't be a good [Class] B league. They are going to force all the strength into the International, American Association, Texas League, and Southern Association." He then asked, "What major league club would send a player to the Coast league, when they know there is no chance of buying that player back?"[13]

But the PCL stood pat. President Pants Rowland insisted that every Coast league club owner would be able to buy all the good players he needs. "Most every big league club has a flock of players it can't send to the International

League or American Association because both of those circuits have salary limits. Already they're being offered to Coast league clubs. . . . We'll get the necessary number of right kind of players to give our clubs the balanced competition. After all, that's what makes baseball class," he declared.[14]

Bill Starr, president of the PCL's San Diego club, agreed the rule should not be rescinded. He said,

> When the open classification was first created, it resulted in a great deal of scoffing and ridicule. Some questioned that any player would waive his selection rights. Who would want to play in the Pacific Coast League if they could go to the majors? . . . Well, exactly 197 Pacific Coast League players signed such a waiver in the first year. What these people overlooked was that the criterion of advancement for a player is not merely exchanging one uniform for another, but what goes into his paycheck. As long as the Pacific Coast League can satisfy its players, they will continue to cast their lot with us.[15]

What the Adlai Stevenson campaign could not escape was the millstone that was the legacy of the incumbent administration. President Truman wrote the governor a congratulatory note the morning after Stevenson was nominated, but the candidate did his best to distance himself from the notion that Truman had handpicked his successor. George Ball remembered that his friend Adlai "was affronted by the indifferent morality and untidiness of the Truman administration and was frantic to distance himself from Truman." The president reacted curtly. In a letter he never sent, he wrote that "I have come to the conclusion that you are embarrassed by having the President of the United States in your corner."[16]

The Truman administration had been plagued by numerous scandals, and when a newspaper in Oregon asked if Stevenson could clean up "the mess in Washington," the candidate took the bait. "I would bespeak the careful scrutiny of what I inherited in Illinois and what has been accomplished in three years," he wrote. Truman was riled, and he was further miffed when Stevenson suggested that Secretary of State Acheson should announce his retirement.[17]

More damaging to Stevenson was the charge that the Democrats, going back to before Yalta in 1945 and maybe as far back as the start of the New Deal in 1933, had been "soft on communism," appeasing the Soviet Union after World War II, allowing Communists to infiltrate the government, and implementing a lax foreign policy that had led directly to war in Korea. The right wing of the Republican Party led the charge. Joe McCarthy deliberately misspoke "Adlai" as "Alger" [Hiss] and expressed his desire to "get onto Stevenson's campaign train with a baseball bat and 'teach patriotism to little Ad-lie.'"[18]

Dwight Eisenhower shied away from participating directly in this redbaiting, but he did nothing to rein in either McCarthy or Richard Nixon. The "soft on communism" charge dominated the Republican campaign that was neatly summarized by a symbol that stuck—K_1C_2—for "Korea, Communism, Corruption." Eisenhower fully embraced the sentiment behind this phrase. While conceding that Stevenson was a skilled orator with a sense of humor, Ike asked a crowd,

> Is it amusing that we have stumbled into a war in Korea; that we have already lost in casualties 117,000 of our Americans killed and wounded; is it amusing that the war seems to be no nearer to a real solution than ever; that we have no real plan for stopping it? Is it funny when evidence was discovered that there are Communists in government and we get the cold comfort of the reply, "red herring"?[19]

On October 8, the peace delegations met at Panmunjom for the first time in a while. General Nam Il rejected the suggestions General Harrison had offered in September regarding non-repatriates and insisted that all Chinese prisoners, regardless of their wishes, be returned to Communist control. Harrison then read from a prepared statement and unilaterally adjourned this plenary meeting. The UN side had no further proposals to offer. Both delegations left the talks for the winter.[20]

A week later, Acheson addressed the UN General Assembly in New York. He said that the UN needed to demonstrate its resolve, and that the US would continue to fight for a just armistice. The American delegation offered a resolution signed by twenty other countries calling upon China and North Korea to recognize prisoners' rights to non-forcible repatriation. But nothing happened. In December, the Red Cross in Switzerland urged the two sides to exchange the sick and the wounded. General Clark agreed, but the Chinese and the North Koreans said no.[21]

By the middle of October, the war had become a fully partisan issue in an election campaign that looked one-sided. Speaking in Hartford, Connecticut, Truman challenged Eisenhower to offer a plan to end the war and save American lives. A week later, Ike responded with an electrifying promise. "That task," he told a crowd in Detroit and a national television audience, "requires a personal trip to Korea. . . . I shall make that trip. . . . I shall go to Korea."[22]

Truman reacted angrily, saying that if Ike had a plan to end the war, he should divulge it now, but the Detroit speech jolted the nation and pretty much settled the election. As Smith wrote, "The country was ready for a change, and Eisenhower seemed the ideal candidate to provide that. The most successful military commander of World War II, he never romanticized war. . . . In 1952, the issue was Korea, and who better to lead the United States to victory than the man who had defeated Hitler and the Third Reich."[23]

On November 4, Election Day, more than sixty-one million Americans, thirteen million more than in 1948, went to the polls. Stevenson got 27.3 million votes, 3.1 million more than Truman had four years before, but Eisenhower got 33.9 million votes, 55.4 percent of the total. He carried thirty-nine states and won the Electoral College tally, 442 to 89. Moreover, Ike cracked the Democrats' hold on the solid South, winning Florida, Tennessee, Texas, and Virginia. Catholics, especially those with roots in Eastern Europe, voted for the GOP. So did large numbers of farmers, blue-collar workers, and suburbanites, a new demographic. The Republicans also squeaked out slim majorities in both houses of Congress, giving them control of two branches of government for the first time since the election of 1930.[24]

Truman wired his congratulations to the president-elect and put the presidential airplane at his disposal for his trip to Korea. Eisenhower demurred, saying that one of the military services could provide suitable transport, and then he began a ten-day vacation at Augusta National.[25]

Earlier in the year, Congress had slashed the budgets of the agencies in charge of wage and price controls. The administration had been forced to eliminate hundreds of jobs, and when prices spiked a bit in the fall, candidate Eisenhower had called these controls an unworkable sham. In December, the results of a strike by the United Mine Workers put the last nail in the coffin of economic controls. Coal mine operators and the union had negotiated a wage increase of $1.90 per day, but the Wage Stabilization Board had authorized only $1.05, and the miners walked off the job. Truman was forced to get involved, as he had during the steel strike, and he undermined the wage board by granting the $1.90 increase.[26]

On November 29, Eisenhower flew to Korea, as he had promised. Before he departed, he met with the Joint Chiefs. They presented two options: to continue the fighting indefinitely or seek a military victory through a significant increase in the number of American troops. Eisenhower rejected both. He spent three days in Korea, primarily visiting frontline commanders and their troops. He also took a reconnaissance flight along the entire length of the front. He gave neither Syngman Rhee nor Clark a chance to present their separate plans for renewed offensives, telling Clark that "I have a mandate from the people to stop the fighting." He later wrote, "My conclusion as I left Korea was that we could not stand forever on a static front and continue to accept casualties without any visible results."[27]

And yet Eisenhower knew that a negotiated settlement would fall far short of the goals the Republican Party had set for itself. On his way back to the United States, Ike stopped at Pearl Harbor where he told the press, "We face an enemy whom we cannot hope to impress by words, however eloquent, but only by deeds—executed under circumstances of our own choosing." Smith wrote that "the implication was clear. Unless the Chinese accepted an armistice in Korea, the new administration would escalate the war."[28]

Responding to criticism aimed at schedule maker Clement Schwener, both major leagues assigned composing their 1953 schedules to committees composed of three club officials in the National League and four in the American. Working together, these groups devised a plan that would cost clubs more to travel but also, they hoped, boost revenues. In the National League, western clubs coming east had, in the past, visited the Dodgers and the Giants consecutively, but in 1953, they would squeeze in games in either Philadelphia or Boston between playing in Brooklyn and New York. Similarly, the Dodgers would no longer immediately follow the Giants on their western swings, so that fans would "be given more time to save additional money and also recover from crucial series in which the home team participated."[29]

In the American League, the new schedule provided for a more balanced division between home and road games in August and September. In addition, the four western clubs would visit New York and Boston, or vice versa, consecutively during only two of their four eastern trips. Opening Day was set for Tuesday, April 14, but two games, Pittsburgh at the Cincinnati Reds and the Yankees at the Washington Senators, with President Eisenhower expected to attend, were set for the day before.[30]

Just before the arrival of more than a thousand league and club officials in Arizona for the winter meetings, Robinson rocked the baseball world by charging the Yankees with racial discrimination. Speaking on a New York radio and television show, the Dodgers' star said, "I think the Yankee management is prejudiced. They haven't a single Negro on the team and very few in the Yankee organization." New York general manager George Weiss fired back. "The Yankees are not going to promote a Negro player to the Stadium simply in order to be able to say that they have such a player," he pointed out. "If Robinson can get me a Negro free agent who is capable of taking the job of any Yankee regular, I would be only too glad to establish a Negro player on our club. . . . Robinson's allegation was silly."[31]

The agendas for the Phoenix meetings were full, including at least twenty-nine proposed amendments to rules governing relations between the majors and the minors, and seventeen suggested changes to the agreement binding the minor leagues together. The minors met first. The Dallas club in the Texas League introduced a proposal to establish a committee to replace the existing major-minor league agreement with a new one that would reduce the number of minor leaguer players any major league club could control. After debate, the resolution failed with only sixteen minor leagues voting in favor and twenty-seven opposed.[32]

St. Louis Browns owner Bill Veeck went next, proposing on behalf of his San Antonio club, also in the Texas League, that no major league club be allowed to sign any player without previous professional experience. In other words, only minor league clubs would be able to sign first-year players, all of whom would be eligible for the draft after completing their first season. Veeck's resolution would have solved the bonus problem, but it, too, was voted down.[33]

The minors got some satisfaction on their complaint that major league clubs were allowed to option players to minor league clubs subject to twenty-four-hour recall, thereby limiting the ability of minor league clubs to plan. The rule was amended to require optioned players to remain with their minor league clubs for a minimum of ten days and for players optioned after July 31 to stay in the minors until the end of the minor league season.[34]

Answering complaints that teams involved in pennant races were abusing the waiver system, the rule by which teams in one major league could move players to the other league was adjusted. The National League opposed the original proposal that would have pushed the trading deadline from June 15 to July 15, but both leagues approved extending the waiver system to interleague transactions. That is, after the trading deadline, a club would have to obtain waivers from all clubs in both leagues before transferring a player to a club in the other league.[35]

The most important rules change was the approval of a new bonus rule. The committee deliberating how to reinstitute some control over clubs' paying first-year players huge bonuses introduced a proposal declaring that any first-year player would be designated as a bonus player if he signed a contract for more than $4,000 with a major league club or a minor league club above Class B or for more than $3,000 if he signed with a Class B, C, or D club. Major league bonus players would have to remain on the major league roster for two years, and minor league bonus players on the roster of the team that signed them for one year. The new rule, which went into effect immediately, granted the commissioner the right to fine or suspend violators.[36]

On December 15, the Pirates became the first club to sign a bonus player under the new rule, knowing that he would have to remain on the roster for the entirety of the 1953 and 1954 seasons. He was Vic Janowicz, who had won college football's Heisman Trophy in 1950 as an Ohio State junior and gone on active duty with his National Guard unit after finishing college. Even though Janowicz had not played any baseball in college, Pittsburgh signed him for a reported $25,000.[37]

Two items not resolved at the winter meetings were baseball's continuing television problem and the growing concern that one or more major league teams might use the sport's economic woes as a reason to move to new cities. Just before the meetings opened, Cardinals owner Fred Saigh fired an opening salvo by suggesting that National League clubs forsake televising all games for a year "to see if TV really is as harmful as we think." In Phoenix, American League owners defeated Veeck's proposal to guarantee visiting clubs a share of home team television revenue. Although this would have benefited the Browns and other clubs at the expense of the Yankees, none of the other clubs were willing to risk incurring the Yankees' wrath. In the National League, a few clubs signed separate deals to pay visiting clubs, but no league-wide policy emerged, and there was no sense that the television tiger had been tamed.[38]

The minors, of course, continued to complain about major league games being televised into minor league cities. Senator Edwin Johnson (D-CO), president of the Western League, proposed that all money accrued from televising such games be deposited in a trust fund to aid the minors. The majors rejected this proposal but agreed to establish a committee to study the matter. Simultaneously, NL president Warren Giles argued that the best way for the minors to survive would be to contract to no more than twenty leagues.[39]

En route to Phoenix, Brooklyn president Walter O'Malley suggested that one or two teams in two-team cities, the Braves and the Browns, might be ready to move. Indeed, two months before, Braves president Lou Perini had put Boston on notice, saying that he had no plans to move the Braves, 'but I wouldn't be so stubborn as to go along this way for ten years." Similarly, Veeck had expressed doubts that the Browns could prosper in St. Louis and turned his gaze to Milwaukee where he once owned a minor league team.[40]

"I think there is a call to action on our part," O'Malley said. No major league club had moved since 1903, and the existing rule governing relocation required approval from a majority of clubs in both leagues. A new rule approved in Phoenix said that if a major league club wanted to move to a city that did not already have a major league team, approval would be confined to the clubs in that league. A club wanting to move to a city that already had a team would require unanimous approval from all sixteen clubs.[41]

In November, Selective Service rendered yet another decision on Mickey Mantle's draft status. His local board again found him ineligible for military service, not because of his osteomyelitis, but because of the knee injury he had suffered during the 1951 World Series. Mantle had been reexamined at Fort Sill, Oklahoma, where he had been previously classified 4-F. This time, his medical record was sent to Washington from where the new verdict was rendered.[42]

A week or so later, Ted Williams got his orders to report by January 2 to the Marine Air Station at El Toro, California, prior to being shipped overseas. According to his biographer, Leigh Montville, Williams reportedly told a friend that he thought he was going to die in Korea. Jerry Coleman got similar orders at roughly the same time. Lloyd Merriman, who was already in Hawaii where his heavy flying schedule permitted him to play ball with the Waikiki club in the Hawaii Baseball League only on Sundays, got his orders for Korea too. "Flying a jet was quite a thrill," he recalled years later. "I met Ted Williams at El Toro, and [future astronaut] John Glenn was in our group too."[43]

The worst moment of Bob Kennedy's training as a jet pilot at Cherry Point came when he was flying a Grumman F9F Panther at 20,000 feet and found a scorpion perched on his knee. "I asked for advice by radio from other members of the squadron," he said. "They advised me to go up to 35,000 feet and kill it by lack of oxygen. But I didn't want it with me that long." Kennedy landed his plane and told the first mechanic on the scene to get the scorpion out of there. "He looked at me and gave me a flat 'Nuts' and then added 'Sir.' I guess they killed it later." A few weeks later, Kennedy received word that he would not be going to Korea after all, the Marines deciding that he should be discharged because he had so many dependents.[44]

One more professional-ballplayer-turned-soldier died near the end of the year. Erwin "Ace" Adamcewicz played in the Cardinals' organization as an outfielder from 1947 through 1950 after which he was drafted into the Army and assigned to the 179th Infantry Regiment, Forty-Fifth Infantry Division. Adamcewicz was wounded in action on May 14, 1952. He returned to a military hospital at Fort Devens, Massachusetts, where he died of his wounds on November 21.[45]

13

The Braves Move to Milwaukee, January–March 1953

In the weeks between the 1952 winter meetings and the start of spring training in 1953, Organized Baseball's officials, from the commissioner down to minor league club owners, had time to reexamine the business of baseball and propose solutions for its problems. No unified vision emerged, and none of these executives was prepared as the map of major league baseball changed dramatically before anyone threw a pitch on Opening Day.

Acting upon authority given to him in Phoenix, Commissioner Ford Frick appointed a committee to study baseball's relationship with television and to recommend a policy. "I do not know what our policy should be with regard to television," Frick said. "But we are going to try hard to find out." He named two representatives from the American League, New York Yankees general manager George Weiss and Chicago White Sox general manager Frank Lane; two from the National League, New York Giants vice president Chub Feeney and St. Louis Cardinals vice president William Walsingham; and two from the minors, International League president Frank Shaughnessy and Western League president Edwin Johnson, with Shaughnessy serving as the committee's chair.[1]

Johnson was far from a neutral member. He had testified before the Celler subcommittee about the majors' dominance over the minors. At the annual dinner hosted by the New York chapter of the BBWAA in January, he sounded a Paul Revere-like alarm about television, telling the minors to "wake up; the majors are coming to your ballpark. . . . They are no longer satisfied with the bloodletting in their own territory; they are conniving with a super salesman [television] to take the last drop of blood in the minor league territory, also. Who will fire the first shot to be heard 'round the baseball world'?"[2]

The television committee had already resolved to conduct a nationwide survey of the effects of radio and television on baseball and to present a final report when major league owners convened during the All-Star break. "Then we shall be in position to decide on a remedy," Weiss said. But Johnson refused to stop sounding the alarm. "The Federal Communications Commission right now has applications for more than 1,000 new television stations," he said. "Can you imagine how baseball would be affected if these stations were permitted to hook up with the major leagues and broadcast into our territory?"[3]

Intruding upon this already tense situation was an idea hatched by Tom McMahon, sports director of the DuMont television network, to televise a "game of the week" on twenty-four regular-season Saturdays over DuMont's fifty-eight stations with games blacked out in the local markets. The *Sporting News* said this plan "would deal further financial blows to hard-pressed minor league clubs," even though McMahon intended to set up a corporation to which minor league clubs could subscribe and reap part of the network's profits. To avoid antitrust difficulties, McMahon had to negotiate with each major league club separately, and that proved his plan's undoing. Many club owners expressed interest in this new scheme, but no one wanted to be the first to sign on.[4]

St. Louis Browns president Bill Veeck continued to insist that league rules be amended to require teams televising home games to share revenue from these telecasts with visiting teams. American League owners had voted down Veeck's idea in Phoenix, saying that broadcasting deals should be negotiated on a team-by-team basis. Veeck retaliated by proclaiming that he would withhold the right to allow visiting teams to broadcast games from St. Louis until the Browns received a cut of home team television money when they played on the road.[5]

Three clubs, the Boston Red Sox, the Cleveland Indians, and the Yankees, fired back, telling the Browns that eight games originally scheduled as night games, two in Boston, four in Cleveland, and two in New York, would be rescheduled as day games. Since night games generally drew larger crowds than day games, Veeck's share of ticket revenue would be reduced, costing him, he bristled, "Not too much. Maybe $15,000 to $20,000, not much more." Besides, he added, teams he denied the right to televise home games against the Browns would be losing much more. "If they get $5,000 per game [for each of eleven games in St. Louis], that is $55,000 each of them will lose in their beloved TV fee alone. Stubborn people, aren't they?"[6]

Veeck put his case to his fellow owners at a meeting on January 31, but league president Will Harridge refused to allow the dispute to come to a vote. Veeck then appealed to Frick but got no satisfaction. The Browns' owner, struggling financially and hoping to put a winning team on the field, said he was "forced into action. When the Yankees get $500,000 to televise their home games, they're not only more than compensating financially for their loss in attendance, but they're depriving us of an ordinary share of road receipts."[7]

The Browns earned no home television revenue since St. Louis had only one television station, and it was unwilling to clear time to show baseball games. Veeck's situation got worse when the Indians and the Yankees also refused to allow any of the Browns' forty-four games against them to be broadcast on the radio. Harridge called a league meeting to revisit the entire dispute but not until April 21, too late, in the Browns' view, to do anything about 1953. "All I have done," Veeck summarized, "is tell these other clubs, 'Don't televise us.' I have never asked for a nickel. I have said, though, that if they go ahead and arrange telecasts, after our request not to put us on TV, that we expect we should be recompensed, since we are half the entertainment."[8]

Cardinals president Fred Saigh shared Veeck's concerns about television, but his world turned upside down on January 28 when a federal district court judge sentenced him to fifteen months in prison and fined him $15,000 on two counts of tax evasion stemming from his personal tax returns from 1944 through 1950 and the Cardinals' tax returns for 1948 and 1949. Despite Saigh's protestations, the judge ordered him to settle his business affairs within three months and to "turn [himself] in on May 4 and depart immediately."[9]

Stunned by the severity of the sentence, Saigh said, "This means I must dispose of the Cardinals. I cannot stay in baseball." He was correct. A meeting the next day with Frick and National League president Warren Giles confirmed Saigh's baseball fate. He planned to appoint three trustees to operate the club and oversee its sale, but that proved unnecessary. Interest in buying the Cardinals was intense with bids coming from groups in Houston, Milwaukee, Washington, and Detroit. But Saigh wanted the Cardinals to remain in St. Louis, and on February 20, he sold the club to the Anheuser-Busch brewery for $3.75 million, including assumed debt.[10]

August Busch Jr. was destined to become president of the ball club, but there were two wrinkles to iron out. Anheuser-Busch was a publicly traded company, and all other major league clubs were privately held. Frick insisted that the brewery set up a wholly owned subsidiary, August A. Busch Inc., to own the St. Louis National Baseball Club. In addition, the brewery's stockholders had to approve the purchase. When they did so on March 10, their number included Saigh, who had purchased 28,000 shares of Anheuser-Busch stock just before closing the deal to sell the club and saw that stock rise two dollars a share the day after the stockholders' vote.[11]

The sale of the Cardinals did not bode well for the Browns. Even though Veeck owned Sportsman's Park where both teams played, he was now convinced that St. Louis could not support two major league clubs, and Anheuser-Busch and the Cardinals were obviously not going away. But Veeck's earlier interest in moving the Browns to Milwaukee was suddenly stymied when Lou Perini announced on March 3 that his Braves would be leaving Boston to play in the brand new Milwaukee County Stadium.[12]

Together with his two partners in a massive construction business, Perini had bought control of the Braves in 1944. The team had long been moribund on the field, finishing in the first division only five times since winning the 1914 World Series. The "Three Little Steam Shovels," as the trio of co-owners was called, pumped some life into the team, and the Braves won the 1948 pennant, only to decline again. Perini bought up most of the team's stock and absorbed significant losses.[13]

Perini also owned the Milwaukee Brewers in the American Association, and when Milwaukee County built a new ballpark to replace ancient Borchert Field, the city became a legitimate candidate for major league baseball, and Perini's appetite was whetted. The new park had thirty-two thousand seats and parking for ten thousand cars. In advance of the 1953 minor league season, ticket sales exceeded $75,000. Perini said he was "sick of pounding my head against a stone wall. . . . Boston simply is not a two-club city." National League owners approved the Braves' move to Milwaukee on March 16, just a month before Opening Day.[4]

The Braves' quick transfer, the first such move since the American League's Baltimore Orioles had moved to New York for the 1903 season, turned Veeck's attention to Baltimore whose political and civic leaders wanted to acquire a major league team. Veeck and Mayor Thomas D'Alesandro had shaken hands on a tentative deal late in 1952, and Harridge indicated that the league's owners would approve the move. But on March 16, the same day the National League approved Perini's move, Veeck's partners in the American League nixed his. The Browns would play at least one more season in St. Louis.[15]

In January, 264 members of the BBWAA cast ballots in the annual election to select new members of the Hall of Fame. Before the votes were cast, speculation was that Joe DiMaggio might become the second player, after Lou Gehrig, to be elected immediately after his retirement. That did not happen. DiMaggio received only 117 votes, the eighth highest total and far short of the 198 needed for election. At the top of the tally stood two new members of the Hall, Dizzy Dean and Al Simmons. Dean got 209 votes, and Simmons 199, just one more than required for election. Bill Terry, who had finished third in 1952, finished third again, seven votes short. The *Sporting News* suggested that "his bluntness, his refusal to co-operate, cost him many potential friends among the writers who traveled with his club."[16]

Immediately after the votes were counted, Frick suggested that the Hall should amend its rules to create "what we might call automatic elections," including players who batted .400 in a season and pitchers who completed perfect games. Frick noted that twenty-nine batters had hit .400 but only twelve of them were in the Hall and six pitchers had thrown perfect games but only one, Cy Young, had been enshrined in Cooperstown.[17]

Another cold winter without an armistice meant another cold winter during which American prisoners held by the North Koreans and the Chinese were subject to great deprivation, both physical and psychological, including, as Rees wrote, "a systematic attempt at mass conversion to Communism." Prison camps in the north were divided into two groups: North Korean transit camps near Pyongyang "where the living conditions were unspeakable" and eight permanent camps set up during the winter of 1950–51 and run by the Chinese.[18]

Captured Americans were forced marched to these camps, sometimes clad in summer fatigues during winter and often deprived of any food beyond boiled corn or millet. Medical care was primitive at best. The North Koreans, Rees wrote, killed prisoners by calculated brutality, and the Chinese did so by deliberate neglect. One British war correspondent, captured in September 1950 along with nearly eight hundred soldiers, missionaries, nuns, diplomats, and other journalists, estimated that by February 1951, 60 percent of his group had died from deprivation. With the temperature dropping sometimes to as low as thirty or forty degrees below zero, starvation and cold claimed some while others surrendered to a complete lack of will to live.[19]

Rees estimated that most of the Americans who died in captivity succumbed during the war's first winter. "With this terrible winter in mind," he wrote, "for those who wished to escape the mass graves on the Yalu, the lesson was obvious," and that was to submit to lectures on communist theory. "Study hard, comrades, with open minds," exhorted the commandant of the most notorious camp, "and you will get home soon. But if you don't, we'll dig a ditch for you so deep that even your bourgeois bodies won't stink."[20]

The Chinese called the war a product of imperialist aggression and branded all UN soldiers as war criminals. But, under their "Lenient Policy," a skewed version of the Geneva Convention, prisoners who proved themselves progressive and not reactionary were spared the death they all deserved. Compulsory lectures often lasted until ten o'clock at night and bore such titles as "Corruption of the UN by the American Warmongers" and "Churchill, Tool of the Truman-MacArthur-Dulles Fascist Clique." Complementing these talks was a regimen controlling prisoners' lives completely and, regardless of American military rank, privileging those who proved themselves open to reeducation.[21]

So-called voluntary study groups eventually replaced compulsory talks, but the psychological techniques undergirding this indoctrination remained the same: repetition, harassment, humiliation. The campaign was relentless, and yet postwar analysis showed that the Chinese succeeded in converting only about one in every twenty-five of their prisoners and that just a few, twenty-one Americans and one Briton, opted after the war to live in China.[22]

One of Eisenhower's first acts as president-elect was to entrust two key aides, retired general Lucius Clay and attorney Herbert Brownell, with helping him pick his cabinet, and one of their first choices was John Foster Dulles for secretary of state. The author of the foreign policy section of the 1952 Republican Party platform was a Princeton graduate, a successful lawyer, and an internationalist who, as a critic of containment, never missed an opportunity to urge rolling back the Iron Curtain.[23]

Dulles had supported Truman's decision to intervene in Korea. On the Fourth of July 1950, he had given a speech in which he said, "What we are doing today is in keeping with the tradition of our past. We can say with pride that our spirit today is the spirit of '76 and that our living today is faithful to the principles on which our nation was founded." Two years later, he still supported the president's decision, but in a *Life* magazine article called "A Policy of Boldness," he spoke of the "treadmill policies of containment" and, more positively, of "liberation."[24]

As Rees wrote, "Liberation was supposed to work by exercising unrelenting political, economic, and moral pressure on the Communist bloc from outside, and by attempting to initiate the same pressures inside the Iron Curtain." But it also included "using the threat of atomic retaliation to prevent local Communist aggression." This strategy, which would later be called "Massive Retaliation," was missing from the Republican platform, but both Dulles and Eisenhower believed that if the Communists had been warned beforehand that North Korean aggression would be met by American force, the invasion across the parallel might never have occurred.[25]

Thus, according to Dulles, speaking in May 1952, "The only effective way to stop prospective aggressors is to convince them in advance that if they commit aggression, they will be subjected to retaliatory blows so costly that their aggression will not be a profitable operation."[26]

When Eisenhower left Korea, he flew to Guam and then boarded the cruiser *Helena* to sail to Hawaii. Dulles was onboard. Together, according to reporter Robert J. Donovan, they "determined to make it clear to the Communists that to delay the truce indefinitely would be to invite the United States to enlarge the war and to strike at China not only in Korea but on two or three other fronts of its own choosing." Indeed, giving indication that this strategy, hinting at the use of atomic weapons, owed much to General MacArthur's thinking, Eisenhower and Dulles conferred with the retired general upon their return home, and MacArthur believed this threat would be enough to end the war.[27]

In the weeks after the inauguration on January 20, Eisenhower made no direct threat to use atomic weapons. But on February 2, in his first State of the Union address, the president said that the Seventh Fleet would no longer shield the Chinese mainland from attacks by Chiang Kai-shek's forces on Taiwan. Eisenhower implied no aggressive intent, he said, but according to Rees, "here was a first warning . . . that Taiwan might be used for larger operations against the mainland unless a truce was coming in Korea."[28]

The minor leagues approached the season down five leagues from the year before. All forty-three leagues had finished the 1952 season, but the Interstate League, the Southwest International League, the Coastal Plain League, the Kansas-Oklahoma-Missouri League, and the Western Carolina League soon went out of business. The Coastal Plain League, operating in North Carolina, suspended operations on February 2 when three clubs objected to Wilmington and Elizabeth City replacing Tarboro and Rocky Mount. The proposed additions would have made it difficult for some road teams to return home each night, violating a league compact.[29]

Gerald Nugent, president of the Interstate League and one-time owner of the Philadelphia Phillies, complained that minor league clubs located close to major league cities were bound to die out. In his league, he said,

> the towns are so close to the Phillies and the Athletics . . . that the people developed a major league interest at the expense of our clubs. Radio broadcasts, . . . together with the Game of the Day and telecasts of some of the home contests all contributed. The sports editors of the local papers also gave the big leaguers the main spot in the paper.[30]

The Pacific Coast League began the year by reducing roster size from twenty-three to twenty-two. League president Pants Rowland said the cut was not an economy move but rather preparation for returning servicemen that might boost a team's roster by as many as five players. He added, "When a club carries more than twenty-one players, it breeds dissension. . . . No minor league club needs more than two catchers, six infielders, five outfielders, and eight pitchers." Some owners also wanted home clubs to share their television revenue with visiting clubs. "It takes two clubs to make the show, and both should share in whatever profits come from it," Rowland said, echoing Veeck. But Oakland president Brick Laws disagreed. "TV and radio," he said, "should be sold by the individual club just like peanuts and popcorn and the receipts retained by each."[31]

San Francisco Seals owner Paul Fagan saw the Braves' move to Milwaukee and the Browns' attempted shift to Baltimore as good news for the PCL. "The majors have to do one of two things—nationalize themselves by moving into Los Angeles and San Francisco, or sectionalize themselves by putting clubs in Baltimore and Milwaukee," he said. "Now it looks as if they are sectionalizing themselves. . . . The fear of major league invasion of the Coast's larger cities has now vanished." He argued that the PCL's next move should be a demand to be put under the commissioner on the same basis as the two major leagues, paving the way for equal trading rights and eventual major league status. Hollywood Stars vice president Bob Cobb agreed. "Our league can and will remain intact," he said. "We have had the ambition for years to become a third big league and that is a goal quite possible to reach in the not-too-distant future."[32]

Earl Mann, president of the Southern Association's Atlanta Crackers, a club that televised no games in 1952, attacked the television problem in an unusual way. He agreed to televise home games on Mondays and Wednesdays and Sunday doubleheaders if members of the Atlanta Junior Chamber of Commerce bought twenty-five thousand television game books for $5 each with each book containing four tickets good for any Crackers home game. The president of the Jaycees said that "the project by no means represents a contribution. Most televiewers see four games a year at least, anyway."[33]

Mann's minor league neighbors raised a stink when he announced this plan. Owners of clubs within two hundred miles of Atlanta, the radius of

WSB-TV's signal, squawked about Atlanta's invasion of their territory. "Why yell about the major leagues eating up their young with television," one owner said, "when the minor league towns with television stations are going to do the same thing? Does it make any difference who gobbles you up?"[34]

Frick was content to leave the television debate to others, but he did weigh in on two other economic issues. In January he suggested that baseball on radio and television was being hurt by an inundation of advertising. "I have a recording of a game that ran one hour and fifty-eight minutes. . . . Would you like to guess how many commercials, how many blurbs they jammed into this broadcast of less than two hours? A total of 106!" Of course, as sportswriter Harold Rosenthal pointed out, radio and television revenue had become an important part of every major league club's budget. "Whether radio or TV may be the reason for gate declines," he wrote, "the revenue received represents the difference between red and black ink."[35]

A week later, Frick argued that major league clubs should raise ticket prices significantly. "Since 1947," he noted, "major league attendance figures have been going down and costs of operation have been going up. . . . While all other sports have hiked their rates, the majors still have fifty-cent bleacher and dollar grandstand charges." Frick said he had been studying operating costs and revenues from ticket sales and other sources and was surprised to find out that "whereas a club owner may be a hard-headed businessman in some industry or other non-baseball enterprise, he runs his diamond venture without too much business acumen." He pointed to the new bonus rule as one way to control costs. In 1952, he noted, clubs paid young players with uncertain futures $4.5 million in bonuses. "If we can direct even half of that bonus money into baseball channels, the benefit will be tremendous," he said.[36]

But spending on bonuses did not stop. The Red Sox, habitual big spenders, became the second club after the Pittsburgh Pirates to sign a player under the new rule. He was 18-year-old Billy Consolo, the most sought-after young position player in the country. Consolo signed for $65,000 on February 2. Former pitcher Dutch Ruether, scouting for the Giants, hardly cared that he lost out. "If you didn't have to put the bonus boy on the big league roster, the Red Sox would buy 'em all. The rule is bad for the boy, but it seems the only way to square the deal," he complained.[37]

Johnny and Eddie O'Brien were twins who played both baseball and basketball at the University of Seattle. They sought a package deal to sign baseball contracts, and at least seven teams, including the Giants, the Yankees, and the Pirates, courted them. The Pirates won out, signing the brothers on March 19 and ordering them to report to spring training in Havana, Cuba, right away. "We paid them more than $4,000 [actually, $40,000 each] to sign," said general manager Branch Rickey. There would be more signings once school let out in the spring.[38]

Jerry Coleman reached Korea in mid-January and Ted Williams early in February. Coleman was assigned to the "Death Rattlers" squadron in the First Marine Air Wing. "Our insignia was a coiled snake perched above the silhouette of a flying Corsair, its propeller spinning," he remembered. Coleman flew his first combat mission on January 30, knocking out a railway bridge on a supply route south of Pyongyang. "It seems like old times," he said. "We did a lot of interdiction-type strikes that were not close to the front, attacking a concentration of this, a concentration of that, and all these targets were marked and, I guess, approved by somebody."[39]

"I had two close calls," Coleman recalled in his memoir. On one mission his radio went out as he was returning to base in the clouds. Unable to see other planes, he landed successfully, only to have another F-86 come in over his head and go off the runway. That plane hit the hills beyond, and the pilot was killed. On another occasion, Coleman hit a bump on the runway as he was taking off. His plane's engine cut out, and he knew he would have to stop before reaching the end of the runway or crash. Coleman released his bombs on the ground. As one bomb hit the tail wheel, the plane flipped upside down. An emergency crew rescued him.[40]

Williams took two familiarization flights in Korea before flying his first mission on February 18. The raid involved two hundred planes attacking a troop and supply center about fifteen miles south of Pyongyang, so far from base that they would need to land at an Air Force base on the way home to refuel. Williams's plane reached the target. He dove down to less than two thousand feet, released his bombs, and climbed back to altitude. He did not realize that his plane had been hit, but trouble developed with the landing gear, the stick, and the radio. He was flying a wounded plane fifteen miles from the North Korean capital.[41]

Landing in the Yellow Sea was not an option because of ice, and neither was ejection since Williams was so tall that he risked injury being propelled out of the cockpit. Fortunately, a young pilot named Larry Hawkins, trained and experienced in jets, saw the trouble. Using hand signals, he motioned to Williams to follow him, but then Hawkins noticed smoke from the back of Williams's plane. If this were fuel, and if it pooled at the bottom of the engine, the jet would explode. Hawkins took Williams up to twenty-five thousand feet to burn off as much fuel as possible, and the pair headed toward the Air Force base.[42]

As they descended, Hawkins radioed ahead, but fuel in the wheel wells of Williams's plane caught fire. Unsure of his landing gear, Williams prepared to crash land. Again, luck was with him. The landing strip at the Air Force base was eleven thousand feet long, and Williams needed all of that. He landed going more than two hundred miles per hour, hit the brakes hard, skidded for maybe nine thousand feet, and stopped. Hawkins, right behind him, saw "this tall figure getting out of the cockpit as fast as he could." The plane did not explode because there was no fuel left. "It was an act of God that the plane didn't blow up when it caught on fire. I'd hate to go through those minutes again," Williams admitted.[43]

Bobby Brown and Lloyd Merriman were also in Korea. Brown was assigned as a surgeon with the 160th Field Artillery Battalion, Forty-Fifth Division, and Merriman, like Coleman, was with the First Marine Air Wing. "I flew eighty-seven combat missions in an F9F Panther jet," and "I saw quite of bit of Jerry Coleman." Brown planned a March reunion of the four ballplayers in Seoul, but on the day selected, he was the only one on hand. Coleman flew two missions that day, Williams was on duty, and Merriman's flight to Seoul turned back because of bad weather.[44]

14

The "Game of the Week," April–June 1953

As major league clubs opened spring training, almost all of them had in camp one or more players who had recently completed military service and were eager to play ball again. Some of these returnees, nearly forty in all, were prospects ready—or perhaps not—for the big leagues, but others had played in the majors before being called to duty and were keen to resume their careers. In assessing their talent, clubs had some leeway since all ex-servicemen, players on the Armed Forces Service Rules List, could be carried on major league rosters for a year after reinstatement without being counted against the roster limit.[1]

A *Sporting News* survey identified nearly two dozen returning major leaguers who wanted to reclaim a roster spot, including New York Yankees pitcher Whitey Ford. He had last pitched in the 1950 World Series, and manager Casey Stengel was counting on him to buttress his team's starting rotation. The Cleveland Indians had six returning veterans in camp, most prominently outfielders Bob Kennedy and Jim Lemon and pitchers Al Aber and Dick Weik. Red Friend was in camp with the Detroit Tigers, hoping to start at second base. In the National League, players returning included Carl Sawatski and Preston Ward to the Chicago Cubs and catcher Del Crandall to the soon-to-be Milwaukee Braves.[2]

Minor league club owners also anticipated the return of players-turned-soldiers, but as usual, the minors had to deal with larger challenges than roster construction. As the Pacific Coast League season opened to good crowds on March 31, the *Sporting News* agreed editorially with San Francisco Seals owner Paul Fagan that the Braves' move from Boston to Milwaukee presented the PCL with "the biggest challenge in its history . . . free to march forward as a unit toward major [league] status."[3]

Would the PCL, the weekly wondered, be up to the task at hand? "Can the Coast clubs build up and maintain adequate farm and scouting systems?" the editorial asked. "Can the fans of the Coast league be counted on to support their heroes in a manner which not only will justify bigger budgets for the present, but which will make large-park construction in the reasonably near future seem feasible?" If not, the editorial continued, the league's optimism might prove to be misplaced. "If they can move into Milwaukee on a few weeks' notice," came a warning, "there is no reason to suppose that the majors will hesitate to set up shop in Los Angeles or San Francisco when and if they can see an economic advantage."[4]

Broadcasting, especially the growing threat posed by major league games being shown in minor league territory, also continued to bedevil the minors. Figures supplied by an executive at one of the country's largest advertising agencies allowed sportswriter Hugh Brown to calculate that major league and minor league clubs would be receiving upwards of $10 million for broadcast rights to their 1953 games, even as television stations were "sprouting like cypress trees in a Georgia swamp." One report had the Braves selling their radio rights alone to Miller Brewing for upwards of $1 million.[5]

Compounding this news was word that Gordon McLendon had formed a new business venture, the Knickerbocker Network, which planned to broadcast on radio one major league game, either a day game or a night game, every day of the season. Once again, McLendon would use the technique called recreation, bolstered by a recent court ruling that once a club's own broadcast went on the air, that broadcast became public property. McLendon hoped the minors would consider his project "free advertising for baseball," but Dick Burnett, owner of the Texas League's Dallas Eagles, said, "I don't think the fans in our territory would prefer listening to a 'canned' major league broadcast over those of the local team."[6]

In May a Senate subcommittee held several days of hearings on a bill introduced by Senator Edwin Johnson (D-CO) that would have allowed Organized Baseball to reinstate Rule 1(d) and ban broadcasts or telecasts by one club in the home territory of another. Johnson's goal, of course, was to rescue the minor leagues, and several baseball officials, including Commissioner Ford Frick, National League president Warren Giles, and National Association president George Trautman, spoke in its favor. "We want to restore order where there is chaos," Johnson said, and Frick agreed, saying, "The destruction of minor league baseball eventually would result in the destruction of major league baseball."[7]

Harold E. Fellows, president of the National Association of Radio and Television Broadcasters, opposed the bill, writing in a letter to the subcommittee, "Anything that would lessen broadcasters' ability to bring major league baseball to the American people would be contrary to the public interest." Pittsburgh Pirates general manager Branch Rickey fired back. "Destruction of the minor leagues is not just eating our young but eating ourselves," he said. But Johnson's bill went nowhere.[8]

St. Louis Browns owner Bill Veeck also continued to struggle with broadcasting. Just a week after being defeated in his attempt to move his club to Baltimore, he relented on his demand that Browns' road games be kept off home teams' telecasts. Cleveland, one of three clubs that had retaliated against Veeck by switching night games to day games, thus reducing the Browns' cut of paid attendance, immediately announced that two contests against the Browns would revert to night games, and the Boston Red Sox soon did the same thing.[9]

Veeck's financial troubles did not disappear, and on April 9, he sold Sportsman's Park to Anheuser-Busch for $800,000 plus an additional $300,000 in moving expenses. The Browns agreed to pay $175,000 in rent for each of the next five years, and the brewery announced a $400,000 commitment for much-needed renovations to the ballpark, starting immediately. "Fans will see many improvements during the season," said St. Louis Cardinals president August Busch Jr., "since I have given the contractors the full-speed-ahead sign. Basic improvements will be made first. Many others will follow as the season gets under way." Included in the first changes was a new name, Busch Stadium.

Veeck admitted his club had lost $396,000 in 1952, but, he said, if "people are so upset about it, why aren't they buying tickets for our games?"[10]

"When Harry S. Truman handed the reins of government to Dwight Eisenhower," wrote historian Paul G. Pierpaoli Jr., "the nation was in enviably good shape. Its economy was booming, its rearmament program was nearing its peak, and its ability to uphold domestic and global national security had never been stronger or more sophisticated." The new president felt committed to eliminating wage and price controls, even though public opinion polls showed that more than 60 percent of those polled favored continuation.[11]

Ike moved slowly. "Not until two days before his State of the Union Address," Pierpaoli wrote, "did he decide to scrap controls, bowing to pressure from business and other Republican-oriented groups that had helped get him elected." In his speech, he ordered the relevant agencies to end controls no later than April 20. In fact, once the ball got rolling, everything happened by March 18, and the Truman administration's control of the wartime economy was finished.[12]

Change came in Korea, too. "Some time between March and May," Rees wrote, "the Chinese decided to write off the war." Why? Several reasons stand out. After peace talks were suspended in October 1952, Panmunjom no longer served as a ready outlet for Communist propaganda, and the war was having an adverse effect on the Chinese economy. Moreover, Stalin's death on March 5 suggested to China that it might want to spend more time working on its relations with the Soviet Union. In addition, the United States' hint that it might use atomic weapons unless a truce was signed seemed to have an effect. The US tested a tactical nuclear weapon in January, and the Soviets, Hastings wrote, "feared Dulles and were disposed to believe he meant business."[13]

Late in February, General Clark wrote a letter repeating the December proposal that sick and wounded prisoners be exchanged. This time, Kim Il Sung and General Peng Teh-huai responded positively, suggesting that such an exchange might "lead to the smooth settlement of the entire question of prisoners of war." Liaison groups from both sides met in early April, and the Communists brought with them a statement from Chou En-lai in which he approved a neutral nation repatriation scheme. That is, Chou said that "both parties . . . should undertake to repatriate immediately after the cessation of hostilities all those . . . in their custody who insist upon repatriation and to hand over the remaining prisoners of war to a neutral state so as to ensure a just solution to the question of their repatriation." The Soviets endorsed Chou's suggestion, too.[14]

At last, the deadlock was broken. Liaison groups met soon, and Operation "Little Switch" began on April 20. Three days before, General Harrison had suggested to General Nam Il that Switzerland be appointed as the neutral custodial nation and that the Swiss be given sixty days following a cease-fire to determine the status of all those whose attitude toward repatriation was unclear. On April 26, the two sides held their first plenary session at Panmunjom since October.[15]

Simultaneously, the war continued at sea, in the air, and on the ground. After Inchon, the UN command had realized that naval power could be used not only for amphibious landings but also to blockade traffic to North Korea from Chinese and Soviet ports. This blockade was successful, forcing both China and the Soviet Union to attempt delivering supplies either by air or over land. Moreover, naval superiority meant that six of every seven UN personnel arriving in Korea throughout the war came by sea.[16]

American airpower, both fighters and bombers, had enjoyed superiority from the beginning. Over the course of the war, the air campaign had four objectives: destroy the North Korean air force and its infrastructure; support UN ground troops in their operations; interdict supplies and destroy supply lines; and cripple North Korea's manufacturing. The second pair of these objectives proved difficult to achieve. As the Allies had discovered during World War II in Europe and as the United States would rediscover in Vietnam, bombing campaigns, however damaging, give rise to ingenuity and resilience, and no tonnage of bombs, however large, can drive a settlement at the peace table.[17]

On the ground, the early months of 1953 saw fighting "simmer down," in Rees's words, "to routine patrolling and small-scale attacks." Immediately after the peace talks had adjourned in October, the heaviest fighting since Heartbreak Ridge had broken out along the front line. Chinese infantry attacks, designed to influence the outcome of the American presidential race, were not successful, nor was Operation SHOWDOWN, a subsequent counterattack by US forces. Casualties on both sides were high.[18]

In the spring, each side continued to barrage the other with loudspeaker announcements deemed psychological warfare or psywar, to use the phrase of the day. The UN command's messages praised the way it was treating POWs and insisted that the Soviet Union had manipulated North Korea and China into the war. From the other side came a steady stream of American pop tunes performed by Chinese bands and vocalists, including "There's No Place Like Home."[19]

But even as it looked like the war was finally winding down, the fighting did not cease. The Communists staged a series of small assaults on a variety of UN outposts, each designed to move, if slightly, the boundaries of "no man's land" and affect the eventual location of the demilitarized zone when peace did arrive. In this context came the most famous battle of the war's end game, the fight for Pork Chop Hill, nicknamed for its shape and later remembered in a motion picture starring Gregory Peck. The Chinese attacked Hill 255, its formal name, on April 16, but after some initial success, they were repulsed by US infantry supported by nine artillery battalions that fired a record 77,349 rounds in just two days.[20]

When talks resumed at Panmunjom in April, disagreement still raged over how to implement Chou's suggestion for a general exchange of prisoners. Both sides made proposals that the other rejected. Late in May, the Eisenhower administration sent Clark what Rees called "final proposals." All prisoners would be transferred to a neutral nations repatriation commission that would be staffed by India alone. After sixty days allowed for voluntary repatriation and an additional period of three to four months during which both sides could try to convince the non-repatriates, all those remaining would be released as civilians.[21]

The Communists tabled this plan at first, but after some minor adjustments, they consented to come to an agreement. After eighteen months of on-and-off negotiations, all that remained between the two sides was finalizing the line of demarcation. Clark later wrote that had the Communists rejected the May proposal, "I was authorized to *break off* [italics in original] the truce talks rather than to recess them, and to carry on the war in new ways never yet tried in Korea." Apparently, the administration's threat to use atomic weapons, real or not, did the trick.[22]

BBWAA members participating in the annual poll conducted by the *Sporting News* picked the Brooklyn Dodgers and the Yankees to repeat as pennant winners. The Dodgers received 148 first-place votes from 195 voters while New York, less heavily favored, got 109 votes. The writers picked the Philadelphia Phillies, New York Giants, and the Cardinals to fill out the National League's first division and the Indians, Chicago White Sox, and Philadelphia A's to finish behind the Yankees.[23]

On April 9, just a few days before the start of the season, Cincinnati's general manager Gabe Paul announced that his club would prefer to be called the Redlegs and not the Reds. Paul gave no explanation for the change, but the author of a note in the *Sporting News* remarked that "some observers believed that the political significance of 'Reds' in international affairs was responsible for the change." Unstated was the fact that the Ohio General Assembly, mimicking the US Congress, had its own Un-American Activities Committee.[24]

The opening week of major league play was pockmarked by postponements because of rain and cold weather. Before the presidential opener, New York at Washington on Monday, April 13, was rained out, Eisenhower had committed a public relations gaffe when he told Senators owner Clark Griffith that he would be unable to throw out the ceremonial first pitch because he would be at Augusta National on a golf holiday. Vice President Richard Nixon volunteered to step in, but when the opening game was postponed until Thursday, Eisenhower flew back to Washington in the morning, gave a speech, and attended the start of the game. After an inning and a half, he left the ballpark and flew back to Georgia for several more days of golf.[25]

In the National League, the scheduled Opening Day game was switched from Pittsburgh at Cincinnati to Milwaukee at Cincinnati to accommodate the Braves' move from Boston. The franchise shift had come so close to the start of the season that league officials, working with Harry Simmons, decided that the easiest way to adjust the schedule was to have the Braves and the Pirates simply exchange schedules. Milwaukee thus became one of the league's four western teams while Pittsburgh shifted from a western club to an eastern club.[26]

Milwaukeeans marked the arrival of their new team with both pomp and circumstance, the pomp being a massive parade on April 8 that drew 60,000 spectators and the circumstance being an enormous number of tickets sold. After defeating the Redlegs in Cincinnati on April 13, the Braves staged their home opener on April 14 before a sellout crowd of 34,357. They defeated the Cardinals, 3–2, in ten innings with rookie center fielder Billy Bruton hitting a game-winning home run. On May 20, the Braves, in second place, played their fourteenth game at home. They lost, but the crowd of 23,450 pushed their attendance above 1952's season total in Boston.[27]

Despite the Braves' sellout, the opening games of the sixteen major league clubs drew a total of 328,528, a drop of 67,226 from the year before. The eight National League clubs attracted 166,789, just a tad more than the year before. American League clubs drew 161,739, down 70,269 from 1952, with every AL club selling fewer Opening Day tickets than it had the year before. Cold, wet weather cut attendance throughout the first week of play, down from 852,812 in 1952 to 459,554. On April 17, total attendance for four American League games was 10,218, with only 972 watching the Browns at the White Sox.[28]

So many early season games were postponed that National League officials met on May 4 to discuss changing the schedule in future seasons. Various ideas floated about, including eliminating early season night games; opening the season—and closing it—a week later; or opening later but scheduling more doubleheaders. After Giles presented data from the previous fifteen years showing that there had not been more postponements early in April than early in May, club officials took no action.[29]

The AL opener also marked, in a way, the coming to fruition of Tom McMahon's idea for a DuMont television "game of the week." But it was not the DuMont network that carried this revolution in television programming. Instead, it was the nascent American Broadcasting Company (ABC) that put McMahon's plan into practice. ABC had planned to televise the Yankees-Senators game over a network of fifty-eight stations. When Opening Day was scrubbed, the network scaled back, and the game was shown only on local television. But ABC persisted, signing three clubs, the A's, the Indians, and the White Sox, to a contract to broadcast seventeen games, beginning with a Memorial Day doubleheader, the Indians at the White Sox. ABC's network was small, but the seed for significant change was planted.[30]

Inaugurating the "game of the week" had its rough spots. In Schenectady, New York, WRGB, a new addition to the ABC network, was forced to cancel televising the sixteen Saturday afternoon games because the neighboring Albany Senators in the Eastern League played Saturday home games at 2:30 p.m. Senators owner Tom McCaffrey said he did not intend to block telecasts of major league games, but he expected the local station to adhere to ABC's contract with its sponsor, Falstaff Beer, and decline to show major league games when minor league teams would be playing at home.[31]

The PCL was also none too pleased with the "game of the week." A station in northern California showed the inaugural telecast on Memorial Day, but pulled away from the game at 1 p.m., local time, because the San Francisco and Oakland clubs were going to play home games at 1:30 p.m. That gave fans watching the televised game only thirty minutes to get to the ballpark and get into their seats, and attendance plummeted. "This thing is hurting us," league president Pants Rowland said. "The majors recognize television hurts their own attendance. . . . They've agreed among themselves not to telecast their games in other major league cities. But, for a few thousand dollars, they are willing to kill off minor league attendance."[32]

Yet two of the PCL's clubs in southern California seemed not to mind the competition from the "game of the week." On June 13, Los Angeles moved its home game from 2:30 p.m. to 1:00 p.m., directly competing with the conclusion of a Yankees-Indians game on television and still drew 4,990, about an average crowd for a Saturday afternoon. Club president Don Stewart said that "the Los Angeles club welcomes the opportunity to have our citizens compare Pacific Coast League baseball with that played in the eastern cities." Hollywood took a different tack, moving the starting time of its Saturday games from 2:15 p.m. to 3:00 p.m. so that the "game of the week" would be over before the first pitch was delivered at Gilmore Field.[33]

The National League pennant race remained tight throughout the first half of the season. Philadelphia and Milwaukee set the pace early with Brooklyn, seeking to become the league's first repeat champions since the Cardinals in

1942–44, not far behind. A ten-game winning streak at the end of May lifted the Dodgers into first place, but the Braves bounced back. They went 16–7 during one stretch of June, but then lost eight in a row, including three straight to the Dodgers, and they surrendered first place. At the end of June, Brooklyn led Milwaukee by a half game.[34]

The Yankees had it easier. After losing on Opening Day, New York won nine of its next ten. The Indians stayed close and even took over first place on May 10 but only for a day. On May 27, the Yankees won the first of eighteen straight games, including four in Cleveland, and seized control of the race. By the end of June, New York led the Indians by five games.[35]

Two legendary home runs highlighted play in the season's first half. On April 17, 21-year-old Mickey Mantle cemented his status as one of the game's great young sluggers by hitting a home run out of the park over the left-field wall at Washington's Griffith Stadium. According to reports at the time, Yankees press and promotions director Arthur Patterson dashed out of the ballpark, found the teenager who retrieved the ball, and measured its distance from home plate at 565 feet. When reporters asked Mantle what kind of pitch he hit, he said, "It was a chest-high fast ball."[36]

On April 29, Braves first baseman Joe Adcock hit a two-run homer into the left-center-field bleachers in New York's Polo Grounds, some 475 feet from home plate. No one had ever reached the bleachers before in a National League game although Luke Easter had hit one into the right-center-field bleachers while playing for the all-Black Cincinnati Crescents in 1946. Adcock's third-inning blast gave Milwaukee a 2–0 lead in a game they won, 3–2. "I never expected to hit a ball that far, and I never expect to hit one again to equal it," he said.[37]

Two more minor leagues in the South integrated peacefully, but in a third, trouble brewed. The South Atlantic League saw two Black players on the roster of the Savannah Indians and three, including Henry Aaron, playing for the Jacksonville Braves. "It has been a gradual movement, but one that was inevitable," said one Savannah fan. "What's the difference if the boy is a good ballplayer?" The Piedmont League also ended its color barrier, adding more African American players to several of its rosters than any other league previously.[38]

The Cotton States League resisted change. When the Hot Springs (Arkansas) Bathers announced their intention to sign two African American pitchers, brothers Jim and Leander Tugerson, the other club owners voted to seize the franchise and put Hot Springs out of business. The Bathers retreated, but in May, they needed pitching and brought up Jim Tugerson. The league forfeited Hot Springs' next game, and the club backed down again. Tugerson sued, alleging a conspiracy to deprive him of his rights and challenging the legality of the league's segregation policies. A federal district court judge dismissed the suit, and Tugerson did not appeal.[39]

Near the end of its term, the Supreme Court announced that it had scheduled oral arguments in the fall on three cases concerning the reserve clause and baseball's status under antitrust law. The three cases, bundled together, were the lawsuits brought by players George Earl Toolson and Walter Kowalsk plus a third suit brought by minor league club owner Jack Corbett. In 1949, Corbett had signed seven players under contract with clubs in the Mexican League. He sued after Commissioner Happy Chandler invalidated these contracts on the grounds that Organized Baseball and the Mexican League had agreed to respect each other's contracts.[40]

Willie Mays remained a private at Ft. Eustis, playing military ball during the week and semipro ball for the Newport News Royals when he was free on weekends. One road trip saw his Army team play a Marines team from Camp Lejeune in North Carolina. After the game, Mays drove back in his white convertible with four other players, three Black and one White, when the local sheriff stopped them. Only their military ID cards saved them from serious Jim Crow difficulties.[41]

The rigors of flying in wartime caught up with Jerry Coleman. After his own crash landing, "things got to the point where they probably worked on me emotionally," he recalled. Soon thereafter he watched his roommate crash and die after a bombing run deep into North Korea and was deeply affected. "I started to hyperventilate, and I was missing on my midair join-ups. . . . So they grounded me." After flying his last mission in May, he was assigned to a forward air control unit, living in a tent near the front.[42]

Ted Williams's flying career also ended because of medical problems. On one run, explosions from the bombs dropped by a plane in front of him sent rocks so high into the air that one pierced his fuselage. On another mission, his rockets fired late and nearly hit some other pilots. Williams's respiratory system could not stand the Korean cold. Pneumonia put him in the hospital for twenty-two days, and after he was released, he had problems with his ears and nose. After thirty-nine missions, he, too, was grounded.[43]

Lloyd Merriman endured his own crash. Antiaircraft fire hit his jet, disabling the hydraulic system, which meant no brakes and no way to stop upon landing. The ground crew rigged a wire across the runway so he could hook on, like landing on an aircraft carrier, but Merriman missed the wire and kept going. He needed to circle around and try again, but his speed had dropped to 120 knots, too slow to stay airborne. Merriman hit the ground near the end of the runway and ripped through several rice fields. The plane broke in half, but the pilot emerged unscathed.[44]

Two more former players gave their lives for their country during these months. Carl Tumlinson, known by his middle name, Duane, signed a contract with the Dodgers' organization in 1950 for $6,000 and played in the minors for two seasons and parts of a third before being drafted in July 1952. Sent to Korea to join Company A, First Battalion, Fifth Infantry Regimental Combat Team, he was killed in action on April 7.[45]

Gil Shirk starred in baseball, basketball, and football in high school in Elizabethtown, Pennsylvania, and is generally regarded as one of the best athletes from Lancaster County. After a year of college, he signed with the Dodgers' organization, playing minor league ball in 1950, 1951, and 1952. On July 16, 1952, while playing for Pueblo (Colorado) in the Western League, Shirk stole three bases on three consecutive pitches. He was drafted into the Army after that season and assigned to the Aberdeen Proving Ground in Maryland. On May 20, while driving a car on US Route 40, three miles north of Perryville, Maryland, he crashed into the rear of a tractor trailer truck and was instantly killed.[46]

Epilogue: Armistice at Last, July–September 1953

Early in June, the *Sporting News* took an analytical look at the sport it chronicled on a weekly basis. The editorial did not focus on the game's economics or its problems with television or the challenges presented by the ambitious Pacific Coast League. Instead, the weekly pinpointed lack of competitive balance in both major leagues as a situation "so serious that some sort of a solution must be found before the 1954 races begin."[1]

The editors noted that the pennant races unfolding in both major leagues were lopsided. The American League was "confronted by the disturbing likelihood that the pennant race will be over before the Fourth of July," and several National League teams were "so far behind there is little possibility they will get back into contention even for the first division." Acknowledging that the transplanted Milwaukee Braves were a success, both on the field and at the box office, the weekly asserted that "drastic measures must be taken at least by the trailing clubs in order to halt a continued decline of interest by the fans and consequent damaging effect on the majors as a whole." Yet what these "drastic measures" should be was not spelled out beyond such generalities as "the fallacy of standing pat," "other shifts in weak franchises," and "more aggressive efforts to strengthen teams."[2]

If lack of competitive balance was a problem, the standings at the All-Star break provided some evidence. At the conclusion of play on Sunday, July 12, the Boston Red Sox were in fourth place in the American League, eleven games out of first place, and the last-place Detroit Tigers were already thirty games behind. The National League race, on the other hand, was much closer. The Brooklyn Dodgers were in first place, the Braves in second, the Philadelphia Phillies and St. Louis Cardinals tied for third, and the New York Giants in fifth, just 6½ games behind.

The twentieth All-Star Game, originally scheduled for Braves Field on July 14, was moved to Crosley Field in Cincinnati despite Braves owner Lou Perini's request to play the game in Milwaukee. The National League won the game, 5–1, earning its fourth straight victory, but the American League still led in overall All-Star Game competition, twelve wins to eight. Three NL pitchers, Warren Spahn of the Braves and Robin Roberts and Curt Simmons of the Phillies, shut out the American Leaguers for eight innings while National League hitters scored runs off Allie Reynolds of the New York Yankees, Mike Garcia of the Cleveland Indians, and Satchel Paige of the St. Louis Browns.[3]

The *Sporting News* noted that tickets for the All-Star Game were more expensive, seven dollars for a box seat and five dollars for a reserved seat, and called this increase "a realistic approach to the economic problems which beset all baseball. No doubt," the editorial continued, "the modest advance foreshadowed a hike in World's Series prices and probably a general scaling upward when the clubs set their rates for regular season games in 1954." Indeed, in September, Commissioner Ford Frick announced that box seats for the Series would go up from eight to ten dollars, reserved seats from six to seven and bleacher seats from one dollar to two. Only the price for standing room, four dollars, remained the same.[4]

Meeting during the All-Star break, major league owners were most concerned with a request from players to raise the major league minimum salary from its current $5,000. In May, Reynolds, the American League player representative said, "The most urgent thing requested by the players is a higher minimum salary. The present minimum of $5,000 finds quite a few players in the major leagues who cannot make a decent living. . . . The least a big league player should get is $8,000. There are many players who believe it should be $10,000."[5]

Given the strictures of the reserve clause, owners were under no pressure to accede to this request. In advance of the meeting, Frick reacted dismissively, saying, "Are there any chances that the players will accept a maximum?" Owners "listened politely," veteran sportswriter Fred Lieb wrote, and they did offer lunch to the players in attendance. But they took no action on the request for a higher minimum salary or on any of the players' other grievances. Instead, they offered Reynolds and National League player representative Ralph Kiner the chance to appear at a meeting during the World Series "and repeat their recommendations."[6]

After this rebuff, a reporter asked Reynolds what he might do if the players were turned down on everything. "Would you try to start something like one of the old ballplayers' unions?" the writer queried. "I don't think so," Reynolds replied. "I would be as much opposed to a labor boss in baseball as would the owners." And yet when Reynolds and Kiner met with the owners in the fall about another concern, the financial stability of the players' pension plan, they arrived with J. Norman Lewis, a lawyer skilled in pension issues.[7]

Charles P. Korr, in his history of the Major League Baseball Players Association, explained what happened next. He wrote, "The owners responded that Lewis was welcome to be part of the discussions as long as he would sit in the hall outside the room." Years later, Korr wrote, Kiner was still furious. "In the 1950s, we were powerless," he told Korr. "There was a general feeling that they would ship you out if you were disruptive."[8]

Frick took exception to any notion that the pension plan was unstable. "There is absolutely no doubt about the financial strength and stability of the pension fund," he said. "However," he added, "the fund emphatically could not dispense with revenues received for the television and radio privileges of the World's Series and the All-Star Game." Charley Segar, baseball's secretary-treasurer, concurred, saying that "the contributions of the players and the baseball clubs would not come close to financing the plan and that, were it not for the additional money we get from television at the All-Star Game and World's Series telecasts, the pension could pay less than a third of what it now pays."[9]

Some minor league players wanted a voice in the game too, including some sort of representation at league and National Association meetings. A number of players, speaking to various sportswriters, expressed support for elected player representatives, like the majors, a minimum salary, especially for the minors' lower classifications, and a pension plan, but there was no mechanism in place to make these things happen.[10]

After Dodger minor leaguer Don Zimmer was hit in the head by a pitched ball on July 1, and Dodger right fielder Carl Furillo was beaned on July 20, the Brooklyn club ordered all its players to wear batting helmets or "safety caps," as they were called, every time they came to bat. Pittsburgh Pirates general manager Branch Rickey had introduced batting helmets in 1952 and made their use mandatory for his club. The *Sporting News* agreed with the Dodgers' decision, saying that "aside from all the humanitarian factors, . . . sheer economic common sense should move the owners to insist that their players wear the helmets."[11]

Seething as the two sides at Panmunjom reached agreement, and left out in the diplomatic cold was Syngman Rhee, still the South Korean president. His goal, a reunified Korea under his control, had been shoved aside, but his foreign minister had told the US ambassador that South Korea would demand a price for cooperating with this agreement not to its liking. "Throughout the last days of June," Hastings wrote, "and the early days of July, Rhee spent hours closeted in private talks with Mark Clark and Eisenhower's special envoy, Walter Robertson," haranguing them with his grievances and presenting a list of demands that changed from day to day.[12]

Nor did the fighting in the war's final weeks abate, as the Communists were determined to show South Korea how vulnerable it was. In late June, a hundred thousand Communist troops attacked across the front of five ROKA divisions. The South Koreans were thrown back about five miles, and rescue came only when the UN mounted an artillery counterattack, firing 2.7 million rounds, more than had been fired in any previous month. The UN suffered 17,000 casualties, including 3,333 dead, in the twenty days leading up to Rhee's decision to accept the agreement.[13]

Rhee had control of the South Korean army, but he was a popular leader too. In 1952, he had pushed through the legislature a constitutional amendment to elect the president by direct popular vote, and in August of that year, he had been reelected with over five million votes out of seven million cast. Moreover, many North Koreans had voted for Rhee with their feet, some four million abandoning their homes for life in the South.[14]

The package presented to Rhee to gain his acceptance of the deal was so lavish that Rees called it "an overflowing cornucopia." It included a promise from the sixteen nations that had contributed troops to the UN effort that they would resist Communist aggression again; a US promise to beef up the ROKA to twenty divisions and augment South Korea's naval and air strength; and an offer from the UN for a generous array of postwar economic rehabilitation. The United States further sweetened the pot by offering South Korea a bilateral security pact.[15]

But Rhee was not done, not yet. In the early morning hours of June 18, Americans at Koje-do saw the gates wide open and thousands of prisoners streaming out past their ROKA guards. This was Rhee's doing, and similar events took place at three other prisons around the country. By June 22, only nine thousand North Korean prisoners remained in captivity. Administration officials in Washington feared that Rhee's brazenness might upset the entire apple cart, but the Chinese government soon signaled its acceptance of the American explanation for this mass liberation: blame Rhee, not the United States.[16]

China felt the need to demonstrate its sheer annoyance at Rhee's tactics by launching an attack against ROKA troops and then once again attempting to capture Pork Chop Hill. The Chinese pushed back the South Koreans nearly three miles along an eight-mile front and were halted only when US troops came up from reserve. As for Pork Chop Hill, US troops failed to dislodge the Chinese, and on the fourth day of fighting, the Americans withdrew.[17]

Rhee gave in on July 9, announcing that while he would not obstruct the agreement, he would not sign it. Privately, according to Hastings, the United States assured the Communists that it would not support any independent ROKA offensive. Early on the morning of Monday, July 27, carpenters completed work on the building where the armistice would be signed. The two sides arrived precisely at 10:00 a.m. General Harrison signed nine copies of the agreement, and General Nam Il did the same. The ceremony took twelve minutes. General Clark added his signatures a few hours later, regretting that he was "the first US Army commander in history to sign an armistice without a victory." To the end of his days, Hastings wrote, Clark remained convinced that the better way to peace would have been through military victory. Fighting continued until 10:00 p.m., the time the armistice went into effect, and then the guns went still.[18]

On the following morning, inquisitive Chinese soldiers cut their way through barbed wire and avoided minefields to get a look at their former enemies, who were just as curious. The Chinese offered beer and rice wine as gifts and received cigarettes and chocolate in return. The Korean War was over.[19]

Just as the armistice was taking hold in Korea, the baseball establishment, including Ty Cobb, a member of the Hall of Fame's inaugural class, gathered in Cooperstown to see Dizzy Dean and Al Simmons inducted. Joe Cashman of the *Boston Record* and president of the BBWAA, served as master of ceremonies. He began by asking those in attendance to bow their heads, giving thanks that a truce in Korea had been reached.[20]

National Association president George Trautman gave the induction speech, but he departed from his assigned task to criticize the adverse effect television was having on the minor leagues. "It must be obvious to everybody," he said,

> that professional baseball, if it continues to rely upon its gate admissions for financial underpinning, must be able to exercise reasonable control over its own event. It should be apparent that only flesh-and-blood spectators inside the park will assure the further healthy life of the game, a fact which must be recognized by everybody—even by those who now languidly take their baseball enjoyment seated before a mechanical device.[21]

The day before the ceremony, the Hall's board of directors announced the creation of a new, eleven-person committee to elect veteran players, managers, and umpires. The board appointed *Sporting News* publisher Taylor Spink as the committee's chair. Under revised rules, the BBWAA would consider former players who had been retired for at least five years, while the new committee would meet every two years to consider those who had been out of the game for at least twenty-five years. Spink called for the committee to meet for the first time on September 28 in the city where the World Series would begin.[22]

The pennant races in both major leagues proceeded without any surprises. After the All-Star break, the Dodgers, often regarded as the best of the postwar Brooklyn clubs, reeled off sixteen wins, including three straight against the Braves, in nineteen games. They had an eight-game lead at the end of July, clinched the pennant on September 12, and won 105 games. Brooklyn batted .285 as a team and hit a near-record 208 home runs. Five regulars batted over .300, three had 100 or more RBIs, and two, Duke Snider and Roy Campanella, hit more than forty home runs.[23]

The Braves put an end to their Bostonian streak of mediocrity or worse. They won ninety-two games, more than in any other season since 1914, and finished second. Second-year third baseman Eddie Mathews led both leagues with forty-seven home runs, and he drove in 135 runs, just seven behind Campanella, the league's Most Valuable Player. Milwaukee got solid offensive contributions from Joe Adcock, Billy Bruton, Del Crandall, and Andy Pafko and spectacular pitching from Spahn, who won twenty-three games and finished with a 2.10 earned run average.[24]

Perini's move from Boston proved to be a success off the field as well. Near-capacity crowds at Milwaukee County Stadium were the rule, not the exception. Thirty-seven times (out of sixty-four home dates), attendance exceeded 30,000, with the largest crowd, 37,243, for an August night game against the Chicago Cubs. The Braves' total attendance, 1,826,397, set a National League record.[25]

Perini benefited from a sweet financial deal. His rent for the ballpark was only $1,000 per season, plus he got to keep all concessions' revenues. His estimated net profit was $1.7 million before taxes and $400,000 after taxes. In addition, he sold Braves Field in Boston to nearby Boston University for an amount reportedly between $340,000 and $575,000. Milwaukee County did well, too, and announced a $1.1 million plan to expand the ballpark's capacity by 8,500 seats for the 1954 season.[26]

Major league baseball's success in Milwaukee gave rise to some discussion that the next ballparks to be built, perhaps in cities to which existing franchises would move, would have to be financed with public money. Officials from the Osborn Engineering Company, having designed and constructed facilities for both baseball and football, asserted that construction had become so expensive that only a government entity able to levy taxes and sell bonds could generate enough money to make such projects feasible. Osborn pointed out that the ballparks of the future would be multiuse facilities that could be outfitted with plastic, transparent roofs.[27]

In the American League, the Yankees completed a dream season by winning their fifth consecutive pennant, a feat unprecedented in either league's history. The Indians and the Chicago White Sox hung on doggedly through August and into September, but New York clinched the flag on September 14 and finished 8½ games ahead of Cleveland. Manager Casey Stengel adeptly juggled his lineup. Only two regulars batted over .300, while catcher Yogi Berra led the team with twenty-seven home runs and 108 RBIs. Whitey Ford lived up to his billing and led the pitching staff with eighteen wins.[28]

Browns owner Bill Veeck continued working to move his club, perhaps to Baltimore or Los Angeles. He suggested that his club might be willing to move into an existing ballpark, Wrigley Field in Los Angeles, if he could buy it from Phil Wrigley, owner of both the Cubs and the Los Angeles Angels. Simultaneously, though, Yankees co-owner Del Webb, a real estate developer, contended that if the American League agreed to move the Browns, Kansas City should be the destination. The Yankees owned the Kansas City Blues in the American Association, so, the reasoning went, it would be easy to dislodge the Blues and move them further west, perhaps to Denver.[29]

The PCL reacted to talk that the majors might move west by reiterating its intention to seek status as a third major league. "Given the whole-hearted cooperation of the press, radio, and TV in its member cities," league president Pants Rowland said, the league "could obtain major rating in five years." Asking for support from local businesses, he asserted that the PCL could become the best league in baseball within fifteen years. "No other league," he argued, "is comprised of as many cities with such great possibilities of expansion."[30]

Yet, at the league's annual meeting on September 18, the financial picture was none too rosy. The league announced that its clubs had lost a combined $350,000 during the season, that the Oakland club might go out of business, and that a long-simmering territorial dispute between the Hollywood and Los Angeles clubs had yet to be settled. Moreover, Paul Fagan, owner of the San Francisco

Seals, decided to give up. Saying that he had lost $500,000 over his eight years of ownership, Fagan said he was selling his franchise and his club's players to the league's directors who would operate the team until they found a new owner.[31]

The World Series opened on September 30 with the Dodgers and the Yankees meeting for the fourth time in seven years. The American Leaguers won the first two games at Yankee Stadium, 9–5 and 4–2. In Game Three, Dodgers pitcher Carl Erskine set a World Series record by striking out fourteen Yankees, and Brooklyn won, 3–2. The Dodgers won Game Four, too, 7–3, but the Yankees took both Game Five and Game Six with Billy Martin singling in the Series-winning run in the bottom of the ninth inning.

For Yankees manager Casey Stengel, this was his fifth straight World Series triumph, a record that still stands. For the Dodgers, their loss meant seven modern World Series without a win. When manager Charlie Dressen asked for a new, three-year contract, owner Walter O'Malley gave him a termination notice instead.[32]

When the truce was signed, Jerry Coleman was still in Korea. Bobby Brown called on the telephone from Tokyo, telling him that Yankees general manager George Weiss wanted to know when he could get back to his team. Coleman did not know. As he told the story, Ed McMahon, later a television personality, helped him write a letter to his commanding general, asking for permission to rejoin the Yankees before the conclusion of the season. The general approved his request, saying, "We'll have you out in two days," but the request hit a roadblock in Washington. "So there I was," wrote Coleman, "stuck for another month and having to listen to the World Series on the radio."[33]

A month later, the roadblock suddenly cleared. Coleman wrote, "It [usually] took about two or three weeks to get out of the service," but the general's sergeant major grabbed him and said, "There's a plane leaving for Japan, a Flying Tiger, in one hour." Coleman hopped aboard. He was in Japan for a couple of hours, then on a flight to Hawaii, and then the only passenger on a mail plane to San Francisco, close to home.[34]

Coleman arrived in California on August 23 and flew to New York just twelve hours later. After meeting with Weiss, he rejoined the ball club in

Cleveland. "I'm just another ballplayer looking for a job. I'm not ready to play regularly and, besides, Billy Martin is doing a great job at second base. . . . Maybe I'll be able to pinch run for Johnny Mize once in a while, but I really don't expect to get into high gear again until next year."[35]

The Yankees scheduled "Jerry Coleman Day" for Sunday, September 13. A crowd of nearly fifty thousand came to Yankee Stadium. Webb and partner Dan Topping gave Coleman a Lincoln Capri automobile. The New York chapter of the BBWAA gave him an antique silver tray, and his teammates gave him a second silver tray with their names inscribed on it. Other gifts included a television, silverware, china, and a $500 gift certificate for clothes. Coleman started in that day's game, his first appearance since April 23, 1952. He grounded out in the second inning, and Martin replaced him.[36]

Ted Williams began his journey home and arrived in Tokyo on July 1, preceded by a raft of newspaper stories wondering about his future in the Marines and on the ball field. Like Coleman, Williams traveled to Hawaii before arriving at Moffett Field in Santa Clara County, California, on July 9. The Marines moved Williams to Oak Knoll Naval Hospital and then to Bethesda Naval Hospital near Washington, D.C., for further treatment, but they allowed him to attend the All-Star Game in Cincinnati. Dressed in casual clothes, he made his way from the stands onto the field where other players greeted him. After throwing out the ceremonial first pitch, he watched the game from the American League dugout. On July 28, the Marines discharged Williams, and he went straight to Boston.[37]

Arriving at Fenway Park, Williams was reunited with Red Sox owner Tom Yawkey, who offered the 35-year-old a chance to take some batting practice. "Nah, I'm tired," Williams said. "Nah. I haven't hit in a long time. Nah. I don't think so. Oh, all right." And then to the wonder of collegiate sportswriter George Sullivan, who happened to be at Fenway that day working on a story, Williams started hitting. "He hit a few balls," Sullivan said. "Then he started hitting home runs." One. Two. Three. Four. Five. Six. Seven. Eight. Nine in a row. Blood was dripping through Williams's fingers onto the bat. "It was the greatest thing I'd ever seen," Sullivan said. The war, for Williams, was indeed over.[38]

After Lloyd Merriman was mustered out of the Marines in September, he played winter ball in Cuba, trying to regain his baseball skills prior to spring training with the Reds. But he had lost two full seasons serving his country, and Cincinnati had acquired several good young outfielders in his absence. He played seventy-three games in 1954 and another seventy-three in 1955 with the White Sox and the Cubs. "I am sure the service time hurt our baseball careers. Look what Ted Williams could have done if not for the time he spent in service," he recalled. "As for Jerry [Coleman] and myself, we tried for a couple of years after coming back, but it was all over."[39]

Bobby Brown did not come home until late April 1954. He rejoined the Yankees on May 2, but he had already accepted an appointment as a resident at the City and County Hospital in San Francisco, effective July 1. Brown played twenty-eight games, retired to fulfill his medical commitment, and turned down a chance to play with the Seals on weekends. "The time I spent in Korea," he said later, "essentially ended my career as an active player." After Brown left New York, Stengel said, "I want to thank him, and if I ever want an appendix out, Doc Brown will get my business."[40]

One other former ballplayer had a very different homecoming. Walter Adelmann, born in 1928, had brief trials with three minor league clubs in 1944, 1946, and 1947. He was drafted in December 1950 and arrived in Korea in September 1951. Assigned to the Seventh Regiment, First Cavalry Division, Adelmann was immediately sent to the front where he fought in "the battle of the hills," as he called it, including Pork Chop Hill before it became famous. The Chinese overran his unit's position in November, and Adelmann, twice wounded, lay among the dead for a day or so until he was captured.[41]

Adelmann spent about two weeks in a temporary transit camp before being moved to Camp One, less than ten miles south of the Yalu. "The living conditions were bad," he remembered. "There was body lice, dysentery, intestinal worms, pneumonia, night blindness, beriberi, frostbite, skin disorders, dental problems, starvation, and the threat of death to contend with." Prisoners wore cotton padded pajamas when winter temperatures dropped to forty or fifty degrees below zero, and "in the summer, we would have to shed the padded clothing because the summers were just as hot as the winters were cold."[42]

By late 1952, conditions in the camp had improved somewhat. The Chinese even brought in sports equipment. Adelmann recalled that he wrote to the Cardinals. "I told them that . . . I wanted to try out for the club when I was released. They sent me a letter back and told me that as soon as I got home, they would let me try out. That tryout was at the top of my priority list of things I would do when the war was over."[43]

Adelmann was repatriated in August 1953. Collecting his back pay, he and a friend went to Havana, Cuba, where, he said, "I started drinking pretty heavy. The alcohol really got hold of me." He went back to his Illinois hometown, was admitted to a veterans hospital suffering from battle fatigue, and, as he said, "My drinking problems continued. I never tried out for the baseball team." Adelmann began attending Alcoholics Anonymous meetings in 1962, and "it helped me." In September 1997, he received six combat medals, including two Purple Hearts, for his service in Korea.[44]

Two former ballplayers in service during the war died after the truce went into effect. Jack Leonard was born in Chattanooga in 1930. He played minor league ball in the Kitty League in 1950 before serving in the Air Force. He was diagnosed with leukemia and died on September 15, 1953, at Maxwell Air Force Base in Alabama.[45]

George Reeden (born von Reeden) graduated from high school in Washington, D.C., and played a handful of games in 1950 in the North Carolina State League. By September 1952, he was in the Air Force, first at Greenville AFB in South Carolina and then at Tyndall AFB in Panama City, Florida. On December 11, 1953, he was flying an F-86D Sabre jet that developed a faulty fire warning signal. Reeden declined to eject. He stayed with the plane as it crashed in Saint Andrew Bay, and he did not survive.[46]

One United Nations police action. Three years of fighting. Four baseball seasons disrupted. Twenty-one players or former players giving their lives for their country. Countless other careers altered or ended. As Commissioner Bud Selig said in June 2000, "Major league [and minor league] baseball, like all other sectors of society, sacrificed much in its support of the Korean War effort." Players "stepped up to the plate," he continued. "Each was asked to interrupt his or her private life to serve in harm's way. . . . They served with distinction, prepared and willing to go wherever their country asked in defense of freedom."[47]

And what of Organized Baseball itself? It survived the war, but the problems with which it grappled during these four seasons endured. The challenges television presented persisted. How best to incorporate first-year players into the labor force remained an issue. The minor leagues continued to decline. The Pacific Coast League never became a major league. Before the decade of the 1950s was over, four more major league teams left their traditional homes for greener pastures. And baseball stumbled its way toward incorporating the rest of the country into its vision of what the National Pastime could be.

Notes

Introduction

1   On this point, see, for example, Ima White, "Revisiting the Iconic *M*A*S*H* TV Show: Analysis of Its Impact and Legacy," accessed April 22, 2025, https://tvovermind.com/mash-tv-show-analysis/

2   Herbert Adams to Ron Kaplan, November 1997, in possession of the author.

3   Tony Bartirome to Kaplan, n.d., in possession of the author.

4   Del Crandall to Kaplan, November 1997, in possession of the author.

5   Vernon Law to Kaplan, November 1997, in possession of the author.

6   Rudy Minarcin to Kaplan, March 2004, in possession of the author; Bill Nowlin, "Rudy Minarcin," accessed April 23, 2025, https://sabr.org/bioproj/person/rudy-minarcin/

7   J. W. Porter to Kaplan, n.d., in possession of the author; Dan Taylor, "Jay Porter," accessed April 23, 2025, https://sabr.org/bioproj/person/jay-porter/

8   Bob Ross to Kaplan, April 1, 1988, in possession of the author.

9   Ronnie Joyner, "Bob Neighbors: A Hero Remembered," accessed February 26, 2025, https://web.archive.org/web/20161220073816/http://philadelphiaathletics.org/bob-neighbors-a-hero-remembered/

Prologue

1   Thomas Boswell, "Why Time Begins on Opening Day," in *Why Time Begins on Opening Day* (Garden City, NY: Doubleday, 1984), 287–300.

2   Jeremy Green, "1949: Bonuses, Bargains, and Broadcasts," in *Baseball's Business: The Winter Meetings*, vol. 1, 1901–57, eds. Steven Weingarden and Bill Nowlin (Phoenix: Society for American Baseball Research, 2016), 329.

3   *New-York Tribune,* May 20, 1917, January 26, 1919; *Sporting News,* November 16, 1949.

4   *Baseball Guide and Record Book—1950* (St. Louis: Charles C. Spink & Son, 1950), 81; William Marshall, *Baseball's Pivotal Era, 1946–1951* (Lexington: University Press of Kentucky, 1999), 243–44; J. Ronald Oakley, *Baseball's Last Golden Age, 1946–1960* (Jefferson, NC: McFarland, 1994), 83–85.

5   *1950 Baseball Guide,* 87–88.

6   Ibid., 88–89; Paul Dickson, *Bill Veeck: Baseball's Greatest Maverick* (New York: Walker & Company, 2012), 175.

7   James R. Walker and Robert V. Bellamy Jr., *Center Field Shot: A History of Baseball on Television* (Lincoln: University of Nebraska Press, 2008), 75; *Sporting News,* October 26, 1949. Gillette paid $200,000 for exclusive rights to the Series, more than it paid for the radio rights ($175,000) for the first time. CBS broadcast the Dodgers' home games, and the DuMont network covered the Yankees' home games. Both networks also introduced a split screen, showing both the pitcher and the runner leading off first base. See Walker and Bellamy, *Center Field Shot,* 75, 77.

8   George C. Herring, *From Colony to Superpower: U.S. Foreign Relations since 1776* (New York: Oxford University Press, 2008), 597; James T. Patterson, *Grand Expectations: The United States, 1945–1971* (New York: Oxford University Press, 1996), 82; "Bernard Baruch Coins Term 'Cold War,' April 16, 1947," accessed January 30, 2024, https://www.politico.com/story/2016/04/bernard-baruch-coins-term-cold-war-april-16-1947-221853; James Grant, *Bernard M. Baruch: The Adventures of a Wall Street Legend* (New York: Simon & Schuster, 1983), 323.

9   Odd Arne Westad, *The Cold War: A History* (New York: Basic Books, 2017), 9–10.

10   John Lewis Gaddis, *The Cold War: A New History* (New York: Penguin Press, 2005), 85–87.

11   Westad, *Cold War,* 21–22; "The Fourteen Points," accessed January 30, 2024, https://www.theworldwar.org/learn/peace/fourteen-points; Gaddis, *Cold War,* 16.

12   Ibid., 10–18.

13   See "The Yalta Conference, 1945," accessed January 1, 2024, https://history.state.gov/milestones/1937-1945/yalta-conf; Herring, *Colony to Superpower,* 584–86.

14   Westad, *Cold War,* 58–60.

15   Gaddis, *Cold War,* 20–21, 22, 29, 32–33; Westad, *Cold War,* 80–82, 85–88.

16   "Winston Churchill's Iron Curtain Speech—March 5, 1946," accessed February 1, 2024, https://www.nationalww2museum.org/war/articles/winston-churchills-iron-curtain-speech-march-5-1946; Westad, *Cold War,* 89–92; Gaddis, *Cold War,* 94–95.

17   Ibid., 30–31.

18 Ibid., 33–34; Westad, *Cold War*, 116–20.

19 Gaddis, *Cold War*, 25–26, 35; Westad, *Cold War*, 101.

20 For the agenda and transcript of the joint major league meeting plus associated papers, see Box 6, Folder 13, "Joint Meeting—AL, NL Transcript, December 14, 1949," BA MSS 105, National Baseball Hall of Fame Library, Cooperstown, NY.

21 Jonathan Eig, *Luckiest Man: The Life and Death of Lou Gehrig* (New York: Simon & Schuster, 2005), 40; Hank Greenberg, *Hank Greenberg: The Story of My Life*, edited and with an introduction by Ira Berkow (New York: Times Books, 1989), 18.

22 Steven P. Gietschier, *Baseball: The Turbulent Midcentury Years* (Lincoln: University of Nebraska Press, 2023), 320.

23 Ibid., 321–22; *1947 Baseball Guide*, 146; Brent Kelley, *Baseball's Biggest Blunder: The Bonus Rule of 1953–1957* (Lanham, MD: Scarecrow Press, 1997), 3–4.

24 Oakley, *Last Golden Age*, 102–3; Gietschier, *Baseball*, 322–23; *1950 Baseball Guide*, 90–91.

25 Green, "1949," 330, 333.

26 Oakley, *Last Golden Age*, 82.

27 G. Scott Thomas, *A Whole New Ballgame: Branch Rickey, Bill Veeck, Walter O'Malley and the Transformation of Baseball, 1945–1962* (Jefferson, NC: McFarland, 2022), 66; Walker and Bellamy, *Center Field Shot*, 25–26.

28 Walker and Bellamy, *Center Field Shot*, 25–26; Oakley, *Last Golden Age*, 82; *Sporting News*, December 14, 1949.

29 Dean A. Sullivan, comp. and ed., *Late Innings: A Documentary History of Baseball, 1945–1972* (Lincoln: University of Nebraska Press, 2002), 42–43; Green, "1949," 332–33.

30 Ibid., 331; *Sporting News*, December 14, 1949.

31 Marshall, *Baseball's Pivotal Era*, 378; *Sporting News*, December 21, 1949; Terry Bohn, "Happy Chandler," accessed November 16, 2023, sabr.org/bioproj/person/happy-chandler

Chapter 1

1 House Judiciary Committee, *Hearings before the Subcommittee on Study of Monopoly Power*, Serial No. 1, Part 6, "Organized Baseball," 82nd Cong., 1st sess. (1951), 1253.

2 *Sporting News*, February 5, February 12, 1947.

3 Ibid., February 11, 1948.

4 Ibid., March 10, 1948.

5   Ibid., July 21, 1948.

6   Ibid., February 23, 1949.

7   Ibid., February 1, 1950.

8   Ibid., March 15, 1950.

9   Ibid., March 15, July 19, 1950.

10 "Playing Rules Completely Recodified," *1950 Baseball Guide*, 93.

11 *Baltimore Sun*, February 10, 1949; *Sporting News*, March 2, 1949.

12 Ibid., January 1, 1950.

13 Ibid.

14 Ibid.

15 *Official Baseball Rules Revised for 1949*; *Official Baseball Rules Recodified, Amended and Adopted at New York City, December 21, 1949*.

16 *Official Baseball Rules Recodified*; *Sporting News*, January 18, 1950.

17 Ibid., March 15, 1950.

18 Ibid., March 22, 1950.

19 Gaddis, *Cold War*, 24.

20 Ibid., 24–25, 40–41; Mikiso Hane, *Japan: A Historical Survey* (New York: Charles Scribner's Sons, 1972), 556, 558.

21 Ibid., 556; Robert Whiting, *You Gotta Have Wa* (New York: Macmillan, 1989), 47–48; Robert J. McMahon, *The Cold War: A Very Short Introduction* (New York: Oxford University Press, 2003), 37–38.

22 "The Cairo Conference, 1943," accessed March 12, 2024, https://2001-2009.state.gov/r/pa/ho/time/wwii/107184.htm; Herring, *Colony to Superpower*, 574–78; "Yalta Conference." I have chosen to use the Anglicized version of Chinese names in use at the time.

23 Westad, *Cold War*, 139–40; Sergei N. Goncharov, John W. Lewis, and Xue Litai, *Uncertain Partners: Stalin, Mao, and the Korean War* (Stanford, CA: Stanford University Press, 1993), 5–6.

24 Westad, *Cold War*, 140–41; McMahon, *Cold War*, 43; Gaddis, *Cold War*, 37–38.

25 Westad, *Cold War*, 141–43.

26 Westad, *Cold War*, 145–46.

27 *Sporting News*, February 2, 1949; Associated Press, as seen in *Coshocton* (OH) *Tribune*, January 22, 1949.

28 *Sporting News*, August 3, 1949.

29   "How Hypnotist Swung and Missed in Stint with Browns," accessed December 31, 2023, http://retrosimba.com/2020/06/03/how-hypnotist-swung-and-missed-in-stint-with-browns/; *Sporting News*, March 1, 1950.

30   Ibid., June 7, 1950.

31   *Official Baseball Rules Recodified*; *Sporting News*, February 1, 1950.

32   *New York Times*, February 17, 1950; *Sporting News*, January 25, March 1, 1950.

33   Ibid., January 25, 1950.

34   Ibid., February 1, March 1, March 22, 1950.

35   Ibid., January 11, 1950; Arnold Rampersad, *Jackie Robinson: A Biography* (New York: Alfred A. Knopf, 1997), 226–27.

36   *Sporting News*, January 25, 1950.

37   Ibid., January 25, February 1, February 15, 1950.

38   James N. Giglio, *Musial: From Stash to Stan the Man* (Columbia: University of Missouri Press, 2001), 168; *Sporting News*, February 8, 1950.

39   Ibid., March 1, 1950.

40   Ibid., March 22, 1950.

Chapter 2

1   William B. Mead and Paul Dickson, *Baseball: The Presidents' Game* (Washington, DC: Farragut, 1993), 23–25, 85; David McCullough, *Truman* (New York: Simon & Schuster, 1992), 45; Oakley, *Last Golden Age*, 98.

2   *St. Louis Globe-Democrat*, October 8, 1944; Mead and Dickson, *Presidents' Game*, 83–85.

3   *Sporting News*, April 26, 1950.

4   Lloyd Johnson and Miles Wolff, eds., *The Encyclopedia of Minor League Baseball*, 2nd ed. (Durham, NC: Baseball America, 1997), 98–99, 392–93.

5   Gietschier, *Baseball*, 328–29. For summaries of the proceedings of the winter meetings during these years, see Weingarten and Nowlin, eds., *Baseball's Business*, 305–36.

6   *Sporting News*, March 29, April 5, April 12, 1950.

7   Ibid., April 19, April 26, May 10, May 24, June 10, 1950.

8   Ibid., April 26, 1950.

9   Ibid., March 22, April 12, May 3, 1950.

10   Ibid., May 3, May 17, 1950.

11   Hane, *Japan*, 19–20; David Rees, *Korea: The Limited War* (New York: St. Martin's Press, 1964), 7–8.

12   Hane, *Japan*, 351–55; Rees, *Korea*, 8; Max Hastings, *The Korean War* (New York: Simon & Schuster, 1987), 24–25.

13   Hane, *Japan*, 367–78; Francis Hilary Conroy, *The Japanese Seizure of Korea: 1886–1910* (Philadelphia: University of Pennsylvania Press, 1960), 381.

14   Herring, *Colony to Superpower*, 256–57, 286–87, 357, 359–62.

15   Hane, *Japan*, 405–6; Herring, *Colony to Superpower*, 426; Hastings, *Korean War*, 25.

16   "Syngman Rhee," accessed February 11, 2024, https://archive.ph/20140314010713/http://legacy.wilsoncenter.org/coldwarfiles/index-33794.html; Hastings, *Korean War*, 32–33; Peter Lowe, *The Origins of the Korean War*, 2nd ed. (London and New York: Longman, 1997), 8–9; Westad, *Cold War*, 159–61.

17   Westad, *Cold War*, 159–63; Rees, *Korea*, 11; Lowe, *Origins*, 11–12; Goncharov et al., *Uncertain Partners*, 131.

18   Westad, *Cold War*, 163–64; Hastings, *Korean War*, 27–40; Lowe, *Origins*, 18–20; Rees, *Korea*, 12.

19   Westad, *Cold War*, 163–65; Rees, *Korea*, 12–13; Lowe, *Origins*, 26–47, 54–58.

20   Herring, *Colony to Superpower*, 639–40; Patterson, *Grand Expectations*, 208; Westad, *Cold War*, 166–69; Lowe, *Origins*, 71–80; Goncharov et al., *Uncertain Partners*, 143–54; David Halberstam, *The Coldest Winter: America and the Korean War* (New York: Hyperion, 2007), 48, 54–56; J. Lawton Collins, *War in Peacetime: The History and Lessons of Korea* (Boston: Houghton Mifflin, 1969), 1.

21   *Sporting News*, April 19, 1950; Frederick G. Lieb and Stan Baumgartner, *The Philadelphia Phillies* (New York: G. P. Putnam's Sons, 1953), 221.

22   *Sporting News*, April 19, 1950; Bill Nowlin, *Tom Yawkey: Patriarch of the Boston Red Sox* (Lincoln: University of Nebraska Press, 2018), 142.

23   Donald Dewey and Nicholas Acocella, *The Ball Clubs* (New York: HarperPerennial, 1996), 429; Oakley, *Last Golden Age*, 104–5; Robin Roberts and C. Paul Rogers III, *The Whiz Kids and the 1950 Pennant* (Philadelphia: Temple University Press, 1996), 28, 30–32, 37, 59, 61, 215.

24   *Sporting News*, April 5, 1950.

25   Ibid., June 7, 1950.

26   Ibid., April 12, April 26, 1950.

27   Ibid., April 19, June 14, June 21, June 28, 1950.

Chapter 3

1   *Sporting News*, June 7, 1950.

2   Ibid., July 5, 1950.

3   Ibid. Greenberg, no scientist, might well disagree that water vapor is lighter than air, but later research proved that, if all other factors remain the same, a batted ball will travel further if the humidity is high. See Robert K. Adair, *The Physics of Baseball* (New York: Harper & Row, 1990), 19–20.

4   *Sporting News*, July 12, July 19, 1950.

5   Ibid., July 19, 1950; John P. Rossi, *A Whole New Game: Off the Field Changes in Baseball, 1946–1960* (Jefferson, NC: McFarland, 1999), 73–74; Oakley, *Last Golden Age*, 108–9.

6   Rossi, *Whole New Game*, 70; *Sporting News*, July 12, July 19, 1950.

7   David Vincent, Lyle Spatz, and Davis W. Smith, *The Midsummer Classic: The Complete History of Baseball's All-Star Game* (Lincoln: University of Nebraska Press, 2001), 105–10.

8   *Sporting News*, July 5, 1950.

9   Ibid.

10 Ibid., July 26, 1950.

11 Rees, *Korea*, 3; Patterson, *Grand Expectations*, 210; Hastings, *Korean War*, 52–53, 73; Westad, *Cold War*, 168; Bruce Cumings, *The Korean War: A History* (New York: Modern Library, 2010), 6. In citing Cumings, I note that his account of the war is revisionist, frequently at odds with other narratives and analyses.

12 Cumings, *Korean War*, 11–12; Hastings, *Korean War*, 55–59; Patterson, *Grand Expectations*, 210–11; Rees, *Korea*, 21–23; Herring, *Colony to Superpower*, 640–41.

13 Hastings, *Korean War*, 59–61; Rees, *Korea*, 23–26; Patterson, *Grand Expectations*, 211–13.

14 Rees, *Korea*, 36–54; Patterson, *Grand Expectations*, 215–16.

15 Rees, *Korea*, 77–97; Patterson, *Grand Expectations*, 216–19; Cumings, *Korean War*, 18–19; Hastings, *Korean War*, 105.

16 Rees, *Korea*, 97–104; Herring, *Colony to Superpower*, 641–42; Patterson, *Grand Expectations*, 219–20; Cumings, *Korean War*, 21–22; Harry S. Truman, *Memoirs*, Vol. Two, *Years of Trial and Hope* (Garden City, NY: Doubleday, 1956), 359–60.

17 Hastings, *Korean War*, 61, 83; Patterson, *Grand Expectations*, 213–14.

18 *Newsweek*, July 10, 1950, p. 24, quoted in Patterson, *Grand Expectations*, 214; Hastings, *Korean War*, 83–84; George Q. Flynn, *The Draft, 1940–1973* (Lawrence: University Press of Kansas, 1993), 114.

19 Hastings, *Korean War*, 48–49; Patterson, *Grand Expectations*, 194–96; Rees, *Korea*, 55–65.

20 *Sporting News*, July 19, August 2, 1950.

21 Ibid., July 19, August 16, 1950.

22 Ibid., July 19, August 9, August 16, 1950.

23 Roberts and Rogers, *Whiz Kids*, 243, 287; Edward Veit, "Curt Simmons," accessed March 21, 2024, https://sabr.org/bioproj/person/curt-simmons/; *Sporting News*, August 9, September 27, 1950.

24 *Sporting News*, August 9, 1950.

25 Ibid., August 9, September 16, 1950.

26 Ibid., August 30, 1950.

27 *1951 Baseball Guide*, 9–12; Leonard Koppett, *Koppett's Concise History of Major League Baseball* (Philadelphia: Temple University Press, 1998), 246.

28 *1951 Baseball Guide*, 51–53; Roberts and Rogers, *Whiz Kids*, 281–338.

Chapter 4

1 *Sporting News*, October 18, 1950; Roberts and Rogers, *Whiz Kids*, 339.

2 *Sporting News*, October 11, October 18, 1950.

3 Ibid., October 18, 1950.

4 Ibid., October 11, October 18, November 29, 1950; C. Paul Rogers III, "Whitey Ford," accessed April 4, 2024, https://sabr.org/bioproj/person/whitey-ford/

5 *1951 Baseball Guide*, 95–99.

6 Ibid., 99.

7 Andy McCue, "Los Angeles/Brooklyn Dodgers Team Ownership History," accessed April 5, 2024, https://sabr.org/bioproj/topic/los-angeles-brooklyn-dodgers-team-ownership-history/

8 *Sporting News*, October 25, 1950.

9 *1951 Baseball Guide*, 111; *Sporting News*, October 11, October 18, October 25, November 29, 1950.

10 Patterson, *Grand Expectations*, 219; Rees, *Korea*, 99–103, 107–8.

11 Herring, *Colony to Superpower*, 641–42; Patterson, *Grand Expectations*, 219; Rees, *Korea*, 106–7; Truman, *Years of Trial and Hope*, 362.

12 Rees, *Korea*, 104–5.

13   Patterson, *Grand Expectations*, 220; Herring, *Colony to Superpower*, 642.

14   Patterson, *Grand Expectations*, 220; Truman, *Years of Trial and Hope*, 362–63.

15   Rees, *Korea*, 117–22.

16   Ibid., 119–20; Patterson, *Grand Expectations*, 220.

17   Ibid., 220; Hastings, *Korean War*, 137.

18   Patterson, *Grand Expectations*, 221; William R. Corson, *The Armies of Ignorance: The Rise of the American Intelligence Empire* (New York: Dial Press, 1977), 205, quoted in Cumings, *Korean War*, 26.

19   Lynn Montross and Capt. Nicholas Canzona, *US Marine Corps Operations in Korea*, Vol. III, *The Chosin Reservoir Campaign* (Washington: Historical Branch, USMC HQ, USGPO, 1957), 121, quoted in Rees, *Korea*, 135.

20   Rees, *Korea*, 148, 150.

21   Ibid., 155–61, 166; Patterson, *Grand Expectations*, 221.

22   McCullough, *Truman*, 813; Patterson, *Grand Expectations*, 222–24.

23   Ibid., 222.

24   Ibid., 221–22, 225.

25   Ibid., 225; Rees, *Korea*, 172, 176.

26   Ibid., 176; Patterson, *Grand Expectations*, 226; Hastings, *Korean War*, 188; Halberstam, *Coldest Winter*, 486.

27   *Sporting News*, September 27, October 18, November 8, November 15, November 29, 1950.

28   Ibid., August 23, September 6, September 27, 1950.

29   Ibid., November 29, 1950.

30   Ibid., November 22, November 29, December 6, 1950; Richard Ben Cramer, *Joe DiMaggio: The Hero's Life* (New York: Simon & Schuster, 2001), 295; Brian McKenna, "Lefty O'Doul," accessed April 16, 2024, https://sabr.org/bioproj/person/lefty-odoul/

31   *New York Times*, December 7, 1950.

32   *1951 Baseball Guide*, 102–3.

33   Ibid., 102; *Sporting News*, October 25, 1950.

34   *1951 Baseball Guide*, 103–4; Nick Klopsis, "1950: The Happy Dagger," in Weingarden and Nowlin, eds., *Baseball's Business*, 339–40; Box 6, Folder 13, "Joint Meeting-AL, NL-Minutes, December 11–12, 1950," BA MSS 105, Hall of Fame Library; Box 10, Folder 12, "NL Meetings, Minutes, Conferences, and Financial Ledgers," MSS 55, Hall of Fame Library.

35 *1951 Baseball Guide*, 93–94; "Joint Meeting-AL, NL-Minutes, December 11–12, 1950."

36 Ibid.; *Sporting News*, December 20, 1950.

37 Marshall, *Baseball's Pivotal Era*, 375–79.

38 *Sporting News*, December 13, 1950.

Chapter 5

1 *1951 Baseball Guide*, 94; *Sporting News*, January 10, 1951.

2 Ibid.; Marshall, *Baseball's Pivotal Era*, 385–86; Box 10, Folder 13, "The National League of Professional Base Ball Clubs, Minutes of Special Meeting, March 11, 1951."

3 *Sporting News*, March 21, 1951; *New York Times*, March 13, 1951; Marshall, *Pivotal Era*, 389–91.

4 *Sporting News*, January 31, 1951.

5 Ibid., January 17, 1951.

6 Ibid., January 10, January 31, February 14, 1951.

7 Ibid., February 7, 1951.

8 Ibid., February 28, 1951; "Stan Musial," accessed May 15, 2024, https://www.baseball-reference.com/players/m/musiast01.shtml; "Ted Williams," accessed May 15, 2024 https://www.baseball-reference.com/players/w/willite01.shtml; "Joe DiMaggio," accessed May 15, 2024, https://www.baseball-reference.com/players/d/dimagjo01.shtml

9 *Sporting News*, January 31, 1951.

10 Halberstam, *Coldest Winter*, 486.

11 Patterson, *Grand Expectations*, 226; Halberstam, *Coldest Winter*, 487–88.

12 Hastings, *Korean War*, 188; Halberstam, *Coldest Winter*, 491; Matthew B. Ridgway, *Soldier: The Memoirs of Matthew B. Ridgway* (New York: Harper & Brothers, 1956), 205, quoted in Rees, *Korea*, 177.

13 Matthew B. Ridgway, *The Korean War* (Garden City, NY: Doubleday, 1967), 86, quoted in Hastings, *Korean War*, 189; Patterson, *Grand Expectations*, 226; Halberstam, *Coldest Winter*, 488, 493.

14 Rees, *Korea*, 177; Patterson, *Grand Expectations*, 226.

15 Rees, *Korea*, 180.

16 Ibid., 183.

17 Ibid.

18 Ibid., 185–86; Patterson, *Grand Expectations*, 226.

19 Rees, *Korea*, 190.

20 Patterson, *Grand Expectations*, 226–27; David Halberstam, *The Fifties* (New York: Random House, 1993), 109.

21 *Sporting News*, January 3, January 17, 1951; Marshall, *Pivotal Era*, 384; Walker and Bellamy, *Center Field Shot*, 81.

22 *Sporting News*, January 10, February 21, February 28, March 14, 1951.

23 Ibid., March 14, March 28, 1951.

24 Ibid., February 14, March 14, March 21, March 28, 1951.

25 Ibid., February 7, 1951.

26 Ibid., January 3, January 17, February 14, 1951; Lowell Reidenbaugh, *100 Years of National League Baseball* (St. Louis: The Sporting News Publishing Co., 1976), 143.

27 *Sporting News*, February 14, 1951.

28 Ibid., January 31, 1951.

29 Ibid.

30 Box 10, Folder 13, "The National League of Professional Base Ball Clubs, Minutes of Special Meeting, February 3, 1951."

31 *Sporting News*, January 17, January 24, February 14, February 21, March 14, March 21, and March 28, 1951.

32 Ibid., February 14, March 14, 1951.

33 Ibid., January 10, 1951.

34 Ibid., January 10, January 24, February 14, February 21, 1951; Warren Corbett, "Art Houtteman," accessed August 15, 2024, https://sabr.org/bioproj/person/art-houtteman/

Chapter 6

1 Johnson and Wolff, Encyclopedia of Minor League Baseball, 98–99, 347; Robert L. Finch, L. H. Addington, and Ben M. Morgan, eds., *The Story of Minor League Baseball: A History of the Game of Professional Baseball in the United States with Particular Reference to Its Growth and Development in the Smaller Cities and Towns of the Nation—The Minor Leagues* (Columbus, OH: Stoneman Press, 1952), 87.

2 *Sporting News*, April 4, April 11, April 25, 1951.

3 Ibid., April 11, 1951.

4 Ibid.

5   Ibid., April 4, April 11, 1951.

6   James Lincoln Ray, "Mickey Mantle," accessed September 11, 2024, https://sabr. org/bioproj/person/mickey-mantle/; Marty Appel, *Pinstripe Empire: The New York Yankees from Before the Babe to After the Boss* (New York: Bloomsbury, 2014), 287; Cramer, *Joe DiMaggio*, 298; *Sporting News*, March 14, April 4, 1951.

7   Stew Thornley, "Willie Mays Had a Spectacular—But Short—Stay in Minneapolis," accessed September 11, 2024, https://sabr.org/journal/article/willie-mays-had-a-spectacular-but-short-stay-in-minneapolis/

8   *Sporting News*, April 4, 1951.

9   Ibid., April 25, 1951.

10 Ibid., April 11, June 13, June 27, 1951.

11 Ibid., April 18, 1951.

12 Ibid., May 23, 1951.

13 Rees, *Korea*, 194–95.

14 Ibid., 196; Herring, *Colony to Superpower*, 642, 650.

15 James T. Patterson, *Mr. Republican: A Biography of Robert A. Taft* (Boston: Houghton Mifflin, 1972), 484–87.

16 Patterson, *Grand Expectations*, 227; Truman, *Years of Trial and Hope*, 438–42.

17 Patterson, *Grand Expectations*, 227–28.

18 Truman, *Years of Trial and Hope*, 445–50.

19 Patterson, *Grand Expectations*, 229–30.

20 Hastings, *Korean War*, 206.

21 Ibid., 208; Rees, *Korea*, 243–51.

22 Patterson, *Grand Expectations*, 231; Rees, *Korea*, 264–67.

23 Patterson, *Grand Expectations*, 231–32; Rees, *Korea*, 272–74.

24 Ibid., 251–56.

25 Ibid., 251, 255–63, 284–85; Truman, *Years of Trial and Hope*, 456.

26 *Sporting News*, April 13, 1951.

27 Patterson, *Grand Expectations*, 231; *Sporting News*, May 2, 1951.

28 Richard C. Lindberg, *The White Sox Encyclopedia* (Philadelphia: Temple University Press, 1997), 61–62; *1952 Baseball Guide*, 9.

29 Cramer, *DiMaggio*, 301; Koppett, *Concise History*, 248.

30 *Sporting News*, May 30, 1951; Koppett, *Concise History*, 247.

31 *Sporting News*; John Saccoman, "Willie Mays," accessed September 15, 2024, https://sabr.org/bioproj/person/willie-mays/

32 *Sporting News*, May 30, 1951.

33 Ibid., May 16, June 6, 1951.

34 Ibid.

35 Ibid., May 16, 1951.

36 Gietschier, *Baseball*, 391–92; Ed Edmonds and Frank G. Houdek, eds., *Baseball Meets the Law: A Chronology of Decisions, Statutes and Other Legal Events* (Jefferson, NC: McFarland, 2017), 96.

37 Gietschier, *Baseball*, 393–95; *Sporting News*, May 2, May 9, June 20, 1951.

38 Ibid., January 10, March 28, April 18, June 13, June 27, 1951.

39 Ibid., April 11, 1951; "Eddie Leneve," accessed September 17, 2024, https://www.baseballsgreatestsacrifice.com/biographies/leneve_edward.html; "James Pickett," accessed September 17, 2024, https://www.baseballsgreatestsacrifice.com/biographies/pickett_james.html

40 "George Sulliman," accessed October 7, 2024, https://www.baseballsgreatestsacrifice.com/biographies/sulliman_george.html; "Len Glica," accessed October 7, 2024, https://www.baseballsgreatestsacrifice.com/biographies/glica_len.html; *Sporting News*, July 25, 1951.

Chapter 7

1 Gietschier, *Baseball*, 384.

2 *Sporting News*, July 4, 1951.

3 Ibid., August 15, 1951; *1952 Baseball Guide*, 101.

4 Ibid. *Sporting News*, August 29, September 26, 1951.

5 "Hearings Before the Subcommittee on Study of Monopoly Power of the Committee on the Judiciary," Serial No. 1, Part 6, "Organized Baseball," 82nd Cong., 1st sess. (1951), 30, 82–83.

6 *Sporting News*, July 4, 1951.

7 Hearings, 260, 302, 324.

8 Ibid., 2–4, 468; *Sporting News*, August 8, August 15, 1951.

9 For a short summary of Veeck's life and career, see Warren Corbett, "Bill Veeck," accessed October 2, 2024, https://sabr.org/bioproj/person/bill-veeck/

10 *Sporting News*, July 4, 1951; Dickson, *Veeck*, 184–86.

11 Ibid., 187; Jim Ball, "Frank Saucier," accessed October 1, 2024, https://sabr.org/bioproj/person/frank-saucier/

12 Dickson, *Veeck*, 191–93; *Sporting News*, August 29, 1951.

13 Ibid., July 4, 1951; Jonathan Fraser Light, *The Cultural Encyclopedia of Baseball* (Jefferson, NC: McFarland, 1997), 195.

14 *Sporting News*, July 4, 1951.

15 Ibid., July 18, August 1, August 8, August 22, August 29, 1951.

16 Alonzo L. Hamby, *Beyond the New Deal: Harry S. Truman and American Liberalism* (New York: Columbia University Press, 1973), 415.

17 Ibid., 441; Steven P. Gietschier, "Limited War and the Home Front: Ohio During the Korean War" (PhD diss., Ohio State University, 1977), 58.

18 Truman, *Years of Hope and Trial*, 427–28; Gietschier, "Limited War," 58; Hamby, *Beyond the New Deal*, 446–47; Paul G. Pierpaoli Jr., "Truman's Other War: The Battle for the American Homefront, 1950–53," *OAH Magazine of History* 14 (Spring, 2000), 17–18.

19 Hamby, *Beyond the New Deal*, 449.

20 *Sporting News*, February 7, April 18, 1951.

21 Ibid., April 18, July 11, August 22, 1951; Giglio, *Musial*, 188.

22 Rees, *Korea*, 285; Hastings, *Korean War*, 231–32.

23 Rees, *Korea*, 291; Admiral C. Turner Joy, *How Communists Negotiate* (New York: Macmillan, 1955), 18.

24 Rees, *Korea*, 292–94; Hastings, *Korean War*, 231–32.

25 Rees, *Korea*, 299–300; Hastings, *Korean War*, 232; Harry G. Summers Jr., *Korean War Almanac* (New York: Facts on File, 1990), 134–35.

26 *Sporting News*, August 8, 1951.

27 Ibid., July 4, July 18, July 25, 1951.

28 Ibid., August 1, August 8, 1951.

29 Ibid., August 22, August 29, September 5, September 12, 1951.

30 Oakley, *Last Golden Age*, 132–33.

31 Ibid., 133; Koppett, *Concise History*, 248; Appel, *Pinstripe Empire*, 290–92.

32   Andrew Goldblatt, *The Giants and the Dodgers: Four Cities, Two Teams, One Rivalry* (Jefferson, NC: McFarland, 2003), 26–27.

33   G. H. Fleming, *The Dizziest Season: The Gashouse Gang Chases the Pennant* (New York: William Morrow, 1984), 32, 276–82.

34   Goldblatt, *Giants and Dodgers*, 96–97; Lee Lowenfish, *Branch Rickey: Baseball's Ferocious Gentleman* (Lincoln: University of Nebraska Press, 2007), 460.

35   *Sporting News*, October 10, 1951; Oakley, *Last Golden Age*, 138.

36   Ibid., 138–41.

37   Ibid., 139–40.

38   *Sporting News*, October 17, 1951; Robert L. Tiemann and Pete Palmer, "Major League Attendance," in *Total Baseball: The Official Encyclopedia of Major League Baseball,* ed. John Thorn, Pete Palmer, Michael Gershman, and David Pietrusza, 5th ed. (New York: Viking, 1997), 103–4.

39   "Bill Crago," accessed October 7, 2024, https://www.baseballsgreatestsacrifice. com/biographies/crago_bill.html; "John Lazar," accessed October 7, 2024, https:// www.baseballsgreatestsacrifice.com/biographies/lazar_john.html; "Marcel Poelker," accessed October 7, 2024, https://www.baseballsgreatestsacrifice.com/ biographies/poelker_marcel.html; *Sporting News*, September 12, October 24, 1951, January 9, 1952.

Chapter 8

1   Goldblatt, *Giants and Dodgers*, 110.

2   Ibid., 114–15.

3   Ibid.

4   Koppett, *Concise History*, 249; *Sporting News*, December 19, 1951.

5   Ibid., October 31, 1951.

6   Ibid., October 17, 1951.

7   Hearings, vii–viii.

8   *Sporting News*, October 24, October 31, 1951.

9   Ibid., October 31, 1951.

10   Gietschier, *Baseball*, 303; *Sporting News*, October 17, 1951.

11   Ibid., October 17, 1951.

12   Ibid., October 3, December 19, 1951.

13   Ibid., October 17, October 24, 1951.

14   Ibid., October 24, 1951.

15   Rees, *Korea*, 294–95.

16   Ibid., 295–97.

17   Ibid., 297–98.

18   Ibid., 298–300.

19   Ibid., 300; Hastings, *Korean War*, 232.

20   Ibid., 232–33; Rees, *Korea*, 300–301.

21   Hastings, *Korean War*, 233; Rees, *Korea*, 301; Joy, *How Communists Negotiate*, 301.

22   Rees, *Korea*, 310.

23   *Sporting News*, October 24, October 31, 1951; Rob Fitts, "Joe DiMaggio's Last Hurrah: The 1951 Lefty O'Doul All-Star Tour," accessed November 26, 2024, https://sabr.org/journal/article/joe-dimaggios-last-hurrah-the-1951-lefty-odoul-all-star-tour/#calibre_link-1807

24   *Sporting News*, November 7, November 14, November 21, November 28, 1951; Fitts, "Joe DiMaggio's Last Hurrah."

25   *Sporting News*, December 5, 1951; Johnson and Wolff, *Encyclopedia of Minor League Baseball*, 392–93, 295.

26   *Sporting News*, December 5, 1951.

27   Ibid., October 17, 1951.

28   Ibid., November 28, 1951.

29   Ibid., November 14, 1951.

30   Ibid., October 3, 1951.

31   Ibid., October 31, November 7, 1951.

32   Ibid., November 7, 1951.

33   Ibid., December 5, 1951; Steven Bryant, "1951: Open Classification," in Weingarden and Nowlin (eds.), *Baseball's Business*, 342.

34   *Sporting News*, December 5, December 19, 1951; John P. Carvalho, *Frick*: Baseball's Third Commissioner* (Jefferson, NC: McFarland, 2016), 152.

35   Bryant, "1951," 344.

36   *Sporting News*, December 5, December 19, 1951; Carvalho, *Frick**, 152.

37 *Sporting News*, October 24, December 5, 1951; Greg Erion, "Leo Kiely," accessed November 27, 2024, https://sabr.org/bioproj/person/Leo-Kiely/

38 *Sporting News*, November 28, December 19, 1951.

39 Ibid., October 31, November 14, 1951; "Raymond Jankowski," accessed November 27, 2024, https://www.baseballsgreatestsacrifice.com/biographies/jankowski_ray.html; "Bill Sweiger," accessed November 27, 2024, https://www.baseballsgreatestsacrifice.com/biographies/sweiger_bill.html

Chapter 9

1 Jules Tygiel, *Past Time: Baseball as History* (New York: Oxford University Press, 2000), 144–45.

2 Ibid., 145–48.

3 Ibid., 146, 148–51.

4 *1953 Baseball Guide*, 95–98.

5 *Sporting News*, January 2, 1952.

6 Ibid.

7 Ibid., January 23, 1952.

8 Ibid.

9 Ibid., January 30, 1952.

10 Ibid.

11 Ibid.

12 Ibid., February 13, 1952.

13 Ibid., February 20, March 26, 1952.

14 Ibid., January 30, 1952.

15 Ibid.

16 Ibid., January 16, February 13, 1952; Johnson and Wolff, *Encyclopedia of Minor League Baseball*, 99.

17 *Sporting News*, January 23, January 30, February 20, 1952.

18 Ibid., February 13, 1952.

19 Ibid.

20 Rees, *Korea*, 310; Hastings, *Korean War*, 234.

21   Rees, *Korea*, 311–15.

22   Ibid., 315–17; Hastings, *Korean War*, 305–6.

23   Rees, *Korea*, 318–19.

24   Hastings, *Korean War*, 286–88.

25   Patterson, *Grand Expectations*, 231–34; Public Opinion Archives, Roper Center, University of Connecticut, "Job Performance Ratings for President Truman," accessed January 22, 2025, https://web.archive.org/web/20130208072927/http://webapps.ropercenter.uconn.edu/CFIDE/roper/presidential/webroot/presidential_rating_detail.cfm?allRate=True&presidentName=Truman

26   Truman, *Years of Trial and Hope*, 488–89; McCullough, *Truman*, 770–71, 873–74.

27   Truman, *Years of Trial and Hope*, 489–92; McCullough, *Truman*, 887-90; Hamby, *Beyond the New Deal*, 482–83

28   *Sporting News*, February 13, 1952.

29   Light, *Cultural Encyclopedia*, 378.

30   *Sporting News*, February 6, 1952.

31   Ty Cobb, "The Greatest Player of All Time Says: They Don't Play Baseball Any More," *Life*, March 17, 1952, 136–38, 141–42, 144ff, and March 24, 1952, 63–64, 66ff; Matt Rothenberg, "#Shortstops: Letters from Ty Cobb," accessed January 19, 2025, https://baseballhall.org/discover-more/stories/short-stops/letters-from-ty-cobb; Charles C. Alexander, *Ty Cobb* (1984; repr., Dallas: Southern Methodist University Press, 2006), 224.

32   *Sporting News*, January 23, 1952.

33   Ibid.

34   Ibid., January 23, January 30, February 13, 1952.

35   Ibid., January 16, 1952; Adam Lazarus, *The Wingmen: The Unlikely, Unusual, Unbreakable Friendship Between John Glenn and Ted Williams* (New York: Citadel Press, 2023), 4.

36   Ibid., 9–14.

37   *Sporting News*, January 16, 1952; Lazarus, *Wingmen*, 15.

38   *Sporting News*, January 16, 1952; C. Paul Rogers III, "Jerry Coleman," accessed December 13, 2024. https://sabr.org/bioproj/person/jerry-coleman/; Todd W. Anton. *No Greater Love: Life Stories from the Men Who Saved Baseball* (Burlington, MA: Rounder Books, 2007), 90–101.

39   Warren Corbett, "Lloyd Merriman," accessed December 17, 2024, https://sabr.org/bioproj/person/lloyd-merriman/

40   Ibid.; *Fresno (California) Bee*, January 27, 2004; *Sporting News*, January 16, March 12, 1952.

41   James S. Hirsch, *Willie Mays: The Life, The Legend* (New York: Scribner, 2010), 143–45; *Sporting News*, January 23, 1952.

42   Ibid., January 30, March 5, March 26, 1952.

43   Bill Nowlin, "Owen Friend," accessed December 19, 2024, https://sabr.org/bioproj/person/owen-friend/; *Sporting News*, January 9, March 26, 1952; Warren Corbett, "Bob Turley," accessed December 19, 2024, https://sabr.org/bioproj/person/Bob-Turley/; Gregory H. Wolf, "Carl Sawatski," accessed December 19, 2024, https://sabr.org/bioproj/person/carl-sawatski/

44   *Sporting News*, March 26, 1952.

Chapter 10

1   *Sporting News*, April 16, 1952.

2   Ibid.

3   Ibid.

4   Ibid., May 21, 1952.

5   House Judiciary Committee, *Organized Baseball: Report of the Subcommittee on Study of Monopoly Power*, 82nd Cong., 2nd sess. (1952), 231.

6   Hearings, 1601; *Sporting News*, May 21, 1952.

7   Ibid., April 2, 1952.

8   Ibid.

9   Ibid.

10   Ibid., March 26, April 9, 1952.

11   Clark Griffith, "Letter to the Editor," *Life*, April 7, 1952, 17, quoted in Oakley, *Last Golden Age*, 153; *Sporting News*, April 23, 1952.

12   Ibid., March 26, 1952.

13   Ibid., April 2, 1952.

14   Ibid., April 9, 1952.

15   Johnson and Wolff, *Encyclopedia of Minor League Baseball*, 99, 412–18.

16   Bruce Adelson, *Brushing Back Jim Crow: The Integration of Minor-League Baseball in the American South* (Charlottesville: University of Virginia Press, 1999), 35–47.

17   Rees, *Korea*, 319; Hastings, *Korean War*, 306–8.

18   Ibid., 308-9; Rees, *Korea*, 320–22.

19   Ibid., 319–20.

20   Ibid., 320.

21   Ibid., 322; Hastings, *Korean War*, 309.

22   Rees, *Korea*, 322.

23   Ibid., 323; Hastings, *Korean War*, 310.

24   Rees, *Korea*, 324; Hastings, *Korean War*, 310–13; Department of State, Office of the Historian, "Memorandum for the Record, by the Deputy Assistant Secretary of State for Far Eastern Affairs (Johnson), May 14, 1952," *Foreign Relations of the United States, 1952–1954, Korea*, Volume XV, Part 1, accessed January 27, 2025, https://history.state.gov/historicaldocuments/frus1952-54v15p1/d118

25   Hamby, *Beyond the New Deal*, 454; Maeva Marcus, *Truman and the Steel Seizure Case: The Limits of Presidential Power* (New York: Columbia University Press, 1977), 73.

26   Paul G. Pierpaoli, *Truman and Korea: The Political Culture of the Early Cold War* (Columbia: University of Missouri Press, 1999), 162–63.

27   Pierpaoli, *Truman and Korea*, 163–64; Hamby, *Beyond the New Deal*, 454.

28   Pierpaoli, *Truman and Korea*, 165–68.

29   Hamby, *Beyond the New Deal*, 455–56.

30   Ibid., 456–57; Pierpaoli, *Truman and Korea*, 168–69.

31   Ibid., 170.

32   Ibid., 170–72; Hamby, *Beyond the New Deal*, 457–58.

33   *Sporting News*, April 16, 1952.

34   Ibid.

35   Ibid.

36   Ibid.

37   Ibid., April 23, 1952.

38   Ibid., April 9, April 23, May 7, June 11, 1952.

39   Ibid., April 23, 1952.

40   Johnson and Wolff, *Encyclopedia of Minor League Baseball*, 419.

41   Joel Rippel, "Ron Necciai Strikes Out 27 Batters in a Nine-Inning Game," accessed April 18, 2025, https://sabr.org/journal/article/ron-necciai-strikes-out-27-batters-in-a-nine-inning-game/

42 James R. Walker, *Crack of the Bat: A History of Baseball on the Radio* (Lincoln: University of Nebraska Press, 2015), 193–96; *Sporting News*, April 23, May 21, May 28, 1952.

43 *1953 Baseball Guide*, 53.

44 Ibid., 9; Koppett, *Concise History*, 249–50; *Sporting News*, June 25, 1952.

45 Ibid., April 23, May 7, May 14, 1952; Jerry Coleman with Richard Goldstein, *An American Journey: My Life on the Field, in the Air, and on the Air* (Chicago: Triumph Books, 2008), 106–10.

46 *Sporting News*, May 7, 1952; Leigh Montville, *Ted Williams: The Biography of An American Hero* (New York: Doubleday, 2004), 154–57.

47 *Sporting News*, January 16, February 13, April 30, May 7, May 14, May 28, June 4, July 2, 1952; Philip A. Cola, "Bob Kennedy," accessed February 18, 2025, https://sabr.org/bioproj/person/bob-kennedy/

48 *Sporting News*, April 16, April 23, May 28, June 4, June 25, 1952.

49 Gary Bedingfield, "Jim Hudgens," accessed February 18, 2025, https://www.baseballsgreatestsacrifice.com/biographies/hudgens_jim.html

50 *Sporting News*, October 1, 1952; Gary Bedingfield, "Jim Ferguson," accessed February 19, 2025, https://www.baseballsgreatestsacrifice.com/biographies/ferguson_jim.html

Chapter 11

1 Kelley, *Baseball's Biggest Blunder*, 13–14; "Billy Joe Davidson," accessed February 20, 2025, https://www.baseball-reference.com/bullpen/Billy_Joe_Davidson

2 Kelley, *Baseball's Biggest Blunder*, 14–15; "Ed Urness," accessed February 20, 2025, https://www.baseball-reference.com/register/player.fcgi?id=urness001edw#; Norm King, "Jerry Zimmerman," accessed February 20, 2025, https://sabr.org/bioproj/person/Jerry-Zimmerman/; Paul Geisler Jr., "Frank Baumann," accessed February 20, 2025, https://sabr.org/bioproj/person/Frank-Baumann/; Bill Nowlin, "Marty Keough," accessed February 20, 2025, https://sabr.org/bioproj/person/Marty-Keough/

3 Kelley, *Baseball's Biggest Blunder*, 15.

4 *Sporting News*, July 2, 1952.

5 Ibid., July 16, 1952.

6 Ibid., July 30, 1952.

7 Ibid., August 6, August 20, 1952.

8   Ibid., October 8, 1952.

9   Ibid., August 6, 1952.

10 Ibid.

11 Ibid., August 13, August 20, September 3, September 10, September 24, 1952.

12 Ibid., September 10, September 24, 1952.

13 Ibid., September 3, 1952.

14 Ibid., August 13, August 20, September 3, September 10, September 24, 1952.

15 Ibid., June 11, June 18, July 9, July 16, August 4, 1952.

16 Rees, *Korea*, 325.

17 Ibid.

18 Ibid., 325–26.

19 Patterson, *Grand Expectations*, 252; McCullough, *Truman*, 889–90.

20 Ibid., 889, 891. For details about the January meeting at which Truman invited
    Stevenson to become a candidate, see John Bartlow Martin, *Adlai Stevenson of Illinois*
    (Garden City, NY: Doubleday, 1976), 517–28.

21 Patterson, *Mr. Republican*, 499–506, 514.

22 Stephen E. Ambrose, *Eisenhower: Soldier and President* (1990; repr., New York:
    Simon & Schuster, 2003), 259–63; Jean Edward Smith, *Eisenhower in War and Peace*
    (New York: Random House, 2012), 509.

23 Ambrose, *Eisenhower*, 264–65; Smith, *Eisenhower*, 511–12.

24 Ambrose, *Eisenhower*, 265–66; Smith, *Eisenhower*, 512–13.

25 Ibid., 514–15.

26 Ibid., 516–19.

27 Ibid., 521–22.

28 Conrad Black, *Richard M. Nixon: A Life in Full* (New York: Public Affairs Books
    2007), 129–35; Irwin Gellman, *The Contender* (New York: Free Press, 1999), 282, 303;
    Roger Morris, *Richard Milhous Nixon: The Rise of an American Politician* (New York:
    Henry Holt, 1990), 535, 581.

29 McCullough, *Truman*, 903–4.

30 Ibid., 904–5; Martin, *Adlai Stevenson*, 592–600.

31 Patterson, *Grand Expectations*, 253–54.

32 Smith, *Eisenhower*, 532.

33 Ibid., 532–36; Ambrose, *Eisenhower*, 278–80.

34 Smith, *Eisenhower*, 538–42; Ambrose, *Eisenhower*, 280–81.

35 *Sporting News*, July 23, 1952.

36 Ibid., July 23, August 13, 1952.

37 Ibid., August 27, 1952.

38 Ibid., July 2, 1952.

39 Ibid.

40 Ibid., July 30, August 27, September 10, September 17, 1952; Bill O' Neal, *The Pacific Coast League, 1903–1988* (Austin, TX: Eakin Press, 1990), 105.

41 Hirsch, *Willie Mays*, 152–54.

42 *Sporting News*, July 9, July 23, August 4, 1952.

43 Koppett, *Concise History*, 250; Oakley, *Last Golden Age*, 158–59; *1953 Baseball Guide*, 9–12.

44 Koppett, *Concise History*, 249; Oakley, *Last Golden Age*, 155–56; *1953 Baseball Guide*, 53–56.

45 *Sporting News*, October 22, 1952; Gary Bedingfield, "Walter Koehler," accessed February 25, 2025, https://www.baseballsgreatestsacrifice.com/biographies/koehler_walter.html

46 *Sporting News*, August 27, October 8, 1952; Gary Bedingfield, "John Hrasch," accessed February 26, 2025, https://www.baseballsgreatestsacrifice.com/biographies/hrasch_john.html; Gary Bedingfield, "Charlie Wilcox," accessed February 26, 2025, https://www.baseballsgreatestsacrifice.com/biographies/wilcox_charlie.html

47 *Sporting News*, September 3, 1952; Ronnie Joyner, "Bob Neighbors"; Bill Nowlin, "Bob Neighbors," accessed February 26, 2025, https://sabr.org/bioproj/person/bob-neighbors/; Gary Bedingfield, "Bob Neighbors," accessed February 26, 2025, https://www.baseballsgreatestsacrifice.com/biographies/neighbors_bob.html

Chapter 12

1 Marty Appel, *Casey Stengel: Baseball's Greatest Character* (New York: Doubleday, 2017), 196; *Sporting News*, April 23, April 23, June 25, July 9, 1952. On the "Boys of Summer," see Roger Kahn, *The Boys of Summer* (New York: Harper & Row, 1972).

2 Oakley, *Last Golden Age*, 16; Appel, *Casey Stengel*, 199.

3 Ibid. *Sporting News*, October 22, December 10, 1952.

4   Ibid., October 15, 1952.

5   Ibid., October 22, 1952.

6   Ibid., November 12, November 19, 1952.

7   Ibid., October 15, 1952.

8   Ibid.

9   Ibid., October 15, October 29, November 19, 1952.

10 Ibid., December 24, 1952; Mark Armour, "Emmett Ashford," accessed March 1, 2025, https://sabr.org/bioproj/person/emmett-ashford/

11 *Sporting News*, October 15, 1952.

12 Ibid., October 8, 1952.

13 Ibid., October 29, December 10, 1952.

14 Ibid., December 24, 1952.

15 Ibid.

16 McCullough, *Truman*, 903–4.

17 Ibid., 906–7; Truman, *Years of Trial and Hope*, 497; Martin, *Adlai Stevenson*, 644–45.

18 Patterson, *Grand Expectations*, 255.

19 Ibid., 255–56.

20 Rees, *Korea*, 326–27.

21 Ibid., 327; Hastings, *Korean War*, 320.

22 Patterson, *Grand Expectations*, 260; Smith, *Eisenhower*, 547.

23 Ibid., 546–47.

24 Patterson, 260; Smith, *Eisenhower*, 548; Martin, *Adlai Stevenson*, 760–62.

25 Ibid., 548–49.

26 Pierpaoli, *Truman and Korea*, 197–99, 214–17.

27 Smith, *Eisenhower*, 557–59; Ambrose, *Eisenhower*, 294–95.

28 Smith, *Eisenhower*, 560–61.

29 *Sporting News*, October 29, 1952.

30 Ibid.

31 *New York Times*, December 1, 1952; *Sporting News*, December 10, 1952; Gregory H. Wolf, "1952: Changing Demographics and Broadcast Challenges," in Weingarden and Nowlin, eds. *Baseball's Business*, 347–48.

32 Ibid., 348; *Sporting News*, December 10, 1952.

33 Ibid., December 10, 1952; Wolf, "1952," 348–49.

34 Ibid., 350; *Sporting News*, December 10, December 17, 1952. See also Box 29, Volume 3, "National League Meetings, Brooklyn BBC Copies," BA MSS 55, National Baseball Hall of Fame Library, Cooperstown, NY.

35 *Sporting News*, December 17, 1952; Wolf, "1952," 349; "National League Meetings, Brooklyn BBC Copies."

36 *Sporting News*, December 17, 1952; Wolf, "1952," 349–50; "National League Meetings, Brooklyn BBC Copies"; Kelley, *Baseball's Biggest Blunder*, 19–20.

37 *1953 Baseball Guide*, 97–98; *New York Times*, February 29, 1996; Kelley, *Baseball's Biggest Blunder*, 22; Warren Corbett, "Vic Janowicz," accessed March 12, 2025, https://sabr.org/bioproj/person/vic-janowicz/

38 *Sporting News*, December 3, December 17, 1952; *New York Times*, December 7, December 8, 1952; Dickson, *Veeck*, 207; *1953 Baseball Guide*, 108.

39 Wolf, "1952," 351–52; *Sporting News*, December 17, 1952; "National League Meetings, Brooklyn BBC Copies."

40 *Sporting News*, October 1, 1952; Dickson, *Veeck*, 209.

41 Wolf, "1952," 352; *1953 Baseball Guide*, 106; *Sporting News*, December 17, 1952.

42 Ibid., November 12, 1952.

43 Ibid., October 8, November 19, 1952; Montville, *Ted Williams*, 158; Jim Sargent, "An Interview with Lloyd Merriman: Football Star, War Hero, Big Leaguer," in *Baseball in the Buckeye State*, eds. Mark Stang and Dick Miller (Cleveland: Society for American Baseball Research, 2004), 48.

44 *Sporting News*, December 3, December 31, 1952.

45 Ibid., December 3, 1952; Gary Bedingfield, "Ace Adamcewicz," accessed March 11, 2025, https://www.baseballsgreatestsacrifice.com/biographies/adamcewicz_ace.html

Chapter 13

1 *Sporting News*, December 17, 1952; January 7, 1953; Carvalho, *Frick**, 157.

2 Walker and Bellamy, *Center Field Shot*, 99.

3 Carvalho, *Frick**, 157; *Sporting News*, February 11, 1953; *New York Times*, February 3, 1953.

4 Walker and Bellamy, *Center Field Shot*, 99–100; *Sporting News*, February 18, March 4, 1953.

5   Dickson, *Veeck*, 207

6   *Sporting News*, January 21, 1953.

7   Ibid., February 11, 1953.

8   Ibid., February 25, March 11, 1953.

9   Ibid., February 5, 1953; John Bauer, "Three Weeks in 1953: The Fate of the Cardinals," accessed March 18, 2025, https://sabr.org/journal/article/thre-weeks-in-1953-the-fate-of-the-cardinals/; Mark Stangl, "St. Louis Cardinals Team Ownership History," accessed March 18, 2025, http://sabr.or/bioproj/topic/st-louis-cardinals-team-ownership-history/

10 Bauer, "Three Weeks"; Stangl, "St. Louis Cardinals"; John Snyder, *Cardinals Journal: Year by Year & Day by Day with the St. Louis Cardinals Since 1882* (Cincinnati: Emmis Books, 2006), 397–98.

11 Stangl, "St. Louis Cardinals"; Snyder, *Cardinals*, 398.

12 Dickson, *Veeck*, 209; *Sporting News*, March 25, 1953.

13 Dewey and Acocella, *Ball Clubs*, 42–45.

14 *Sporting News*, March 11, March 18, March 25, 1953; Dickson, *Veeck*, 209.

15 Ibid., 209–10.

16 *Sporting News*, January 14, January 28, February 4, 1953.

17 Ibid., January 28, 1953.

18 Rees, *Korea*, 328–30.

19 Ibid., 330, 332.

20 Ibid., 333.

21 Ibid., 335–36.

22 Ibid., 336–37, 346.

23 Smith, *Eisenhower*, 551–53; Ambrose, *Eisenhower*, 273.

24 Richard Rovere, *The Eisenhower Years: 1950–1956, Affairs of State* (New York: Farrar, Strauss, 1956), 60, quoted in Rees, *Korea*, 388.

25 Rees, *Korea*, 390.

26 Ibid., 391.

27 Robert J. Donovan, *Eisenhower: The Inside Story* (New York: Harper, 1956), quoted in Rees, *Korea*, 404–5.

28 Rees, *Korea*, 405.

29   *Sporting News*, February 11, 1953.

30   Ibid., February 18, 1953.

31   Ibid., January 28, 1953.

32   Ibid., March 25, 1953.

33   Ibid., February 25, 1953.

34   Ibid.

35   Ibid., January 14, 1953.

36   Ibid., January 21, 1953.

37   Kelley, *Baseball's Biggest Blunder*, 25–26.

38   *Sporting News*, January 21, March 25, 1953; Kelley, *Baseball's Biggest Blunder*, 22.

39   *Sporting News*, February 11, February 18, 1953; Coleman, *An American Journey*, 111–12.

40   Ibid., 113–14.

41   Montville, *Ted Williams*, 161–62.

42   Ibid., 161–64.

43   Ibid., 164–65; *Sporting News*, July 8, 1953.

44   Ibid., January 7, February 25, March 18, 1953; Sargent, "Lloyd Merriman," 48.

Chapter 14

1   *Sporting News*, April 1, 1953. In May 1954, when rosters had to be finalized for the balance of the season, there were fourteen reinstated servicemen on the rosters of American League clubs and fourteen with National League clubs. See *Sporting News*, May 19, 1954.

2   *Sporting News*, April 1, 1953.

3   Ibid., April 1, April 8, 1953.

4   Ibid, April 1, 1953.

5   Ibid., April 15, 1953.

6   Ibid., April 22, 1953.

7   Ibid., April 1, May 13, 1953; *New York Times*, March 21, 1953.

8   Ibid., May 9, 1953; *Sporting News*, May 20, 1953; Walker and Bellamy, *Crack of the Bat*, 197.

9   *Sporting News*, April 1, 1953; Dickson, *Veeck*, 211.

10   *Sporting News*, April 15, 1953; Dickson, *Veeck*, 211.

11   Pierpaoli, *Truman and Korea*, 197, 219.

12   Ibid., 219–20.

13   Rees, *Korea*, 406; Hastings, *Korean War*, 319.

14   Rees, *Korea*, 407; Hastings, *Korean War*, 320.

15   Rees, *Korea*, 407; Hastings, *Korean War*, 320–21.

16   Rees, *Korea*, 364–70.

17   Ibid., 370–83.

18   Ibid., 385–86.

19   Ibid., 408–9.

20   Ibid., 409–13; Summers, *Almanac*, 211–12.

21   Rees, *Korea*, 414–17.

22   Ibid., 416–18; Mark W. Clark, *From the Danube to the Yalu* (New York: Harper & Brothers, 1954), 267.

23   *Sporting News*, April 15, 1953.

24   Ibid.; Gietschier, *Baseball*, 339.

25   Ibid.; Oakley, *Last Golden Age*, 166–67; *New York Times*, April 14, 1953.

26   *Sporting News*, April 8, 1953; *Newport* (VT) *Daily Express*, March 19, 1953; David Simmons, "Harry Simmons, Major League Schedule Maker," accessed March 27, 2025, https://www.youtube.com/watch?v=lT6rXvxkPUk

27   *Sporting News*, April 15, 1953; Dewey and Acocella, *Ball Clubs*, 310.

28   *Sporting News*, April 29, 1953.

29   Ibid., May 6, May 13, 1953.

30   Walker and Bellamy, *Center Field Shot*, 100–101; *Sporting News*, April 8, May 13, June 3, 1953.

31   Ibid., June 10, 1953.

32   Ibid.

33   Ibid., June 24, 1953.

34   *1954 Baseball Guide*, 51.

35   Ibid., 9–10.

36 *Sporting News*, April 29, 1953; Appel, *Pinstripe Empire*, 297–98. For a detailed analysis of how far the ball might really have traveled, see Jane Leavy, *The Last Boy: Mickey Mantle and the End of America's Childhood* (New York: HarperCollins, 2010), 85–102.

37 *Sporting News*, May 13, 1953; Justin Murphy, "Luke Easter," accessed March 28, 2025, https://sabr.org/bioproj/person/luke-easter/

38 Gietschier, *Baseball*, 364; Adelson, *Brushing Back*, 83–84, 98.

39 Gietschier, *Baseball*, 364; Adelson, *Brushing Back*, 107–19; *Sporting News*, April 15, April 22, April 29, May 6, May 27, July 22, 1953.

40 Ibid., June 3, 1953; Gietschier, *Baseball*, 392–93.

41 Hirsch, *Willie Mays*, 155–57.

42 Coleman, *An American Journey*, 114–16.

43 Montville, *Ted Williams*, 171.

44 Ibid., 166.

45 Ibid., April 22, 1953; Gary Bedingfield, "Carl Tumlinson," accessed March 23, 2025, https://www.baseballsgreatestsacrifice.com/biographies/tumlinson_carl.html

46 *Sporting News*, May 27, 1953; Gary Bedingfield, "Gil Shirk," accessed March 23, 2025, https://www.baseballsgreatestsacrifice.com/biographies/shirk_gil.html

Epilogue

1 *Sporting News*, June 24, 1953.

2 Ibid.

3 Ibid., April 8, 1953; Vincent et al., *Midsummer Classic*, 124–30.

4 *Sporting News*, July 8, September 16, 1953.

5 Ibid., May 27, 1953.

6 Ibid., July 8, July 22, 1953.

7 Ibid. Charles P. Korr, *The End of Baseball as We Knew It: The Players Union, 1960–81* (Urbana and Chicago: University of Illinois Press, 2002), 19.

8 Ibid., 19–20.

9 *Sporting News*, July 29, September 9, 1953.

10 Ibid., July 1, 1953.

11 Ibid., August 12, 1953; Light, *Cultural Encyclopedia*, 85–86.

12 Rees, *Korea*, 421–27; Hastings, *Korean War*, 322–24.

13 Ibid., 324.

14 Rees, *Korea*, 423–24.

15 Ibid., 422–23, 425.

16 Ibid., 425–27; Hastings, *Korean War*, 323–24.

17 Rees, *Korea*, 428–29; Summers, *Almanac*, 212.

18 Rees, *Korea*, 429–34; Hastings, *Korean War*, 324–26.

19 Ibid., 327.

20 *Sporting News*, August 5, 1953.

21 Ibid.

22 Ibid.

23 *1954 Baseball Guide*, 51–52.

24 Ibid.; Oakley, *Last Golden Age*, 170–72.

25 *1954 Baseball Guide*, 98.

26 Ibid.

27 *Sporting News*, July 15, 1953.

28 *1954 Baseball Guide*, 10–11; Oakley, *Last Golden Age*, 172–75.

29 *Sporting News*, July 22, September 2, 1953.

30 Ibid., August 5, 1953.

31 Ibid., September 30, 1953.

32 Dewey and Acocella, *Ball Clubs*, 99.

33 Coleman, *An American Journey*, 117–18.

34 Ibid., 118

35 *Sporting News*, September 2, 1953.

36 Ibid., September 9, September 23, 1953.

37 Montville, *Ted Williams*, 172–73; *Sporting News*, July 15, July 22, 1953; Vincent, et al., *Midsummer Classic*, 124.

38 Montville, *Ted Williams*, 174–75.

39 Sargent, "Lloyd Merriman," 48–49; Merriman to Ron Kaplan, November 1997, in possession of the author.

40   *Sporting News*, May 5, May 12, June 2, July 7, July 14, July 21, 1954; Brown to Ron Kaplan, November 1997, in possession of the author.

41   Harry Spiller, ed., *American POWs in Korea: Sixteen Personal Accounts* (Jefferson, NC: McFarland, 1998), 31–33.

42   Ibid., 33–34.

43   Ibid., 36; *Sporting News*, August 26, 1953.

44   Spiller, *American POWs*, 37–38.

45   Gary Bedingfield, "Jack Leonard," accessed April 6, 2025, https://www.baseballsgreatestsacrifice.com/biographies/leonard_jack.html

46   Gary Bedingfield, "George Reeden," accessed April 6, 2025, https://www.baseballsgreatestsacrifice.com/biographies/reeden_george.html

47   Master Sgt. Anne Proctor, USAF, "Chairman, Baseball Commissioner Honor Korean War Veterans," American Forces Information Service, June 20, 2000 (printout in possession of author); Thomas E. Mani, "Baseball Goes to Bat for the Korean War," www.koreanwar.net/baseball.net (printout in possession of author).

Bibliography

ARCHIVAL MATERIALS

Joint Major League Meetings. National Baseball Hall of Fame Library, Cooperstown NY.
Papers of the National League. National Baseball Hall of Fame Library, Cooperstown NY.
Ron Kaplan correspondence with former major league players. In possession of the
author.

PUBLISHED WORKS

Adair, Robert K. *The Physics of Baseball*. New York: Harper & Row, 1990.
Adelson, Bruce. *Brushing Back Jim Crow: The Integration of Minor-League Baseball in the
American South*. Charlottesville: University of Virginia Press, 1999.
Alexander, Charles C. *Ty Cobb*. Dallas: Southern Methodist University Press, 2006.
Ambrose, Stephen E. *Eisenhower: Soldier and President*. New York: Simon & Schuster,
1990.
Anton, Todd W. *No Greater Love: Life Stories from the Men Who Saved Baseball*.
Burlington, MA: Rounder Books, 2007.
Appel, Marty. *Casey Stengel: Baseball's Greatest Character*. New York: Doubleday, 2017.
Appel, Marty. *Pinstripe Empire: The New York Yankees from Before the Babe to After the
Boss*. New York: Bloomsbury, 2014.
Armour, Mark. "Emmett Ashford." https://sabr.org/bioproj/person/emmett-ashford/;
accessed March 1, 2025.
Ball, Jim. "Frank Saucier." https://sabr.org/bioproj/person/frank-saucier/; accessed
October 1, 2024.
Baseball Guide and Record Book. St. Louis: Charles C. Spink & Son, 1950–54.
Bauer, John. "Three Weeks in 1953: The Fate of the Cardinals." https://sabr.org/journal/article/
thre-weeks-in-1953-the-fate-of-the-cardinals/; accessed March 18, 2025.

Bedingfield, Gary. "Ace Adamcewicz." https://www.baseballsgreatestsacrifice.com/biographies/adamcewicz_ace.html; accessed March 11, 2025.

Bedingfield, Gary. "Bill Crago." https://www.baseballsgreatestsacrifice.com/biographies/crago_bill.html; accessed October 7, 2024.

Bedingfield, Gary. "Bill Sweiger." https://www.baseballsgreatestsacrifice.com/biographies/sweiger_bill.html; accessed November 27, 2024.

Bedingfield, Gary. "Bob Neighbors." https://www.baseballsgreatestsacrifice.com/biographies/neighbors_bob.html; accessed February 26, 2025.

Bedingfield, Gary. "Carl Tumlinson." https://www.baseballsgreatestsacrifice.com/biographies/tumlinson_carl.html; accessed March 23, 2025.

Bedingfield, Gary. "Charlie Wilcox." https://www.baseballsgreatestsacrifice.com/biographies/wilcox_charlie.html; accessed February 26, 2025.

Bedingfield, Gary. "Eddie Leneve." https://www.baseballsgreatestsacrifice.com/biographies/leneve_edward.html; accessed September 17, 2025.

Bedingfield, Gary. "George Reeden." https://www.baseballsgreatestsacrifice.com/biographies/reeden_george.html; accessed April 6, 2025.

Bedingfield, Gary. "George Sulliman." https://www.baseballsgreatestsacrifice.com/biographies/sulliman_george.html; accessed October 7, 2024.

Bedingfield, Gary. "Gil Shirk." https://www.baseballsgreatestsacrifice.com/biographies/shirk_gil.html; accessed March 23, 2025.

Bedingfield, Gary. "Jack Leonard." https://www.baseballsgreatestsacrifice.com/biographies/leonard_jack.html; accessed April 6, 2025.

Bedingfield, Gary. "James Pickett." https://www.baseballsgreatestsacrifice.com/biographies/pickett_james.html/; accessed September 17, 2024.

Bedingfield, Gary. "Jim Ferguson." https://www.baseballsgreatestsacrifice.com/biographies/ferguson_jim.html; accessed February 19, 2025.

Bedingfield, Gary. "Jim Hudgens." https://www.baseballsgreatestsacrifice.com/biographies/hudgens_jim.html; accessed February 18, 2025.

Bedingfield, Gary. "John Hrasch." https://www.baseballsgreatestsacrifice.com/biographies/hrasch_john.html; accessed February 26, 2025.

Bedingfield, Gary. "John Lazar." https://www.baseballsgreatestsacrifice.com/biographies/lazar_john.html; accessed October 7, 2024.

Bedingfield, Gary. "Len Glica," https://www.baseballsgreatestsacrifice.com/biographies/glica_len.html; accessed October 7, 2024.

Bedingfield, Gary. "Marcel Poelker." https://www.baseballsgreatestsacrifice.com/biographies/poelker_marcel.html; accessed October 7, 2024.

Bedingfield, Gary. "Raymond Jankowski." https://www.baseballsgreatestsacrifice.com/biographies/jankowski_ray.html; accessed November 27, 2024.

Bedingfield, Gary. "Walter Koehler." https://www.baseballsgreatestsacrifice.com/biographies/koehler_walter.html; accessed February 25, 2025.

"Billy Joe Davidson." https://www.baseball-reference.com/bullpen/Billy_Joe_Davidson; accessed February 20, 2025.

Black, Conrad. *Richard M. Nixon: A Life in Full*. New York: Public Affairs Books, 2007.

Blair, Clay. *The Forgotten War: America in Korea, 1950–1953*. New York: Times Books, 1987.

Boswell, Thomas. *Why Time Begins on Opening Day*. Garden City, NY: Doubleday, 1985.

Bryant, Steven Bryant. "1951: Open Classification." In Weingarden and Nowlin, *Baseball's Business*, vol. 1, 1901–57.

Carvalho, John P. *Frick*: Baseball's Third Commissioner*. Jefferson, NC: McFarland, 2016.

Clark, Mark W. *From the Danube to the Yalu*. New York: Harper & Brothers, 1954.

Cobb, Ty. "The Greatest Player of All Time Says: They Don't Play Baseball Any More." *Life*, March 17, 1952, 136–38, 141–42, 144ff.

Cola, Philip A. "Bob Kennedy." https://sabr.org/bioproj/person/bob-kennedy/; accessed February 18, 2025.

Coleman, Jerry, with Richard Goldstein. *An American Journey: My Life On the Field, In the Air, and On the Air*. Chicago: Triumph Books, 2008.

Collins, J. Lawton. *War in Peacetime: The History and Lessons of Korea*. Boston: Houghton Mifflin, 1969.

Conroy, Francis Hilary. *The Japanese Seizure of Korea: 1886–1910*. Philadelphia: University of Pennsylvania Press, 1960.

Corbett, Warren. "Bill Veeck." https://sabr.org/bioproj/person/bill-veeck/; accessed October 2, 2024.

Corbett, Warren. "Bob Turley." https://sabr.org/bioproj/person/Bob-Turley/; accessed December 19, 2024.

Corbett, Warren. "Lloyd Merriman." https://sabr.org/bioproj/person/lloyd-merriman/; accessed December 17, 2024.

Corbett, Warren. "Vic Janowicz." https://sabr.org/bioproj/person/vic-janowicz/; accessed March 12, 2025.

Corson, William R. *The Armies of Ignorance: The Rise of the American Intelligence Empire*. New York: Dial Press, 1977.

Cramer, Richard Ben. *Joe DiMaggio: The Hero's Life*. New York: Simon & Schuster, 2001.

Cumings, Bruce. *The Korean War: A History*. New York: Modern Library, 2010.

Department of State, Office of the Historian. "Memorandum for the Record, by the Deputy Assistant Secretary of State for Far Eastern Affairs (Johnson), May 14, 1952." *Foreign Relations of the United States, 1952–1954, Korea*, Volume XV, Part 1, https://history.state.gov/historicaldocuments/frus1952-54v15p1/d118; accessed January 27, 2025.

Dewey, Donald, and Nicholas Acocella. *The Ball Clubs*. New York: HarperPerennial, 1996.

Dickson, Paul. *Bill Veeck: Baseball's Greatest Maverick*. New York: Walker, 2012.

Donovan, Robert J. *Eisenhower: The Inside Story*. New York: Harper, 1956.

"Ed Urness." https://www.baseball-reference.com/register/player.fcgi?id=urness001edw#; accessed February 20, 2025.

Edmonds, Ed, and Frank G. Houdek, eds. *Baseball Meets the Law: A Chronology of Decisions, Statutes and Other Legal Events*. Jefferson, NC: McFarland, 2017.

Eig, Jonathan. *Luckiest Man: The Life and Death of Lou Gehrig*. New York: Simon & Schuster, 2005.

Erion, Greg. "Leo Kiely." https://sabr.org/bioproj/person/Leo-Kiely; accessed November 27, 2024.

Fehrenbach, T. R. *This Kind of War: A Study in Unpreparedness*. New York: Macmillan, 1963.

Finch, Robert L., L. H. Addington, and Ben M. Morgan, eds. *The Story of Minor League Baseball: A History of the Game of Professional Baseball in the United States with Particular Reference to its Growth and Development in the Smaller Cities and Towns of the Nation—The Minor Leagues*. Columbus, OH: Stoneman Press, 1952.

Fitts, Rob. "Joe DiMaggio's Last Hurrah: The 1951 Lefty O'Doul All-Star Tour." https://sabr.org/journal/article/joe-dimaggios-last-hurrah-the-1951-lefty-odoul-all-star-tour/#calibre_link-1807; accessed November 26, 2024.

Fleming, G. H. *The Dizziest Season: The Gashouse Gang Chases the Pennant*. New York: William Morrow, 1984.

Flynn, George Q. *The Draft, 1940–1973*. Lawrence: University Press of Kansas, 1993.

Gaddis, John Lewis. *The Cold War: A New History*. New York: Penguin Press, 2005.

Geisler, Paul, Jr. "Frank Baumann." https://sabr.org/bioproj/person/Frank-Baumann/; accessed February 20, 2025.

Gellman, Irwin. *The Contender*. New York: Free Press, 1999.

Gietschier, Steven P. *Baseball: The Turbulent Midcentury Years*. Lincoln: University of Nebraska Press, 2023.

Gietschier, Steven P. "Limited War and the Home Front: Ohio During the Korean War." PhD diss. Ohio State University, 1977.

Giglio, James N. *Musial: From Stash to Stan the Man*. Columbia: University of Missouri Press, 2001.

Goldblatt, Andrew. *The Giants and the Dodgers: Four Cities, Two Teams, One Rivalry*. Jefferson, NC: McFarland, 2003.

Goncharov, Sergei, John W. Lewis, and Xue Litai. *Uncertain Partners: Stalin, Mao, and the Korean War*. Stanford, CA: Stanford University Press, 1993.

Grant, James. *Bernard Baruch: The Adventures of a Wall Street Legend*. New York: Simon & Schuster, 1983.

Greenberg, Hank, edited by Ira Berkow. *Hank Greenberg: The Story of My Life*. New York: Times Books, 1989.

Griffith, Clark. "Letter to the Editor," *Life*, April 7, 1952, 17. In Oakley, *Last Golden Age*.

Halberstam, David. *The Coldest Winter: America and the Korean War*. New York: Hyperion, 2007.

Hamby, Alonzo L. *Beyond the New Deal: Harry S. Truman and American Liberalism*. New York: Columbia University Press, 1973.

Hane, Mikiso. *Japan: A Historical Survey*. New York: Charles Scribner's Sons, 1972.

Hastings, Max. *The Korean War*. New York: Simon & Schuster, 1987.

Herring, George C. *From Colony to Superpower: U.S. Foreign Relations Since 1976*. New York: Oxford University Press, 2008.

Hirsch, James S. *Willie Mays: The Life, The Legend*. New York: Scribner, 2010.

Hooker, Richard. *M*A*S*H*. Mattituck, NY: Rivercity Press, 1976.

House Judiciary Committee. *Organized Baseball: Report of the Subcommittee on Study of Monopoly Power of the Committee on the Judiciary*. 82nd Cong., 2nd sess. (1952), H. Report 2002.

House Judiciary Committee. *Study of Monopoly Power: Hearings before the Subcommittee on Study of Monopoly Power*. Serial No. 1, Part 6, "Organized Baseball," 82nd Cong., 1st sess. (1951).

Hunt, Michael H. *The World Transformed: 1945 to the Present*. New York: Oxford University Press, 2014.

"Joe DiMaggio." https://www.baseball-reference.com/players/d/dimagjo01.shtml; accessed May 15, 2024.

Johnson, Lloyd, and Miles Wolff, eds. *The Encyclopedia of Minor League Baseball*. 2nd ed. Durham, NC: Baseball America, 1997.

Joy, Admiral C. Turner. *How Communists Negotiate*. New York: Macmillan, 1955.

Joyner, Ronnie Joyner. "Bob Neighbors: A Hero Remembered." https://web.archive.org/web/20161220073816/http://philadelphiaathletics.org/bob-neighbors-a-hero-remembered/; accessed February 26, 2025.

Kahn, Roger. *The Boys of Summer*. New York: Harper & Row, 1972.

Kelley, Brent. *Baseball's Biggest Blunder: The Bonus Rule, 1953–1957*. Lanham, MD: Scarecrow Press, 1997.

King, Norm. "Jerry Zimmerman." https://sabr.org/bioproj/person/Jerry-Zimmerman/; accessed February 20, 2025.

Klopsis, Nick. "1950: The Happy Dagger." In Weingarden and Nowlin, *Baseball's Business*, vol. 1, 1901–57.

Koppett, Leonard. *Koppett's Concise History of Major League Baseball*. Philadelphia: Temple University Press, 1998.

Korr, Charles P. *The End of Baseball As We Knew It: The Players Union, 1960–81*. Urbana and Chicago: University of Illinois Press, 2002.

Lazarus, Adam. *The Wingmen: The Unlikely, Unusual, Unbreakable Friendship Between John Glenn and Ted Williams*. New York: Citadel Press, 2023.

Leavy, Jane. *The Last Boy: Mickey Mantle and the End of America's Childhood*. New York: HarperCollins, 2010.

Lieb, Frederick G., and Stan Baumgartner. *The Philadelphia Phillies*. New York: G. P. Putnam's Sons, 1953.

Light, Jonathan Fraser. *The Cultural Encyclopedia of Baseball*. Jefferson, NC: McFarland, 1997.

Lindberg, Richard C. *The White Sox Encyclopedia*. Philadelphia: Temple University Press, 1997.

Lowe, Peter. *The Origins of the Korean War*. 2nd ed. London and New York: Longman, 1997.

Lowenfish, Lee. *Branch Rickey: Baseball's Ferocious Gentleman*. Lincoln: University of Nebraska Press, 2007.

Mani, Thomas E. "Baseball Goes to Bat for the Korean War." www.koreanwar.net/baseball.net (defunct; printout in possession of the author).

Marcus, Maeva. *Truman and the Steel Seizure Case: The Limits of Presidential Power*. New York: Columbia University Press, 1977.

Marshall, William. *Baseball's Pivotal Era, 1945–1951*. Lexington: University Press of Kentucky, 1999.

Martin, John Bartlow. *Adlai Stevenson of Illinois*. Garden City, NY: Doubleday, 1976.

McCue, Andy. "Los Angeles/Brooklyn Dodgers team ownership history." https://sabr.org/bioproj/topic/los-angeles-brooklyn-dodgers-team-ownership-history/; accessed April 5, 2024.

McCullough, David. *Truman*. New York: Simon & Schuster, 1992.

McKenna, Brian. "Lefty O'Doul." https://sabr.org/bioproj/person/lefty-odoul/; accessed April 16, 2024.

McMahon, Robert J. *The Cold War: A Very Short Introduction*. New York: Oxford University Press, 2003.

Mead, William B., and Paul Dickson. *Baseball: The Presidents' Game*. Washington, DC: Farragut, 1993.

Montross, Lynn, and Capt. Nicholas Canzona. *The Chosin Reservoir Campaign*. Vol. III. US Marine Operations in Korea, 1950–53. Washington: Historical Branch, USMCHQ, USGPO, 1957.

Montville, Leigh. *Ted Williams: The Biography of an American Hero*. New York: Doubleday, 2004.

Morris, Roger. *Richard Milhous Nixon: The Rise of an American Politician*. New York: Henry Holt, 1990.

Nowlin, Bill. "Bob Neighbors." https://sabr.org/bioproj/person/bob-neighbors/; accessed February 26, 2025.

Nowlin, Bill. "Marty Keough." https://sabr.org/bioproj/person/Marty-Keough/; accessed February 20, 2025.

Nowlin, Bill. "Owen Friend." https://sabr.org/bioproj/person/owen-friend/; accessed December 19, 2024.

Nowlin, Bill. *Tom Yawkey: Patriarch of the Boston Red Sox*. Lincoln: University of Nebraska Press, 2018.

Oakley, J. Ronald. *Baseball's Last Golden Age, 1946–1960*. Jefferson, NC: McFarland, 1994.

O'Neal, Bill. *The Pacific Coast League, 1903–1988*. Austin, TX: Eakin Press, 1990.

Patterson, James T. *Grand Expectations: The United States, 1945–1971*. New York: Oxford University Press, 1996.

Patterson, James T. *Mr. Republican: A Biography of Robert A. Taft*. Boston: Houghton Mifflin, 1972.

Pierpaoli, Paul G., Jr. *Truman and Korea: The Political Culture of the Early Cold War*. Columbia: University of Missouri Press, 1999.

Pierpaoli, Paul G., Jr. "Truman's Other War: The Battle for the American Homefront, 1950–53." *OAH Magazine of History* 14, Spring (2000): 15–19.

Proctor, Master Sgt. Anne. "Chairman, Baseball Commissioner Honor Korean War Veterans." American Forces Information Service, June 20, 2000.

Public Opinion Archives, Roper Center, University of Connecticut. "Job Performance Ratings for President Truman." https://web.archive.org/web/20130208072927/http://webapps.ropercenter.uconn.edu/CFIDE/roper/presidential/webroot/presidential_rating_detail.cfm?allRate=True&presidentName=Truman; accessed January 22, 2025.

Rampersad, Arnold. *Jackie Robinson: A Biography*. New York: Alfred A. Knopf, 1997.

Ray, James Lincoln. "Mickey Mantle." https://sabr.org/bioproj/person/mickey-mantle/; accessed September 11, 2024.

Rees, David. *Korea: A Limited War*. New York: St. Martin's, 1964.

Reidenbaugh, Lowell. *100 Years of National League Baseball*. St. Louis: The Sporting News Publishing Co., 1976.

Ridgway, Matthew B. *Soldier: The Memoirs of Matthew B. Ridgway*. New York: Harper & Brothers, 1956.

Ridgway, Matthew B. *The Korean War*. Garden City, NY: Doubleday, 1967.

Rippel, Joel. "Ron Necciai Strikes Out 27 Batters in a Nine-Inning Game." https://sabr.org/journal/article/ron-necciai-strikes-out-27-batters-in-a-nine-inning-game/; accessed April 18, 2025.

Roberts, Robin, and C. Paul Rogers III. *The Whiz Kids and the 1950 Pennant*. Philadelphia: Temple University Press, 1996.

Rogers, C. Paul. "Jerry Coleman." https://sabr.org/bioproj/person/jerry-coleman/; accessed December 13, 2024.

Rogers, C. Paul, "Whitey Ford." https://sabr.org/bioproj/person/whitey-ford/; accessed April 4, 2024.

Rossi, John P. *A Whole New Game: Off the Field Changes in Baseball, 1946–1960*. Jefferson, NC: McFarland, 1999.

Rothenberg, Matt. "#Shortstops: Letters from Ty Cobb." https://baseball.org/discover-more/stories/short-stops/letters-from-ty-cobb; accessed January 19, 2025.

Rovere, Richard. *The Eisenhower Years: 1950–1956, Affairs of State*. New York: Farrar, Straus, 1956.

Saccoman, John. "Willie Mays." http://sabr.org/bioproj/person/willie-mays/; accessed September 15, 2024.

Sargent, Jim. "An Interview with Lloyd Merriman: Football Star, War Hero, Big Leaguer." In *Baseball in the Buckeye State*, edited by Mark Stang and Dick Miller, 45–49. Cleveland: Society for American Baseball Research, 2004.

Smith, Jean Edward. *Eisenhower in War and Peace*. New York: Random House, 2012.

Snyder, John. *Cardinals Journal: Year by Year & Day by Day with the St. Louis Cardinals Since 1882*. Cincinnati: Emmis Books, 2006.

Spiller, Harry, ed. *American POWs in Korea: Sixteen Personal Accounts*. Jefferson, NC: McFarland, 1998.

"Stan Musial." https://www.baseball-reference.com/players/m/musiast01.shtml; accessed May 15, 2024.

Stangl, Mark. "St. Louis Cardinals Team Ownership History." http://sabr.org/bioproj/topic/st-louis-cardinals-team-ownership-history/#_ednref441; accessed March 18, 2025.

Sullivan, Dean A. comp. and ed. *Late Innings: A Documentary History of Baseball, 1945–1972*. Lincoln: University of Nebraska Press, 2002.

Summers Jr., Harry G. *Korean War Almanac*. New York: Facts on File, 1990.

"Ted Williams." https://www.baseball-reference.com/players/w/willite01.shtml; accessed May 15, 2024.

Thomas, G. Scott. *A Whole New Ballgame: Branch Rickey, Bill Veeck, Walter O'Malley and the Transformation of Baseball*. Jefferson, NC: McFarland, 2022.

Thorn, John, Pete Palmer, Michael Gershman, and David Pietrusza, eds. *Total Baseball*. 5th ed. New York: Viking, 1997.

Thornley, Stew. "Willie Mays Had a Spectacular—But Short—Stay in Minneapolis." https://sabr.org/journal/article/willie-mays-had-a-spectacular-but-short-stay-in-minneapolis/; accessed September 11, 2024.

Tiemann, Robert L., and Pete Palmer, "Major League Attendance." In *Total Baseball*, edited by John Thorn, Pete Palmer, Michael Gershman, and David Pietrusza, 101–5. 5th ed. New York: Viking, 1997.

Truman, Harry S. *Memoirs. Vol. Two: Years of Trial and Hope*. Garden City, NY: Doubleday, 1956.

Tygiel, Jules. *Past Time: Baseball as History*. New York: Oxford University Press, 2000.

Vincent, David, Lyle Spatz, and David W. Smith. *The Midsummer Classic: The Complete History of Baseball's All-Star Game*. Lincoln: University of Nebraska Press, 2001.

Walker, James R. *Crack of the Bat: A History of Baseball on the Radio*. Lincoln: University of Nebraska Press, 2015.

Walker, James R. and Robert V. Bellamy Jr. *Center Field Shot: A History of Baseball on Television*. Lincoln: University of Nebraska Press, 2008.

Weingarden, Steve, and Bill Nowlin eds. *Baseball's Business: The Winter Meetings*. Vol. 1, 1901–57. Phoenix: Society for American Baseball Research, 2016.

Westad, Odd Arne. *The Cold War: A History*. New York: Basic Books, 2017.

White, Ima, "Revisiting the Iconic M*A*S*H TV Show: Analysis of Its Impact and Legacy," https://tvovermind.com/mash-tv-show-analysis/; accessed April 22, 2025.

Whiting, Robert. *You Gotta Have Wa*. New York: Macmillan, 1989.

Wolf, Gregory H. "Carl Sawatski." https://sabr.org/bioproj/person/carl-sawatski/; accessed December 19, 2024.

Wolf, Gregory H. "1952: Changing Demographics and Broadcast Challenges." In Weingarden and Nowlin, *Baseball's Business*, vol. 1, 1901–57.

Index

About the Author

Steven P. Gietschier is a public historian whose career has included archival work, teaching, consulting, and publishing. He established the corporate archives for the *Sporting News* and managed the *Sporting News* Research Center from 1986 until 2008. Thereafter, he taught American history, sport history, and the history and culture of baseball at a midwestern university. He is a 2023 recipient of the Society for American Baseball Research's Henry Chadwick Award and the author of *Baseball: The Turbulent Midcentury Years* (2023), which won the Seymour Medal, given by SABR to the author of the year's best baseball history or biography.